*The Art of*
CRITICISM

# The Art of
# CRITICISM

## ESSAYS IN FRENCH LITERARY ANALYSIS

### EDITED BY PETER H. NURSE

## EDINBURGH
### at the University Press

©
1969
EDINBURGH UNIVERSITY PRESS
22 George Square, Edinburgh
*North America*
Aldine Publishing Company
529 South Wabash Avenue, Chicago
*Australia and New Zealand*
Hodder & Stoughton Limited
*Africa*, Oxford University Press
*India*, P. C. Manaktala & Sons
*Far East*, M. Graham Brash & Son
85224 068 6
Library of Congress Catalog Card Number 74–77156
Printed in Great Britain
by W. and J. Mackay and Co. Ltd, Chatham

# CONTENTS

CONTENTS

# ACKNOWLEDGEMENTS

The Edinburgh University Press is grateful to the publishers of the various works from which extracts have been reproduced in this volume. In particular the Press wishes to extend thanks to Gallimard, Paris, for permission to reproduce extracts from the works of Apollinaire, Proust, Breton, Éluard and Camus; and to Mercure de France, Paris, for permission to reproduce the extract from Jouve.

*Peter H. Nurse*

# INTRODUCTION

THIS VOLUME CONTAINS a collection of pieces of practical criticism of French literary texts, on the lines of the celebrated exercise, known in France as *explication de textes*, which was made an official part of the teaching programme in French schools following a ministerial decree in 1902.

The purpose of the exercise, as originally devised, was to counter-act the existing tendency to teach French literature almost exclusively through lectures which concentrated on giving capsulated generaliza-tions about authors and literary movements, and to re-direct atten-tion to the all-too-frequently neglected texts themselves. Such an exercise, calling for a detailed commentary on a given passage drawn from one of the great authors, was meant not only to test the ability of the student to apply the knowledge derived from secondary sources (lectures or manuals), but also to sharpen his personal judge-ment and make him critical of all *a priori* generalizations.

Stated thus, the theory of *explication* must seem unexceptionable, but in practice it often failed to live up to the expectation of many critics; and, in its traditional form, – as developed and somewhat dogmatically systematized by a generation of men who dominated the French academic community during the first half of this century – it has been increasingly subject to suspicion and challenge. In this sense, it is possible for Roland Barthes, one of those who have been most vocal in making the challenge, to write of 'une *crise générale du Com-mentaire*, aussi importante, peut-être, que celle qui a marqué, relative-ment au même problème, le passage du Moyen Age à la Renais-sance.'[1] Hence the new 'querelle des Anciens et des Modernes' (the title of the first part of Serge Doubrovsky's: *Pourquoi la Nouvelle Critique*?)[2] now being fought out with a passion that would rarely be found outside the confines of the French intellectual world.

In this encounter, the *Anciens* are essentially represented by the latter-day followers of Gustave Lanson and Daniel Mornet – both former Sorbonne Professors – and a survey of the main grievances of their 'modernist' adversaries will perhaps form a convenient frame-work for a discussion of the problems involved in *explication de textes*.

At the heart of most theories of criticism, irrespective of the differences between them, is the belief that what distinguishes genuine creative literature is a coherent, personal vision of life which gives to the artist's work a fully organic structure. When we read a poem, a novel or a play by a great writer, we are ultimately conscious that, somewhere behind all its complexity of detail, there is a principle of organization which provides a focus and binds all the separate elements into a total pattern. This point has been made by countless critics, but it is particularly well explained by T. S. Eliot when he relates this unity of the artistic product to the synthesizing activity of the poet's mind:

> When a poet's mind is perfectly equipped for its work, it is constantly amalgamating disparate experience; the ordinary man's experience is chaotic, irregular, fragmentary. The latter falls in love, or reads Spinoza, and these two experiences have nothing to do with each other, or with the noise of the type-writer or the smell of cooking; in the mind of the poet, these experiences are always forming new wholes.[3]

Eliot's conception of the 'unified sensibility' of the poet is thus closely linked with the notion of the intrinsic coherence of the text which we seek to elucidate, and traditionally the explicator has sought to relate each element of his text to some central motif or *intérêt dominant*. Normally, he begins by formulating an initial *impression d'ensemble*, the validity of which is subsequently put to the test in an analysis of individual details of form and content. The criterion for judging the validity of the 'focus' is its comprehensiveness and correspondence with all the data of the passage, and it is frequently the case that during the analytical process, the initial formulation is modified or extended to embrace a deeper synthesis.

At the same time, this deepening of the ultimate synthesis will also result from another vital stage of the explication, namely the placing of the text in a wider perspective or *context*. Thus, if the passage for analysis is only part of a larger work, it must be situated with regard to the overall structure of that work, and if it is itself a formal entity, such as a sonnet, it still needs to be envisaged as taking its place in a more comprehensive totality, represented by the writer's complete *œuvre*. When Jean-Pierre Richard claims for 'la nouvelle critique' that it is *totalitaire*, it is this extra comprehensiveness of the critic's range of search for the unifying principle to which he draws attention:

> Toute la critique moderne . . . croit . . . que la partie – ici telle phrase, telle image, telle pensée détachées de l'œuvre – ne peut se comprendre qu'une fois mise en rapport avec le tout dont elle fait partie, et que ce dernier est lui-même bien plus que la simple

somme de ses parties, qu'il en constitue l'horizon, l'au-delà, ou la synthèse . . . Il y aura donc entre la partie et le tout, entre chaque morceau, chaque phrase, chaque mot même d'une œuvre et le sens global de cette œuvre une relation d'interdépendance et de réciprocité. *Entendre résonner ce ton, cette note unique et globale de l'œuvre, en chaque phrase lue, tel serait l'idéal d'une parfaite explication de textes.*[4]

I think most critics would accept this as a perfectly acceptable statement of the ideal function of the explicator, and it is not profitable here to dwell on the particular novelty of this approach. It echoes in all essentials the long-standing view that each author has what has variously been called his individual 'faculté maîtresse' or 'forme d'esprit originelle' (Taine) or his own 'dynamisme spirituel' (Ramon Fernandez). Thus, when M. Richard sums up the object of his quest as 'quelques grandes permanences, quelques façons uniques de s'exprimer et de sentir, quelques attitudes primordiales d'existence', he is still in line with statements made by nineteenth-century critics like Paul Bourget who wrote: 'Dans l'arrière-fond de toute belle œuvre littéraire se cache l'affirmation d'une grande vérité psychologique.'[5]

However, it is this reference to 'psychological truths' that perhaps holds the key to the main differences that separate the 'moderns' from 'ancients' in to-day's controversy. For, when Barthes refers to a watershed in critical theory as big as that which marks the transition from the medieval to the Renaissance worlds, he means that the modern era has for the first time fully understood the degree to which literature is a product of the imagination, with all its mysterious sub-conscious roots, rather than of the logical processes of the conscious mind. There is, once again, a substantial element of over-exaggeration in this claim. Freud himself always denied having 'discovered' the sub-conscious, and already in many pre-Freudian critics (we can again quote Paul Bourget, writing in the 1880s) the modernist theses are largely anticipated:

Les œuvres de la littérature et de l'art . . . ne sont pas le produit artificiel d'un travail de la réflexion. Des hommes vivants les ont composées, pour lesquels elles étaient un profond besoin, une intime et nécessaire satisfaction de tout l'être . . . L'exemple de tous les siècles prouve que la grande ouvrière des créateurs de génie est l'inconscience.[6]

Yet it was especially with the development of psycho-analysis by Freud and Jung, and the parallel literary phenomenon of the Surrealist movement, at its height between 1925 and 1935, that the new insights into the subconscious elements in the creative process achieved wide-spread recognition. By giving undue emphasis to the logical structure of conscious thought, the tendency of *lansonisme* was to assimilate the *explication de textes* to the kind of exegesis used by the medieval schoolmen in their glosses of religious texts: what mattered most was the ideological content and the critic's main job was sometimes thought to be done once he had elucidated this and demonstrated its grammatical structure. It is true that this method of approach is more suitable for literature which is above all designed to *persuade*, and such a view of the writer's function was predominant in the pre-Romantic era. It is reflected in the stock divisions of the old treatises on rhetoric where the three major components of literary discourse are singled out as *inventio* (what to say); *dispositio* (in what order to say it); and *elocutio* (how to say it). Provided the critic gave due place in his analysis to this third element, style, he was not radically failing in his task.

The trouble is, of course, that great literature cannot be reduced to this category of ideological persuasion: even before the Romantic revolution, before the concept of art as self-expression came to predominate, conceptual thinking was rarely the foremost characteristic of genuinely imaginative literature. Certainly, in the metaphysical poets like Donne in England, or like his French counterparts, Scève or Sponde, a firm logical, linear architecture is more clearly discernible, but there too the 'meaning' of the work transcends any kind of direct, abstract statement, through absorption into the oblique suggestiveness of concrete language with its sensuous properties of rhythm and imagery.[7] How much greater, then, is the gap between logical statement and global meaning where, as in so much art, the linear or syntactical progression is renounced in favour of a series of juxtaposed images. This is particularly the case with so much post-Symbolist poetry, but it is by no means a modern phenomenon: critics of Molière's work, to take but one example, have found that their understanding of the unifying principles of many of his plays is increased by abandoning the idea of a linear plot, or of a central character, as the key to structure, and by concentrating on the way a dominant theme is orchestrated in a succession of juxtaposed situations (the 'situation' being the equivalent, in drama, of the image in poetry, both representing what Eliot called the 'objective correlative'.)[8] Certainly, it is only with the application of this approach that so apparently disorganized a work as *Dom Juan* has revealed its inner coherence.

It would be idle to generalize either on the exact relationship of thought and emotion in art or on the degree of consciousness present in the artist's creative process: each case will be different from the others. Yeats, for example, illustrates the visionary poet in whom the process is akin to a mystical state, and he once remarked that 'anyone who has any experience of any mystical state of the soul knows how there float up into the mind profound symbols whose meaning . . . one does not perhaps understand for years.' It is notably when dealing with writers like this, therefore, that an awareness of the dangers of over-rationalizing is of value, and this will be especially apparent in the commentaries on the more modern poets in this volume. They represent an extreme form of the contention that literature is 'une psychologie vivante' and that its ultimate unity of vision must be rooted in, and communicated through, sensuous experience; for, to quote Tolstoy, 'art is a human activity consisting in this, that one man consciously, by means of external signs, hands on to others *feelings* he has lived through, and that others are infected by those feelings and also experience them.' When the more traditional explicator sought his focus in an *idée dominante*, his method always ran the danger of over-conceptualizing and he could well have been reminded of J.S. Mill's *Thoughts on Poetry and its Varieties* of 1859, which contains the following type of comment:

> Whom, then, shall we call poets? Those who are so constituted that emotions are the links of association by which their ideas, both sensuous and spiritual, are connected together. . . . Thoughts and images will be linked together, according to the similarity of the feelings which cling to them. A thought will introduce a thought by first introducing a feeling which is allied with it. At the centre of each group of thoughts or images will be found a feeling; and the thoughts or images will be there only because the feeling was there. The combinations which the mind puts together, the pictures which it paints, the wholes which Imagination constructs out of the materials supplied by Fancy, will be indebted to some dominant *feeling*, not as in other natures

to a dominant *thought*, for their unity and consistency of character, for what distinguishes them from incoherencies.[9]
This extract helps one to understand why so much modern criticism, both in English and French studies, has concentrated on the study of imagery as giving the key to the inner structure of a work, for it is the formal image which is the most tangible example of the essentially symbolic nature of language in imaginative literature: hence the view which equates the literary product with an extended metaphor.

But if this more modern tendency to avoid the less explicit facets of literature and to stress the more obscure, affective elements has undoubtedly enriched our critical understanding, it has also made the problems of interpretation increasingly more complex. For, once the symbolic nature of all literary statements is accepted, and where the roots of the symbolism are so often, as with Yeats, buried so deep that even the writer 'does not perhaps understand for years' the full sense of his meaning, how are we, as critics, to decipher it? Must we be content with a purely subjective reading and with the notion that 'il n'y a pas de vérité', that a work can have as many interpretations as there are readers? It is this that raises the problem of the value of all the aids of literary scholarship to which the *lansonien* regularly resorted in order to pin down an objective sense in the text, – such factors as the opinions and biography of the author, the nature of the milieu in which he lived and wrote, and the 'sources' from which he worked. On most of these points, there is no absolute consensus of views among the 'moderns'unless it be the premise – perfectly reasonable, and by no means novel – that it is only after exhaustive interrogation of the text itself that 'outside' help is to be sought, either as confirmation of internal evidence or as a hypothetical solution to what otherwise defies analysis.

Once again, the rule must be to avoid dogmatism. For instance, I personally find it impossible automatically to discount the value of an author's testimony as to his intentions, and the thesis of *intentionnalité inconsciente* seems to me to be misleading as an absolute dogma. Gaëton Picon puts it in the following terms:

La Création est pour elle-même une activité assez obscure . . .
On ne sait quel décalage, douloureux ou ironique, existe entre les intentions de l'auteur et la vérité de sa création. . . . A peine prennent-ils la plume qu'une force mystérieuse dévie leur main:

l'œuvre se substitue à la sincérité . . . La *Préface de Cromwell* n'est pas la préface de *Cromwell*.[10]

Against this, I would put the fact that some artists' work is so highly organized, in terms of conscious goals, that they are frequently the best equipped to shed light on their creations. Such would seem to be the case, for instance, with a writer like Henry James, Baudelaire or Valéry,[11] all of whom could hardly be further from applying the method counselled by André Breton in his *Premier Manifeste de Surréalisme* of 1924: 'Placez-vous dans l'état le plus passif ou réceptif que vous pourrez. Faites abstraction de votre génie, de vos talents. . . . Ecrivez vite sans sujet préconçu.'[12] Another relevant factor here is that many post-Freudian writers ( Jouve seems to be a case in point), are themselves so fully conversant with the theories of psychoanalysis that their choice of symbols often seems to be highly deliberate.

Again, on the question of the study of 'sources', there is need of flexibility. It is perfectly true that once we adopt the view that great art is the expression of a unique, coherent vision, then every great work is necessarily totally distinct from any historical prototype. If we list the sources of Racine's *Phèdre* and show what elements he took from Euripides, Seneca, Garnier or Gilbert, we are merely engaged on literary history, and if our comments stop short at the juxtaposition of the source with the Racinian text, there is no real literary criticism involved. Indeed, it would be to miss the point that even a phrase which is borrowed word for word from a previous author will take on a new significance by being transplanted into a different structure. What distinguishes the literary critic's handling of this kind of historical scholarship is therefore that he always uses it as a means to an end: namely, the further elucidation of the total meaning of his author. For that reason, I subscribe wholly to the sentiments of Professor H. B. Charlton, when he outlines his approach to Shakespearian criticism:

> A traditional aid of scholarship has frequently been sought for the purpose of supplementing deficiency in critical intuition. A mere scholar seldom has the gift of perceiving directly what are the distinctive traits of artistic genius. He needs all the pointers and sign-posts which he can find. Hence, wherever there is a non-Shakespearian source of a Shakespeare play, it has generally been called in to help. It has, one hopes, never entered merely as a fact

of erudition. Its function has been purely critical. If one can see the specific and concrete raw material which a genius had on his table while he was transmuting it into a masterpiece, one may be able to catch glimpses of the way in which his mind was working. One may even be able to speculate on the conscious or unconscious motives for the changes by which the sublimation came.[13] It was in this spirit that Jean Pommier studied the sources of *Phèdre*, and the method produced valuable critical insights contained in such phrases as: 'Chez Racine, la Phèdre d'Euripide a honte de celle de Sénèque.'[14]

Similar caution is necessary when we seek help from either a writer's biography or his historical milieu in order to throw light on the 'distinctive traits of artistic genius'. There are some modern critics who would reject the value of either of these factors as potential 'sign-posts', and Roland Barthes is probably taking the most extreme position when he proclaims the work of art to be free from all situational contingencies:

L'œuvre est pour nous sans contingence. . . . L'œuvre n'est entourée, désignée, dirigée par aucune situation.[15]

Most reasonable critics, bearing in mind that 'all categories are a compromise with chaos', would almost certainly reject this position as too rigid. Where the majority of the representatives of 'la nouvelle critique' are concerned, they are content to use such extraneous information, but only after it has been interpreted in the light of the latest thinking in the other modern sciences such as phenomenology, psycho-analysis or structural anthropology. Jean-Pierre Richard, for example, who is always in search of what he calls 'isomorphisms' (i.e. structural interconnections between all domains of man's experience as revealed both in life and art) is inspired by Lévi-Strauss's work. M. Richard instances the way the French social anthropologist demonstrated that the patterns of face-decorations of the primitive Brazilian tribes reproduced the geographical lay-out of their jungle villages, and the literary critic then illustrates equivalent correlations between the work and life of Mallarmé:

Mallarmé s'hallucine, on le sait, sur l'azur inaccessible et sur l'irrémédiable *fané* de l'existence: et il épouse alors une femme aux yeux bleus, plus âgée que lui, déjà usée par la vie, qui sera comme la princesse de ce fané . . . Plus tard rêvera-t-il au feu, à l'azur vaincu, à l'existence activement et lumineusement jaillie de son

cerveau, ce sera pour rechercher alors une femme joyeuse et plantureuse, à la chair d'or et aux cheveux de feu.[16]
Correlations of this kind are equally sought between literary works and the historical milieu in which they flourished, and this is inevitably given strongest attention by Marxist critics like Lucien Goldmann, following the famous declaration by Marx that 'It is not the consciousness of men that determines their existence, but, on the contrary, their social existence determines their consciousness.' Goldmann thus relates the tragic vision of Jansenism, as reflected in the work of Racine and Pascal, to the economic and social structures of seventeenth-century France, when the *officier* class, or *noblesse de robe*, (with which so many of the leading Jansenists were closely connected) was the chief victim of the alliance of the monarchy and the *tiers état*.[17] An older historical variant of Richard's idea of isomorphisms is the Hegelian notion of a *Zeitgeist* which penetrates all the levels of activity in a given period of history. It provides the inspiration for Oswald Spengler's book: *The Decline of the West*, where we can read the following profession of Hegelian faith:

> Between the differential calculus and the dynastic principle of politics in the age of Louis xiv, between the Classical city-state and the Euclidean geometry, between the space perspective of Western oil-painting and the conquest of space by railway, telephone and long-range weapon, between contrapuntal music and credit economics, there are deep uniformities.[18]

This is the kind of attitude, albeit shorn of its excesses, that lies behind the work of a critic like Jean Rousset, when he sets out to determine the essence of baroque sensibility by demonstrating the aesthetic and psychological common denominator of European art – music, sculpture, architecture and literature – in the late sixteenth and seventeenth centuries.[19] Many of us will no doubt treat with suspicion such wide-ranging syntheses, yet as long as we are content to go on using in our critical terminology labels like 'classical', 'romantic', and 'baroque', we cannot afford to ignore the kind of work done by Rousset.[20]

And lastly, among these potential aids to a better critical vision, there is the perhaps less disputed importance of a knowledge of the historical evolution of aesthetic forms such as *genres* or versestructure: one is reminded of Valéry's remark that 'en poésie les conditions métriques et musicales restreignent beaucoup l'indétermination'. [21] To know what was innovation and what was convention in the formal structure of a given work can be of considerable significance. Baudelaire, for instance, was a most conscious artist in his use of verse forms and rhythms, and was at pains to remind the literary critics of his day how they failed in their duty if they neglected the study of the stylistic mechanics of art:

Il est évident que les rhétoriques et les prosodies ne sont pas des tyrannies inventées arbitrairement, mais une collection de règles réclamées par l'organisation même de l'être spirituel. Et jamais les prosodies et les rhétoriques n'ont empêché l'originalité de se produire distinctement. Le contraire, à savoir qu'elles ont aidé l'éclosion de l'originalité, serait infiniment plus vrai. [22]

The impact of Baudelaire's own poetry is immeasurably increased if our eye and ear are trained to pick out the shifts in rhythm in the alexandrine, to detect, for example, the shift to the swinging cadences of the *trimètre* in the following lines of *Le Beau Navire*:

Quand tu vas balayant l'air de ta jupe large
Tu fais l'effet d'un beau vaisseau qui prend le large.

Lines such as these re-inforce the point made by Valéry that it is courting disaster in critical practice to separate form and content:

Distinguer dans les vers le fond et la forme; un sujet et un développement; le son et les sens; considérer la rhythmique, la métrique et la prosodie comme naturellement et facilement séparables de l'expression verbale même, des mots eux-mêmes et de la syntaxe: voilà autant de symptômes de non-compréhension ou d'insensibilité en matière poétique. [23]

Many a critical *contre-sens* concerning the 'meaning' of a La Fontaine fable would have been avoided had the critic's ear been better attuned to the presence of irony and parody in the style. Similarly with Molière, many an apparently serious passage reveals its burlesque tonality through the semi-mechanical lilt of the verse or through the mock-heroic level of the vocabulary.

From time to time, poets and other eminent men of letters have made statements which seem to call in question the whole practice of literary explication. Goethe, for instance, is on record as saying that 'the more incomprehensible a literary work is, the better it is'. Coleridge in turn remarked that the best poetry remains only 'generally and not perfectly understood'. And lastly, Montaigne, in *De l'Experience*, seems to issue the ultimate warning against the explicators:

Qui ne dirait que les gloses augmentent les doutes et l'ignorance, puisqu'il ne se voit aucun livre, soit humain, soit divin, auquel le monde s'embesogne, duquel l'interprétation fasse tarir la difficulté? Le centième commentaire le renvoie à son suivant, plus épineux et plus scabreux que le premier ne l'avait trouvé . . . Il y a plus à faire à interpréter les interprétations qu'à interpréter les choses, et plus de livres sur les livres que sur autre sujet: nous ne faisons que nous entregloser. Tout fourmille de commentaires; d'auteurs, il en est grande cherté . . .

It is appropriate that Montaigne should be quoted here since none has written more tellingly than he of the dangers of dogmatism in any shape or form; and the first lesson that the literary critic needs to learn is perhaps that of humility in front of the work of art: that *soumission au texte* which has long been the watch-word of the ideal explicator. No doubt, as Goethe said, the masterpieces of creative art will always retain something of their mystery, and the dogmatic affirmation of any one interpretation can only reduce their resonance. Thus, when Barthes says that 'une œuvre est "éternelle", non parce qu'elle impose un sens unique à des hommes différents, mais parce qu'elle suggère des sens différents à un homme unique',[24] he provides a valid reminder that to cling to the notion of a totally 'objective' meaning to be extracted from a work of the imagination, where 'l'Indécis au Précis se joint', is a form of folly. Where the personal response is missing, all exegesis is condemned to sterility.

On the other hand, it is no less part of the critic's humility that he should set limits to his own subjectivity and seek every available aid to *extend* his own understanding. It was the method of 'absolute subjectivity' of the kind preached with fervour by Anatole France – 'Le bon critique est celui qui raconte les aventures de son âme au milieu des chefs-d'œuvre. Il n'y a pas plus de critique objective qu'il n'y a d'art objectif, et tous ceux qui se flattent de mettre autre chose qu'eux-mêmes dans leur œuvre sont dupes de la plus fallacieuse illusion'[25] – which was responsible for the patently false, Romantic interpretations of Molière's *Le Misanthrope* as being a work of tragic tonality, glorifying the heroic solitude of Alceste in his fight against the corruption of society. As such, pure 'impressionism' is a travesty of genuine literary analysis, and the only possible justification for it is that its author is himself of such creative genius that we are prepared to forget the work he is supposedly criticizing in order to enjoy the play of the critic's personality.

To delineate any more precisely the frontiers between the objective and subjective elements in literary criticism would certainly lead to over-simplified generalizations. Moreover, the purpose of this introductory survey of some of the issues involved in the practice of *explication de textes* was not to formulate a new position, nor too obviously to take sides in the current critical debate, for that would have been contrary to the whole spirit of this volume. The novelty of the enterprise lies precisely in the fact that our book, unlike its better-known predecessors in the field,[26] does not present its series of *explications* as illustrations of any one approach to the art of commentary. For this reason, all the pieces are by different hands and each contributor, who is a British-, or American-based academic, specializing in the study of French literature, has been left entirely free from any editorial directives.

The reader will therefore find here considerable variety of critical approach, but the volume as a whole will, I hope, prove to reflect the ideal once so well expressed by Sainte-Beuve when, after restating the point that some aspects of literary genius will probably always defy analysis, he nevertheless saw the *point d'honneur* of the critic as lying in an unflagging effort to *mieux comprendre*:

Nous tous, artisans et serviteurs d'une même science que nous cherchons à rendre aussi exacte que possible, sans nous payer de notions vagues et de vains mots, continuons donc d'observer sans relâche, d'étudier et de pénétrer les conditions des œuvres diversement remarquables et l'infinie variété des formes de talent; forçons-les de nous rendre raison et de nous dire comment et pourquoi elles sont de telle ou telle façon et qualité plutôt que d'une autre, dussions-nous ne jamais tout expliquer et dût-il rester, après tout notre effort, un dernier point et comme une dernière citadelle irréductible.[27]

Special thanks are due to Professor Alan Steele for his invaluable help in the preparation of this book: whenever there were editorial problems, he never failed to give most generously of his time and advice.

P.H.N.

NOTES

1 *Critique et Vérité,* Editions du Seuil, 1966, p. 48.
2 Mercure de France, 1966. For brief surveys and analyses of the different representatives of *la nouvelle critique,* see the articles by Jean-Pierre Richard: 'Quelques aspects nouveaux de la critique littéraire en France', in *Le Français dans le Monde,* March 1963, pp. 2–9; and by Jean Starobinski: 'Les Directions nouvelles de la Recherche critique', in *Preuves,* June 1965, pp. 23–32. For a hostile rejoinder to the 'new critics', see Raymond Picard: *Nouvelle critique ou nouvelle imposture,* Pauvert, 1965.
3 *Selected Essays,* 1932; p. 287 of the 1948 edition (Faber & Faber).
4 Art. cit., p. 5 (my italics).
5 *Essais de psychologie contemporaine: Flaubert,* quoted in Roger Fayolle: *La Critique,* Armand Colin, 1964, p. 128.
6 Fayolle, op. cit., pp. 303–4.
7 Cf. Mallarmé's words to Degas: 'Ce n'est pas avec des idées qu'on fait des sonnets, Degas, c'est avec des mots.' Quoted by R. D. D. Gibson in *Modern French Poets on Poetry,* CUP, 1961, p. 150.
8 Here is Eliot's definition of the objective correlative: 'The only way of expressing emotion in the form of art is by finding an "objective correlative"; in other words, a set of objects, a situation, a chain of events which shall be the formula of that *particular* emotion; such that when the external facts, which must terminate in sensory experience, are given, the emotion is immediately evoked.' (*Selected Essays,* 1948, p. 145.)
   As regards the structure of Molière's plays, see the perceptive comments of W. G. Moore in chapter 5 of his *Molière,* OUP, 1962; cf. pp. 78–9: 'Molière has in this play [*Le Malade Imaginaire*] illustrated an alternative to the usual step-by-step method of building up a dramatic action. The new principle of structure might be said to depend on suffusion rather than on deduction. The loosely linked scenes all stand in direct relation to the master concept; they build up a vision not of a person nor of a plot, but of a choice of attitudes. . . . Perhaps one of the unexplained secrets of our enjoyment of Molière is his art of relating each detail and episode to the complete picture.'
9 *English Critical Essays: Nineteenth Century* (1916), 1945, pp. 415–17.
10 *L'Écrivain et son ombre,* NRF, 1953, p. 14.
11 While Valéry's own pronouncements on this question lack consistency, one might note his following remarks: 'La critique, en tant qu'elle *jugerait,* consisterait dans une comparaison de ce que l'auteur a entendu faire avec ce qu'il a effectivement fait. Tandis que la *valeur* d'une œuvre est une relation singulière et inconstante entre cette œuvre et quelque lecteur, le *mérite* propre et intrinsèque de l'auteur est une relation entre lui-même et son dessein . . . Une critique elle-même idéale prononcerait uniquement sur ce mérite, car on ne peut exiger de quelqu'un que d'avoir accompli ce qu'il s'était proposé d'accomplir.' Quoted in R. D. D. Gibson, op. cit., pp. 18–19.
12 Kra, Paris, 1929, p. 51.
13 *Shakespearian Tragedy,* CUP (1948) 1961, pp. 16–17.
14 *Aspects de Racine,* Nizet, 1954, p. 321.

5 Op. cit., p. 54.

6 Art. cit., p. 6. Charles Mauron, author of *L'Inconscient dans l'œuvre et la vie de Racine*, 1957; *Des métaphores obsédantes au mythe personnel*, 1963, etc., has coined for this kind of criticism the term: *psychocritique*. Both his and M. Richard's approach are severely criticized by Raymond Picard; cf. op. cit., pp. 127, 130 *et passim*: ' "S'enfoncer dans les en-dessous de l'œuvre", comme le recommande M. Richard (*Mallarmé*, p. 17) c'est se mettre en mesure de trouver, peut-être, la source de ce que l'écrivain aurait dit sans le vouloir, mais c'est aussi s'exposer à ne pas comprendre ce qu'il a dit en le voulant. . . . Les "nouveaux critiques", on le sait, ne disposent ni quantitativement, ni qualitativement du matériel qui les autoriserait à tenter cette exploration avec des garanties scientifiques. L'inconscient de l'auteur devient ainsi pour eux l'alibi de leur fantaisie; c'est une sorte de pays d'*Utopie* où, sans craindre d'être contredits, ils situent la justification de leurs interprétations les plus déconcertantes.'

7 *Le Dieu caché*, NRF, 1955.

8 *The Decline of the West*, Allen and Unwin, n.d., vol. 1, p. 7.

9 *La Littérature de l'âge baroque en France: Circé et le Paon*, Corti, 1954.

10 The dangers inherent in Rousset's method are well picked out in a passage of Jean Starobinski's *L'Œil vivant* (Gallimard, 1961). The author makes the point that good criticism has to move constantly between two positions: first, identification with the text ('la participation passionnée à l'expérience sensible et intellectuelle qui se déploie à travers l'œuvre'), and second, a deliberate distancing of the self from the text: this is *le regard surplombant*, which reveals relationships between the text and its *alentours* (historical, social, biographical). But here is the problem: 'Or voici l'écueil: le contexte est si vaste, les relations si nombreuses que le regard se sent saisi d'un secret désespoir; jamais il ne rassemblera tous les éléments de cette totalité qui s'annonce à lui . . . L'œuvre s'évanouit à mesure que le regard prétend embrasser, dans le monde social ou dans la vie de l'auteur, davantage de faits corrélatifs' (pp. 25–7).

1 Quoted in Gibson, op. cit., p. 253. Cf. also Picard, op. cit., p. 144: 'Ce dont nous avons besoin, ce n'est pas d'un répertoire de complexes, si nuancé soit-il, c'est d'une étude détaillée des structures littéraires.'

2 Quoted in Gibson, op. cit., p. 207 n. (*Salon de 1859*).

3 'Question de poésie', in *Variété* III, Gallimard, 1936, p. 54.

4 Op. cit., pp. 51–2.

5 Quoted in Fayolle, op. cit., p. 130.

6 For a fuller list, see the Bibliography; but perhaps the two most famous are M. Roustan's *Précis d'explication française*, Mellottée, 1911; and G. Rudler's *L'Explication française*, Armand Colin, 1948. Both are fairly severely criticized by Professor E. Vinaver in his remarks on *explication* in the inaugural address he gave as President of the Modern Language Association, reprinted in *Modern Languages*, March, 1961. A similar line is more fully developed by P. Mansell Jones in *The Assault on French Literature*, Manchester Univ. Press, 1963.

7 *Nouveaux Lundis*, May 30, 1864: 'Taine'.

*Grahame Castor*

# RONSARD

*Les Amours* 'Quand en songeant ma follastre j'acolle . . .'

Quand en songeant ma follastre j'acolle,
  Laissant mes flancz sus les siens s'allonger,
  Et que d'un bransle habillement leger,
  En sa moytié ma moytié je recolle:
5 Amour adonq si follement m'affolle,
  Qu'un tel abus je ne vouldroy changer,
  Non au butin d'un rivage estranger,
  Non au sablon qui jaunoye en Pactole.
  Mon dieu, quel heur, & quel contentement,
10   M'a fait sentir ce faux recollement,
  Changeant ma vie en cent metamorphoses:
  Combien de fois doulcement irrité,
    Suis-je ore mort, ore resuscité,
    Parmy l'odeur de mile & mile roses?

I HAVE CHOSEN this particular sonnet for comment because it seems to me to be characteristic in a number of ways of Ronsard's most successful poetry. Principally, perhaps, it expresses that mood of joyous delight which is one of the most marked features of Ronsard's poetry in the 1550s – odes, sonnets, and hymns alike. But the sonnet also exhibits a quality which is manifested in Ronsard's poetry at all stages of his career, in his early odes no less than in the sonnets he wrote in the last year of his life – namely the capacity to weave almost transparently simple language and imagery into a richly sensuous texture which makes the reader particularly aware of what Valéry has called the 'forme sensible' of poetic language.[1]

The sonnet first appeared in the collection entitled *Les Amours de P. de Ronsard Vandomoys*, which was published in 1552.[2] In 1560, in the first collected edition of Ronsard's poetry, it formed part of the first book of *Amours*, and it remained in that section in the later collected editions until 1578, when it was transferred (along with half-a-dozen other sonnets from the 1552 *Amours*) to a new section entitled *Les Amours Diverses*. Finally, in the collected edition of 1584, the last to be published before Ronsard's death, it disappeared entirely.[3] But it is important not only to 'place' the poem in terms of the dates of its publication and of the editions in which it appeared, but also to recognize the context of literary tradition in which it is set, and to be aware of the conventional themes which Ronsard is using as foundations for the building of his own poem.

The theme of the *songe amoureux* is in fact one that occurs quite frequently in poetry with which Ronsard was well acquainted. It is used on a number of occasions in the *Greek Anthology*; it appears in the work of Italian petrarchist poets, and it appears also in neo-Latin poetry.[4] The lover dreams that his desire for the woman whose beauty enslaves him – a desire which in real life remains unfulfilled – is nevertheless fulfilled for one brief and delightful period, in the dream. Clearly, the poet can give various emphases to this theme. He may dwell on the fleeting nature of the dream and the insubstantiality of the happiness which it brings. He may emphasize the bittersweet quality of his happiness, in as much as it is inevitably mingled with an awareness that this is a transitory happiness and, moreover, that it is illusory and false; or the relief and delight that the dream brings may be emphasized in contrast with the *peine* which the lover normally suffers as a result of his love for a *fiere et cruelle maistresse*.

The imagined physical presence of the woman may be evoked with great vividness, in order to accentuate the difference between her remoteness in real life and her friendly complaisance in the dream; and sometimes the ecstasy experienced in the dream is taken as an indication of how infinitely more delightful will be the union of the lovers when it takes place in reality. On the other hand, the woman may remain more of a spiritual than a physical presence, an object of reverent adoration, but one who now acknowledges and reciprocates the poet's love.

Ronsard himself uses several of these possibilities. The *songe amoureux* is a recurring theme in his love-poetry, both as the principal subject of a number of sonnets, and also as a minor theme, briefly alluded to or evoked, in other poems. In sonnet XXIX of the 1552 *Amours*, for instance ('Si mille œilletz, si mille liz j'embrasse . . .'), he presents first in metaphorical and then in generalized terms the joy which he owes to his 'Songe divin', and ends by stressing the disappointment which supervenes when the dream disappears, 'comme au vent s'esvanouit la nuë'.[5] The theme appears again in the next sonnet of the collection, but here the poet wonders whether the image of his 'Dame' which he sees and embraces is reality or illusion; and he appeals to the vision to linger a while, so that even if not in fact, at least in his dream he can embrace her 'Toute une nuict'.[6] Sonnet CLIX, on the other hand, evokes very powerfully the physical delights of the poet's dream; there is no direct reference to its possible illusoriness, nor is the poet presented as awaking into disappointment.[7] As Henri Weber notes, this is a poem which conveys very beautifully 'la chaleur d'une après-midi d'été qui invite au sommeil et favorise le rêve voluptueux'.[8] Finally, we have the opposite extreme in one of the *Sonets pour Helene* (II, xxiii), where the falseness of the dream-image is very heavily stressed. Hélène's coming to the poet in his sleep brings him relief from torment: 'Je fusse mort d'ennuy sans ta forme douteuse', but he is quite clear that this is all so much illusion and deceit. A deliberately flat, almost bitter tone dominates the sonnet, culminating in the last line in a thoroughly ironical *sententia*: 'S'abuser en amour n'est pas mauvaise chose'.[9]

In the present sonnet Ronsard is clearly concerned to convey above all the delights which the poet's dream brings. There is no sense of any contrast between the dream and waking reality – the poet accepts his dream, in an almost matter-of-fact tone: 'Quand en songeant ma follastre j'acolle', and does not question its validity. Throughout the poem the only kind of reality to be presented is the poet's dream, a product of his imagination made real in words.

Indeed, a certain 'realism' forms the keynote of the opening quatrain, where the poet presents the erotic content of his dream in a disarmingly direct and straightforward manner. The mood established is in large part one of languorous ease. The participial phrase in the second line, extending and particularizing the implications of 'j'acolle', contributes importantly to the creation of an atmosphere of extreme relaxation, as the poet yields, almost passively, to the pull of his senses, 'Laissant [ses] flancz sus les siens s'allonger'. But the quatrain also expresses the poet's exuberant delight. It is conveyed for instance in the playful word *follastre*, with which the poet's mistress first appears in the poem,[10] and which the use of the possessive adjective makes into a gentle, caressing endearment. There is delight, too, in the poet's lingering over the most intense moment of his experience, taking pleasure in his own skill as a lover (l. 3). And there is delight in the neatly turned joke at the end of the quatrain, where with delicious wit the poet uses a word taken from the terminology of neo-platonic theories of love in order to add precision to the account of his physical love-making.[11]

The whole of the first quatrain leads up syntactically and emotionally to the climax in the fifth line – 'Amour adonq si follement m'affolle'. The full and rounded sounds, forming intricate patterns of repetition, help to suggest an atmosphere of rich sensuousness.[12] The line reduplicates, and thereby enriches (in the technical sense) its own rhyme, 'si follement m'affolle'; and in the process it echoes the rather similar near-reduplication of line 1, 'ma follastre j'acolle', recalling and reinforcing for the reader all the delight evoked in the earlier line. Indeed the verbal texture of the poem is particularly closely woven at this point, so that each vowel and each consonant echoes in varying degrees an earlier sound, and the whole line seems to intensify and prolong the mood created by its predecessors.[13]

This mood is sustained throughout the remainder of the quatrain in the poet's expression of preference for his dream over all the rich plunder brought back from a distant land, or over all the gold that brightly gleams in the bed of the river Pactole.[14] These things, representing the highest imaginable point of material wealth, he rejects. Yet through this figure of paralipsis (i.e. the device of drawing attention to something by affecting to pass it by without notice) the poet incorporates into his poem all the suggestions of magnificence and luxury surrounding precisely those things which he claims he would *not* exchange for his dream, 'abus' though it may be.[15] By being caught up into the argument of the poem in this way, the richly visual associations of these two lines help to express the sumptuous aura of the dream itself.

The sonnet has now completed the first part of its development. It has risen through the narrative presentation of the poet's dream in the opening quatrain to the climax of line 5, and this climax has been sustained, in the poet's expression of the supreme importance of his dream, to the end of the second quatrain. At this point the sonnet changes perspective, and the present tense of the earlier lines becomes a perfect tense, as the poet begins now to reflect upon the nature of his experience.[16] It is clearly an almost ecstatic experience, in which the sensations of the dream and the sensations of the embrace are intertwined and fused. The erotic elements of the experience cannot be separated from the dream. The *recollement* is a 'faux recollement', that is to say it is a dream-experience, and the fact that it is dreamt is an essential part of its total quality. Hence the poet makes no reference here to what the equivalent *actual* erotic experience might be like. What happens in the dream is not used to suggest how much more delightful it would be to embrace 'ma follastre' in reality; nor does the poet present himself as drawing consolation from his dream for the disappointments he suffers in real life; nor does he feel regret that the *recollement* is mere illusion. In this sonnet comparison or contrast with reality has no part to play. The word *faux* seems to have no negating force; it does not destroy the value of the embrace for the poet, but serves rather to bring the two aspects of his experience fully together. It is as though the particular quality of his erotic sensations here can be conveyed to the reader only through a presentation of his dreaming state.

What dream and embrace have in common is the kind of languorous physicality which I have suggested was already present in line 2. In the tercets this sensation becomes completely dominant, as the poet recalls, in an exclamation of pleasure, the delight which he has experienced – 'quel heur [= bonheur] . . . quel contentement'. As in the opening lines of the poem, so here too a participial phrase extends the sense of what has gone before, and helps to create the atmosphere of great languor, particularly through the richly evocative word *metamorphoses*, with all its Ovidian associations. The poet seems to sink into a state in which he is freed from the limitations of his individual self. The sensation of metamorphosis is in part the product of his dream, this half-physical, half-visionary state made up of shifting images and sensations which continually dissolve and reform. But it also describes the precise quality of the ecstatic experience which he is trying to convey. Once more the dream and the embrace are presented as an indissoluble unity.

In the final tercet the poet develops the presentation of his ecstasy even further. He now hovers, uncertainly but delightfully, between activity and relaxation, in an ambivalent state which seems to partake both of sleeping and of waking, neither fully one nor fully the other. The poet relives an experience which is composed of contrasted states. It is both an alternation of the two states, in which the poet is 'ore mort, ore resuscité', and also a simultaneous experiencing of them, for he is 'doulcement irrité', stimulated almost to the point of pain, but gently, delightfully.[17] These opposites are reconciled in the final evocation of ecstasy in line 14, which forms the emotional and sensual culmination of the poem, the fullest and most delicate expression of the poet's *songe amoureux*.

The whole range of the use of rose-symbolism in Western European love-poetry, as expressing an ideal of womanly beauty, lies behind Ronsard's naming of the flower, and some of the rich associations of this image, however imperfectly remembered they may be by the reader, are drawn into the poem, as the word 'roses', the final sound of the final line, echoes through his mind and lingers there, hauntingly. Through the symbolism of the rose the poem returns to the loved woman, whose presence had been so directly evoked in the first quatrain. But here the scent of the roses serves also, very strikingly, as a metaphor for the poet's whole experience of dreaming.

Ronsard brings into his poem a superabundance of roses, but he has chosen to present them only through their scent, perhaps the most intensely sensuous manifestation of their physical presence. The scent of the roses epitomizes and heightens the *languissant* atmosphere in which so much of the poem has been bathed, so that all the sensual richness of the experience which the poet has been evoking becomes concentrated in this one line. Here the roses are not just symbols of beauty, nor simply visual images of beauty; more than this, their presence in the poem seems to create for the reader a very immediate sensation of beauty. The poem seems to move beyond the particular physical world of lovers' embraces and languorous dreams which the poet has been evoking so far, into an infinitely expanding world of sensuously experienced beauty, 'Parmy l'odeur de mile & mile roses'.[18]

As so often in Ronsard's best love-poetry, something vigorously alive and fresh has been made out of themes and images which are in themselves completely conventional. Ronsard, like most sixteenth-century poets, did not try to surprise his readers by offering them the unfamiliar; instead he gave them the pleasure of recognizing in his work elements which they already knew well from their reading of other poetry. Ronsard's supreme skill lies in his ability to clothe the commonplace themes and images in words which then seem to take on a sensuous existence in their own right, embodying in rich and subtle patterns of sound and association the beauty of which the poet writes.

NOTES

1 P. Valéry, 'Poésie et pensée abstraite', in *Variété*, 'Théorie poétique et esthétique' (*Œuvres*, Bibliothèque de la Pléiade edition, 1, 1326). This essay contains a most illuminating discussion of the relation between language as an instrument of practical living, and language as a poetic medium, with its own sensuous properties, independent of the purely intellectual meaning which it may convey.

2 I have used the text given in Paul Laumonier's critical edition of the *Œuvres complètes*, Paris, 1914–67, t. IV, p. 100. All references to Ronsard's works are to this edition.

3 One can only guess at Ronsard's reasons for moving and later suppressing this poem. However, it seems possible to infer from the kind of revision he made in various poems and from his suppression of others that he may have been attempting in 1578, and even more so in 1584, to give each of his collections of love-poetry a certain basic consistency of tone, and that there was no longer a place, in his view, for 'Quand en songeant . . .'. For a full discussion of this question, see F. Desonay, *Ronsard poète de l'amour*, Brussels, 1952–9, t. I, p. 220 ff.

4 Other sixteenth-century French poets besides Ronsard found the *songe amoureux* an attractive theme; see the valuable discussion in H. Weber, *La Création poétique au XVIe siècle en France*, Paris, 1956, t. I, pp. 356–66, where the author analyses and compares poems by Sannazar, Bembo, Magny, Baïf, du Bellay, Ronsard, and Grévin. References to its appearance in neo-Latin poetry can be found in Ronsard, *Oeuvres complètes*, t. IV, p. 33, n. 4.

5 *Œuvres complètes*, t. IV, pp. 32–3.
6 *Œuvres complètes*, t. IV, pp. 33–4.
7 *Œuvres complètes*, t. IV, pp. 151–2.
8 *La Création poétique*, t. I, p. 363.
9 *Œuvres complètes*, t. XVII, pp. 264–5.
10 Littré's definition is particularly apt here: 'qui aime à faire gaiement de petites folies'.
11 The word *moytié*, as the commentators have pointed out, is an allusion to the myth of the androgyne recounted by Aristophanes in Plato's *Symposium*. According to this myth the original human beings were of a double nature; as a punishment for having launched an attack upon the gods, Zeus divided each of them into two separate beings, who thenceforth went through the world in search of their corresponding other halves. For an account of the particular emphases which this myth received during the sixteenth century in France, see R. V. Merrill, 'The Pléiade and the Androgyne', in *Comparative Literature*, 1 (1949), 2, 97–112.
12 This, too, is a line full of neo-platonic associations. For the neo-platonists love, like poetic inspiration, is a fury, a madness in which the soul reaches upwards, aspiring towards that perfect, spiritual realm from which it originally came down into the body. Here the neo-platonic associations do not play against the surface meaning of the line, as they do in line 4, but serve rather to give it greater resonance. (For an account of the neo-platonic theory of love as it was understood in France, see J. Festugière, *La philosophie de l'amour de Marsile Ficin et son influence sur la littérature française au XVI^e siècle*, Paris, 1941.)
13 It is perhaps worth noting that what might crudely be termed the musical effects of this poem are achieved almost entirely through the sound-patterns of the words, and hardly at all through the rhythm, which remains a relatively inconspicuous element. Not that this detracts in any way from the aesthetic merits of the poem; but it does provoke the thought that here is perhaps one of the limitations of the decasyllabic form, at least as it is used by Ronsard, for he seems to handle the alexandrine with much more rhythmical subtlety. (See Ronsard's own discussion of the alexandrine and what the sixteenth century called 'vers communs' in the *Abbregé de l'art poétique François*, *Œuvres complètes*, t. XIV, pp. 23–7.)
14 The river in Lydia whose sandy bed, according to the legend, turned to gold after king Midas had bathed in its waters. '. . . sablon qui jaunoye' (l. 8): 'sablon à reflets jaunes'.
15 'Abus' here has its common sixteenth-century meaning of *erreur, tromperie, illusion*.
16 In making this clear division between the quatrains and the tercets Ronsard is of course following the usual pattern of the French sonnet in the sixteenth century.
17 This phrase may perhaps be taken as a half-echo of a familiar theme in petrarchist love-poetry, namely the paradox that love is *doucement amère, amèrement douce*; and perhaps it was in order to eliminate this allusion that in the 1578 edition Ronsard replaced *irrité* by *agité*, which has much the

same meaning of moved, or roused but without any implication of possible pain. Pain seems to have no part in the experience which Ronsard is presenting in this poem.

18 It is difficult to understand why, as early as 1553, Ronsard should have replaced this last line by 'Entre cent lis, & cent vermeilles roses', where so much is lost by comparison with the earlier version. The repeated 'cent' picks up the 'cent' in line 11, and disconcertingly draws one's attention to the actual number, while 'l'odeur', on which so much of the power of the original line depended, disappears entirely in favour of the distractingly visual 'vermeilles'. It may be, however, that Ronsard felt it important to reintroduce at the climax of the sonnet the nasal vowels which form such a dominant pattern in the first twelve lines.

*Source*
Pierre de Ronsard (1524–85): *Les Amours,* in *Œuvres complètes,* ed. P. Laumonier, Paris, 1914–67, t. IV, p. 100.

M. A. Screech

RABELAIS
Le Tiers Livre de Pantagruel

« . . . Tu seras bien poyvré, homme de bien. – Je seray (respondit Panurge) tes fortes fiebvres quartaines, vieulx fol, sot, mal plaisant que tu es. Quand tous coqus s'assembleront, tu porteras la baniere. Mais dont me vient ce cyron icy entre ces deux doigtz?' Cela disoit
5 tirant droict vers Her Trippa les deux premiers doigtz ouvers en forme de deux cornes et fermant on poing tous les aultres. Puys dict à Epistemon: 'Voyez cy le vray Ollus de Martial, lequel tout son estude adonnoit à observer et entendre les maulx et miseres d'aultruy. Ce pendent sa femme tenoit le brelant. Il, de son cousté, paouvre plus
10 que ne feut Irus, au demourant glorieux, oultrecuydé, intolerable plus que dix sept diables, en un mot πτωχαλαζών, comme bien proprement telle peaultraille de belistrandiers nommoient les anciens. Allons, laissons ici ce fol, enraigé, mat de cathene, ravasser tout son saoul avecques ses diables privez. Je croirois tantost que les diables voulus-
15 sent servir un tel marault. Il ne sçait le premier trait de philosophie, qui est CONGNOIS TOY, et, se glorifiant veoir un festu en l'œil d'aultruy, ne void une grosse souche laquelle luy poche les deux œilz. C'est un tel polypragmon que descript Plutarche. C'est une aultre Lamie, laquelle, en maisons estranges, en public, entre le com-
20 mun peuple, voyant plus penetramment qu'un oince, en sa maison propre estoit plus aveugle qu'une taulpe, chés soy rien ne voioyt, car, retournant du dehors en son privé, oustoit de sa teste ses œilz, exemptiles comme lunettes, et les cachoit dedans un sabot attaché darriere la porte de son logis.' »

To APPRECIATE Rabelais we must first understand him. Then, his genius for handling word, character, situation, idea, myth, can work upon our sensitivity. Four centuries have however obscured what was once common and authoritative knowledge. For an author with less to say this would be less of an obstacle, but Rabelais chose to make a definite religio-philosophical system the backcloth of his comedy. This system, once clear, is by now opaque and recondite. In Rabelais's novels, a Classical-Christian syncretism – embracing most human knowledge, including law and medicine – provides the norms against which all must be judged. Patient erudition and literary sensitivity are required to recognize and elucidate these norms. Without them, one can fall into gross error. One could even take Panurge's eulogy of the codpiece seriously – many have – unless one recognizes the silliness of Galen's ideas when judged against the norm of Hippocratic truth. It is often difficult to understand Rabelais in the most ordinary sense of the verb 'to understand': we do not know enough always to recognize his archaisms, for example, for what they are. This is true, though less so, of literary devices such as lists, satirical eulogies, farcical developments and so on, which ought first to be appreciated in their historical context.

The *Tiers Livre* is Rabelais's most intellectual book, a contribution to polite letters intended for *gens sçavans & studieux*. A work *non moins utile que delectable*, it belongs to that highest category, *qui miscuit utile dulci*, combining pleasure with moral stimulus.[1] Unlike some of his earliest work, it may be judged by the highest standards.

The words quoted are Panurge's reply to Her Trippa, the *mathematicus* of the *Tiers Livre*. Panurge now has little in common with his namesake of 1532, and Rabelais defines his new role in the opening chapters of the book. Some writers, preoccupied with the common man in a way that would have baffled Rabelais, see Panurge as *l'homme moyen sensuel*, treated sympathetically. This is false. He is the butt of the farce, a wordy fool, endued with *scientia* not *sapientia*. His windy rhetoric is always opposed to the normative wisdom of the book. Above all, he is dominated by φιλαυτία (self-love), no single vice but, according to Socrates, the fountain-head of them all. In chapter 5 he is condemned with a verse of St Paul against the norm of ἀγάπη (Christian Love, held to be the contrary of φιλαυτία); in chapter 7, by a normative Stoico-platonic interpretation of Romans, 15:5; in chapter 8, for Galenic sophistry; in chapter 10, for not knowing his will; in chapter 11, for favouring the diabolical use of dice; in chapter 12, for thinking he can flout legal authority and appeal against Fortune; in chapter 13, for superstition; in chapter 14, for failure to interpret his dream aright; in chapter 15, explicitly and on the authority of Æsop and Erasmus, for φιλαυτία;[2] in chapter 16, for superstitious trust in prophetic old women; in chapter 19, for diabolical seduction; in chapter 20, for obstinacy; in 22, for monkish superstition; in 23 and 24, again, for diabolical superstition. The isolation of Panurge is emphasized with the help of the key axiom, *Tout vray à tout vray consonne* (chapter 20). The hero condemns Panurge fundamentally: *L'esprit maling vous seduyt*; and later with punning earnestness: *Philautie et amour de soy vous deçoit*.[3] Rabelais's achievement is to make this awesome condemnation through laughter.

The confrontation with Her Trippa adds a new and subtle comic condemnation. Her Trippa (possibly a caricature of H. C. Agrippa),[4] is a monomaniac *mathematicus*, whose magical lore Rabelais may not sympathize with but does not condemn. There is in this chapter an element of the tug-o'-war which comes when Greek meets Greek. Straightway, Her Trippa recognizes that Panurge has the *metaposcopie d'un coqu* – a good start, which puts him on the side of all the others, quite delightful if one knows that metaposcopy foretells the future by studying the forehead, which bears the horns. The comic setting thus established, the farce develops, with Panurge playing the Pot calling the Kettle smutty. Panurge, the cuckold elect, accuses Her Trippa of just that fate; consistently mocked for that self-ignorance which accompanies self-love, he rounds upon the *mathematicus* he has chosen to consult, accusing him of that very defect. The erudition of Panurge here, which today could seem quite appalling, was quite accessible then. The actual accusations of cuckoldom draw upon contemporary material.

*Tu seras bien poyvré, homme de bien*. With this colloquial expression, Her Trippa ends his judgement of Panurge; like all the others consulted, he sees Panurge as the man to be cuckolded, beaten and robbed by his future wife. Better still, his wife will give him the pox (by strange convention a comic disease) since *être poivré* means to suffer the indignity of a delousing treatment for the pox, an expression borrowed from the practice of dusting hawks with pepper against the scab.[5]

*Je seray (respondit Panurge) tes fortes fiebvres quartaines.* The technique of picking up words from the last speaker is one Rabelais owes to farcical dialogue. It emphasizes that Panurge's first reaction is to make an aggressive retort, since *tes fortes fiebvres quartaines* is only loosely dependent, in sense, on *je seray.* Allusions to quartan fever form part of a well-defined group of serio-comic imprecations. In *Gargantua, Leurs fiebvres quartaines* is evidently so used.[6] The strengthened form, alliterating *fortes* with *fièvres,* has already been used in chapter 6 of the *Tiers Livre.*[7] Other examples in Rabelais suggest that the construction here follows a colloquial formula. In the *Quart Livre,* Dindenault cries, *Tes fortes fiebvres quartaines, lourdault, sot que tu es.* This probably explains why Rabelais inserted the word *sot* in the revised version of his text quoted above, the formula perhaps seeming lopsided without the *sot que tu es.* The expression sounds popular and spoken, but it had its place in traditional farces (in the *Nouveau Pathelin* for example)[8] and consciously recalled olden times. Pasquier writes: 'Quand nous voulons mal à un homme, les plus beaux de nos souhaits, est de luy désirer *ses fièvres quartaines;* ce qui n'a pas été mis en usage sans raison par nos anciens . . .'[9]

The imprecation is immediately followed by another insult, this time not traditional but *à la mode,* echoing a current song. Brantôme knew it: 'Du temps du Roy François fut une vielle chanson, que j'ay ouy conter à une fort honneste ancienne dame, qui disoit:

Mais quand viendra la saison
Que les cocus s'assembleront,
Le mien ira davant, qui portera la bannière;
Les autres suivront aprés, le vostre au darrière . . .'

Brantôme's testimony stops one assuming that this sort of song was merely popular; it was probably known to Margaret of Navarre, to whom the *Tiers Livre* is dedicated. Cuckolds are frequently thought of as forming a *confrerie* (Brotherhood, Guild) – Molière can still get a laugh out of it. The banner is one borne in solemn procession at a religious assembly of the Brotherhood. The idea is intrinsically comic; by alluding to the song, Rabelais profits from the comedy, without having to insist.[10]

In keeping with the farcical tone, we pass from current song to current gesture. With intentional superfluity of detail, Rabelais explains the sign which accompanies Panurge's aggressive question, *Mais dont me vient ce cyron icy entre ces deux doigtz*? The question is aggressive in itself; one pretends 'that a worme makes the place itch, but with a purpose to make hornes at the partie of whom the question is asked'.[11] The laborious explanation is amusing, since the action always went with the question. It would be similarly comic today (though less so, and more wilfully vulgar), if one were to explain in detail to English readers the coarse erotic gesture made with two fingers. Explaining contemptuous or erotic gesture is a technique Rabelais was early attracted to (in *Pantagruel* 13, for example). Here, more than in *Pantagruel*, the comedy lies also in Rabelais's adopting, as storyteller, a mask of naïvety.

So Her Trippa is revealingly answered at first with farcical abuse. The rest of the speech is different in tone, but the essential direction is given: Panurge can think of no more wounding reply than to accuse Her Trippa of his own defects.

Fittingly, when he addresses Epistemon (ἐπιστήμων, learned, wise), Panurge pursues his abuse on a humanistic plane and the comedy is more refined. In its entirety, the erudition is borrowed from Erasmus's *Adagia*. In other words, to make his point clear, Rabelais draws on a common fund of proverbial wisdom authoritatively expounded. It is vital to recognize, not the source itself, but the normative quality of the wisdom Panurge is about to abuse.[12] Panurge comically strives to turn against others notions which plainly condemn him. In one way or another he does this throughout the book. Rabelais exploits no less than four adages, from a section principally concerned with self-love. He had already found here a fifth one – Æsop's fabulous condemnation of this basic vice (*Non videmus manticae quod in tergo est*) – and given it unusual prominence at the end of chapter 15 of the *Tiers Livre*.[13] There it clearly prepares the way for the section we are studying, since it is Epistemon who cites it, correctly, against Panurge.[14] Epistemon rounds it all off with a sharp reminder that only through grace is self-love avoidable. For many pages, Panurge has been the embodiment of this truth. When Rabelais returns to the attack again here, he has prepared the ground well, and if we do not understand him, the fault certainly does not lie with him.

*Puys dict à Epistemon*: we may note in passing how indifferent

Rabelais is to verbs of saying used to introduce speeches; as often as not he is content with *dire, répondre, demander* and so on.

*Voyez cy le vray Ollus de Martial*: here Rabelais is following Erasmus's commentary on *Aedibus in nostris quae prava, aut recta geruntur*, a quotation from the Odyssey meaning, more or less, 'what is done crooked or straight at home', but dear to Socrates as a dark saying instructing us to *nolle alta sapere* and to show forth wisdom 'at home' – in our own lives. Erasmus reminds us that Socrates used it to condemn a study of metaphysics and 'mathematics' and to turn us towards moral philosophy.[15] Her Trippa is, of course, a *mathematicus* (for Rabelais as for others a *mathématicien* was a *faiseur d'horoscopes*).[16] But Rabelais wants to weight the dice against Panurge, not against Her Trippa, so this aspect of the adage is underplayed – the adage itself is not textually cited, although it dominates the whole chapter – and another aspect is brought to the fore: that which condemns Panurge as an indiscreet busybody: 'Quo versu monemur,' writes Erasmus, 'quae ad nosipos pertinent, curemus, externa atque aliena ne inquiramus. Quo vitio festiviter Martialis Ollum quendam notat, qui malorum alienorum erat observator curiosissimus, & taxator acerrimus, cum ipse uxorem haberet adulteram . . .'[17] Ollus was, then, a prototype of the Arnolphe of *L'Ecole des Femmes*.

Rabelais is often treated – in ignorance – as though he were a pedant, incorrigibly overloading his text with obscure learning. When one really examines his 'sources', one is struck rather by his economy of means and his ability to select and reject. Here Rabelais prunes the matter, and expands the means of expression through reduplication (*observer et entendre; maulx et miseres*), a technique which owed much to rhetorical ideas of copiousness.[18] Several of Martial's epigrams are directed against Ollus, so Rabelais explains the allusion, without which the sense would certainly not have been clear. With comic insistence Rabelais outdoes both Martial and Erasmus. Erasmus's *cum ipse uxorem haberet adulteram* is deliberately neutral; Martial's *Uxor tibi moecha est* is pithy but subfusc. The colourful exaggeration of Rabelais is reinforced by the drop in tone from literary allusion and balanced elaboration to the colloquial *Ce pendent sa femme tenoit le brelant*, that is, presided over a disorderly house, an expression drawn from card-playing.[19]

The allusion to Irus, inspired by the adjacent adage, *Iro pauperior*, could seem gratuitous, though probably linked in Rabelais's own mind by its sharing a common Homeric origin with *Aedibus in nostris*. But it is not gratuitous at all. It allows Rabelais to glide easily, via Panurge's odd beggarly garb, to Plutarch's πτωχαλαζών, without losing sight of Panurge himself, the prime butt of the comedy. Of Her Trippa's dress we are told little; Panurge, on the other hand, does clearly merit the reproach he applies to Her Trippa. He is, like Irus, both poor and *gloriosus* (boastful); Rabelais will insist, moreover, on this boastfulness.

The comic exaggeration of Panurge's reply is indicated by the flood of words, and also by the repetition of superlative comparisons introduced by *plus que*: 'plus que ne feut Irus'; 'plus que dix sept diables' and, later on, 'plus . . . qu'un oince' and 'plus aveugle qu'une taulpe'. The grammatical parallelism of the first two serves to throw into relief the contrast between the dignity of the two expressions: the first, recalling Homer; the second, *intolerable plus que dix-sept diables* (apart from Rabelais's affectation of mock numerical precision), falling wilfully into the colloquial bathos of the *passe-partout* comparison.

'*En un mot*, πτωχαλαζών' (braggart beggar) might today raise an uninvited smile. It seems to betray an unconscious pedantry in Rabelais, not Panurge. Once more, the reaction is wrong. There was no barrier here for the reader Rabelais had most in mind. Already Rabelais had alluded, without a smile, to the 'mot vulgaire, ἐχθρῶν ἄδωρα δῶρα', an Erasmian adage stressing that enemies' gifts are no gifts and indeed 'vulgaire' for *gens sçavans & doctes*, however much it may baffle others. [20] In this sort of book Rabelais was as free to strew his text with Classical matter as Montaigne was. And, once more, far from piling up the erudition, Rabelais lightens it. He has now switched to Erasmus's commentary on *Messe tenus propria vive*, by which we are exhorted to live within our own harvest. In place of Erasmus's detailed allusion in his explanation of this adage Rabelais speaks generally of 'les Anciens',[21] so concentrating our attention on the evocative word *peaultraille*, 'scrapings or offals of skinnes, & hence a rascal' (as Cotgrave renders it, in his *Dictionarie of the French and English Tongues*), a word already archaic. This he associates with *belistrandier*, a portmanteau word, of his own creation probably, formed by conflating *belistre* (beggar) with *truand* (beggarly knave). The recourse to archaism and portmanteau neologism within a single phrase leaves us with the impression that language has to be stretched to the limit to accommodate Panurge's folly. This impression is strengthened in the next sentence, where Panurge glosses *fol* (this time with its full sense of raving mad, *enraigé*), by drawing on yet another learned language, Italian.[22] This restoration of the sense of madness to the word *fol* restores also to *ravasser* its meaning 'to rave' – often it was used to mean 'to talke idly' (Cotgrave again). From madness to *diables* is a short step (Rabelais makes the same step five pages later: 'va, fol enraigé, au diable'). We are not dealing with a mere cliché. Throughout the *Tiers Livre*, Panurge talks of the Devil. That he should see Her Trippa preoccupied with familiar spirits is not surprising: he thought even the saintly Raminagrobis was so preoccupied. This is an aspect of his own diabolical seduction, clear in the light of his reiteration of the word *diable* two chapters before this one. Rabelais has brought us from the colloquial imprecision of *dix-sept diables* to the real thing: 'Je croirois tantost que les diables voulussent servir un tel marault'. A *mathematicus* can indeed be an *invocator daemonum*.[23] But Panurge is in no position to mock him – and no one else does. . . .

We now come to the densest and most subtle part. By throwing the Delphic adage CONGNOIS TOY in Her Trippa's teeth, instead of taking it to heart himself, Panurge completes his comic self-condemnation. This adage, Socratic as well as Delphic, reminds us that Socrates, though never named, is never absent from this section. Panurge – of all people – would like to pass for a *Socrates redivivus*, as though the principal obstacle to self-knowledge were not self-love. On *Nosce teipsum* Erasmus comments: 'Nam hinc omnis vitae pestis oritur, quod sibi quisque blanditur, & quantum aliis praeter aequum detrahit, tantum sibi philautiae vitio praeter meritum tribuit'. Moreover, by placing this adage after *In tuum ipsius sinum inspue* and then saying that *Nosce teipsum* pertained *ad eam sententiam*, Erasmus gave an authoritative slant to it.[24] The boastfulness it can also condemn is indicated clearly by Rabelais's using both *glorieux* and *se glorifiant*. Then, without interruption, we are led to the Gospel: *Festucam ex alterius oculum ejicere*. Erasmus saw this as having the same sense as *Non videmus manticae, quod in tergo est*. Rabelais's syncretism – and Erasmus's – is too vast to touch on here. Stylistically one should note how Rabelais elaborates the baldness of Matthew, 7:3, 'but considerest not the beam that is in thine own eye'.[25] The *beam* becomes 'une *grosse* souche'; the singular *eye*, 'les deux œilz'. Renaissance stylists often saw the Bible as being deliberately plain, needing elaboration this way.[26] The verb *pocher* serves another purpose. In place of the barren locative notion of the original, Rabelais introduces a vigorous active verb, which allows him to play on the expression *œil poché*. This raises a smile and, at the same time, anchors the erudition in a contemporary context.

From Socrates and Christ to Plutarch: an excellent Renaissance synthesis. But once more, why dig up *polypragmon*? A large part of an author's task is to place the right word in its perfect context. This Rabelais has done. πολυπράγμων is a word untranslatable into Latin and French, though *curiosus* and *curieux* are made to serve. Because of Aulus Gellius, the notion 'that the Greeks have a word for it' is likely to be present in any reader's mind, when he turns to Plutarch's περὶ πολυπραγμοσύνης.[27] Rabelais was not to know that this particular graecism was not to catch on. Others he used did. Anyway Rabelais wrote for an increasingly Classical public, not one increasingly closed to Classical wisdom. Even now, *Polypragmon* should not bother anyone whose reading extends to *The Water Babies*. It was, until the late nineteenth century, *the* word for a particular sort of busybody.[28]

> Voyez cy le vray Ollus . . .
> C'est un tel polypragmon . . .
> C'est une aultre Lamie . . .

The parallelism is striking, and in each case (since Panurge is an erudite fool), we are given an Ancient literary commonplace to reflect on. The reference to Lamia is again inspired by Erasmus's comment on *Aedibus in nostris*. But Erasmus talks of *Lamiae* in the plural, λαμία meaning enchantress. Since Plutarch uses the word as a singular proper-name, Rabelais was evidently led back to the actual source (which, on other evidence, he can be shown to have known). In Amyot's translation the passage reads:

> Mais maintenant, ainsi comme les fables disent, que la fée Lamia ne fait que chanter quand elle est en sa maison aveugle, d'autant qu'elle a serré ses yeux en un vaisseau à part: mais quand elle sort dehors, elle se les remet & veoit alors: aussi chascun de nous . . .

The meaning is explained thus, and is most relevant to our understanding Panurge here:

Voyla pourquoi le curieux [πολυπράγμων] est plus utile à ses ennemis qu'il n'est pas à luy mesme, d'autant qu'il descouvre, met en evidence, & leur monstre, ce dont il se fault garder, & ce qu'ils doivent corriger, & cependant il ne voit pas la plus part de ce qui est chez luy, tant il est esblouy à regarder ce qui est au dehors . . .²⁹

Rabelais jettisons everything in Erasmus that does not serve his end. Moreover, he inverts the action of Lamia. In both Erasmus and Plutarch it is above all a question of putting in eyes to go outdoors; in Rabelais, with a significant difference of emphasis, eyes are taken out at home. Φιλαυτία, we may remember, is a blind love of oneself, a *caecus amor sui* . . . Erasmus's *foris sunt oculatissimae* is not of course underplayed; quite the reverse ('en maisons estranges'; 'en public'; 'entre le commun peuple'). Similarly Lamia's shrewdness of critical vision is stressed, independently of Erasmus, with the standard Classical comparison, lynx-eyed (the rare form *oince* for *once* being difficult to explain other than as a provincialism like *ouster* (ôter) and *darrière*). This shrewdness is immediately paralleled to her inner blindness: 'en sa maison propre estoit plus aveugle qu'une taulpe'. 'Blind as a mole' is not a *mot de terroir*, but once more a Classical adage. With its help, Rabelais can remind the reader that he is talking of inner, spiritual, blindness. As Erasmus wrote under *Talpa caecior*, it can be used of those who are physically unable to see, but is better applied to those who *minime judicant*. He adds, 'Nam jucundior est metaphora, si quidem ad animum transferatur'.³⁰

In this way – and particularly by means of the inversion – Rabelais gives most emphasis to the blindness at home, so vital in a section drawing upon Socrates' '*Aedibus in nostris* quae prava, aut recta geruntur'. *En sa maison propre – talpa caecior – chés soy rien ne voioyt – retournant du dehors en son privé*: Rabelais points his meaning with the utmost clarity. In the same spirit, the act of taking out the eyes is thrown into relief by the use of the very rare word *exemptile*, and by the total absence of any reference to putting them back again. The resulting blindness is further emphasized by comic precision. In Erasmus the Lamiae simply *domi oculos reconditos habent*. In Plutarch, the eyes are 'serré[s] . . . en un vaisseau à part'. In Rabelais the domestic blindness is complete: the exemptile eyes are not put away, they are hidden, as in Erasmus; the hiding place is unexpected, a clog, suggestive of close rustic avarice;³¹ the clog itself is both secure (*attaché*) and hidden behind the front door – that is, at the very point of homecoming. *Aedibus in nostris,* indeed . . .

This is intellectual comedy at its best. Rabelais has no need of a *raisonneur* to direct our thoughts. What we have here is farce raised almost miraculously to the heights of moral laughter.

NOTES

1 See Francis the First's *Privilège* (*Tiers Livre,* TLF vol. 102, p. 3 seq.). Horace, *Ad Pis.,* 343/4 is the standard form of the highest praise during the Renaissance. The allusion was not applied to Rabelais's work (as far as I know) before this *Privilège.* Although read back into the previous books, it really applies especially to the *Tiers Livre.*

2 Erasmus, *Adagia,* I.VII.XC.

3 *Tiers Livre,* ch. 29.

4 The matter of the chapter is not borrowed from Agrippa. If Rabelais is alluding to him, it is as author of *De occulta philosophia* not of *De vanitate omnium scientiarum et excellentia Verbi Dei.*

5 See Sainéan, *Langue de Rabelais,* Paris 1922, t. 11, p. 367. I borrow from this study at other points also.

6 *Gargantua* (Critical edition) Paris, 1913–, p. 335.

7 Some preachers hate remarriage, we are told: 'Elles sont (respondit Pantagruel) leurs fortes fiebvres quartaines'.

8 Cf. *Gargantua,* ed. cit. (XXXIX, note 42).

9 E. Pasquier, *Œuvres,* Paris, 1723, t. 11, col. 263.

10 Brantôme, *Dames galantes,* Garnier, 1947, p. 128; Molière, *Ecole des Femmes,* Act. IV sc. ix, line 1,276.

11 References in *Tiers Livre,* ed. cit.

12 There has been a reaction against source-hunting, which I partly, but only partly, share. It would certainly be healthier if all those who rejected the pursuit possessed the requisite languages. In Rabelais's case 'sources' are certainly worth tracing, as a means to a great end: they enable us to understand him and, as a bonus, can show us how he set about his work of creation. If one did not know that Rabelais drew heavily at this point on the *Adagia,* it would be much harder to convince a certain type of Rabelaisian enthusiast of Rabelais's meaning here. It is hard enough as it is.

13 *Adagia,* I.VII.XC. The Fable is no doubt best known today through La Fontaine's *La Besace.*

14 Panurge completely exemplifies this condemnation, which Epistemon specifically directs at him.

15 See Erasmus, *Adagia,* I.VI.LXXXV; Odyssey, IV, 392 (ὅττι τοι ἐν μεγάροισι κακόν τ'ἀγαθόν τε τέτυκται). Socrates evidently put the emphasis on the *at home.* Good and ill concern the man *at home,* that is, in himself, in his own character. See also Aulus Gellius, *Attic Nights,* XIV, 6, 5.

16 *Tiers Livre,* ch. 37; p. 258.

M.A. SCREECH

17  *Adagia*, I.VI.LXXXV; Martial, *Epig.*, VII, 10.
18  It was also a means of compensating for the poverty of French when rendering Classical ideas.
19  See Cotgrave, s.v. *brelant*.
20  *Tiers Livre*, ch. 14; p. 115. *Adagia*, I.III.XXXVII.
21  *Adagia*, I.VI.XCI. By eating his *blé en herbe* earlier in the book, Panurge had already been shown as failing to 'live within in own harvest'. The word πτωχαλαζών means, as employed in the *Dipnosophists* and expounded by Erasmus, 'fastum cum paupertate conjunctum'. This is another shaft against Panurge, of course.
22  *Matto da catena*: 'mad enough to be chained up'.
23  See Du Fresne, Du Cange and Carpentarius, *Glossarium manuale*, Halae, 1772, s.v.
24  *Adagia*, I.VI.XCIV: 'Jubent enim hominem aliena vitia taxantem, *in suum ipsius sinum inspuere*, tanquam admonentes, ut domesticorum malorum recordatione desinat arrogantius insectari vitam alienam'. Note, again, the insistence on wisdom *at home*, as in *Aedibus in nostris*. These ideas went so close together at the time, that the same emblem was used to symbolize φιλαυτία, *Nosce teipsum* and *Caecus amor sui*, for example (see A. Henkel and A. Schöne, *Emblemata; Handbuch zur Sinnbildkunst des XVI. und XVII. Jahrhunderts*, Stuttgart, 1967, cols. 1627–8).
25  Rabelais certainly cites Matthew 7 because Erasmus did. He may have had the Vulgate in mind. That would not change the point made here.
26  Amongst hundreds of examples, cf. Garnier's allusion in *Les Juifves* to, 'Eyes have they: and see not; Noses have they: and smell not': 'Il a des yeux *ouverts*, toutefois ne voit goutte. Il a *double* narine, et ne respire l'air', and so on.
27  *Attic Nights*, XI, 16: *Quod Graecorum verborum quorundam difficillima est in Latinam linguam mutatio, velut quod Graece dicitur* πολυπραγμοσύνην. The chapter, which arose out of a reading of the *De curiositate*, is quite delightful and memorably human.
28  I quote from my children's copy: Ch. Kingsley, *The Water Babies* (A Prince Charming Colour Book), Ward, Lock and Co., London, s.d., p. 195: 'Then came Tom to the Island of Polupragmosyne. There everyone knows his neighbour's business better than his own; and a very noisy place it is,' and so on.
29  Plutarch, *Œuvres morales et meslées*, Bâle, 1574, p. 62 (= 515F–516A).
30  *Adagia*, I.III.LV.
31  Plutarch uses simply ἀγγεῖον (vessel, jar).

*Source*

François Rabelais (*c.* 1494–1553): *Le Tiers Livre*, ch. 25,
ed. M. A. Screech, Textes Littéraires Français, Geneva, 1964,
pp. 178–80.

*Errata*

p. 33, l. 17, *for* nosipos *read* nosipsos. p. 35, l. 34, for *oculum* read *oculo*.

*Frank P. Bowman*

---

*MONTAIGNE*
*Du Repentir, Essais,* Book III, chapter 2

« Les autres forment l'homme, je le recite, et en represente un particulier, bien mal formé, et lequel si j'avoy à façonner de nouveau, je
ferois, vrayement bien autre qu'il n'est : mes-huy c'est fait. Or les
traits de ma peinture, ne forvoyent point, quoy qu'ils se changent et
5 diversifient. Le monde n'est qu'une branloire perenne : toutes choses
y branlent sans cesse, la terre, les rochers du Caucase, les pyramides
d'Ægypte : et du branle public, et du leur. La constance mesme, n'est
autre chose qu'un branle plus languissant. Je ne puis asseurer mon
objet : il va trouble et chancelant, d'une yvresse naturelle. Je le prens
10 en ce point, comme il est, en l'instant que je m'amuse à luy. Je ne
peints pas l'estre, je peints le passage. Non un passage d'aage en autre,
ou comme dict le peuple, de sept en sept ans : mais de jour en jour,
de minute en minute. Il faut accomoder mon histoire à l'heure. Je
pourray tantost changer, non de fortune seulement, mais aussi d'in-
15 tention : c'est un contre-rolle de divers et muables accidens et d'imaginations irresoluës et, quand il y eschet, contraires : soit que je sois
autre moymesme, soit que je saisisse les subjects, par autres circon-
stances, et considerations. Tant y a, que je me contredits bien à
l'adventure, mais la vérité, comme disoit Demades, je ne la contredy
20 point. Si mon ame pouvoit prendre pied, je ne m'essaierois pas, je
me resoudrois : elle est tousjours en apprentissage, et en espreuve. Je
propose une vie basse, et sans lustre : c'est tout un, on attache aussi
bien toute la philosophie morale, à une vie populaire et privée, que
à une vie de plus riche estoffe : chaque homme porte la forme entiere,
25 de l'humaine condition. Les autheurs se communiquent au peuple par
quelque marque particuliere et estrangiere : moy le premier par mon
estre universel, come Michel de Montaigne : non come grammairien
ou poête ou jurisconsulte. Si le monde se pleint de quoy je parle trop
de moy : je me pleins de quoy il ne pense seulement pas à soy. Mais
30 est-ce raison, que si particulier en usage, je pretende me rendre public
en cognoissance ? Est-il aussi raison, que je produise au monde, où
la façon et l'art, ont tant de credit et de commandement, des effects
de nature crus et simples, et d'une nature encore bien foiblette ? Est-ce
pas faire une muraille sans pierre, ou chose semblable, que de bastir
35 des livres sans science et sans art ? Les fantasies de la musique, sont
conduictes par art, les miennes par sort. Au moins j'ay cecy selon la
discipline, que jamais homme ne traicta subject, qu'il entendit ne
cogneust mieux, que je fay celuy que j'ay entrepris : Et qu'en celuy-là,
je suis le plus sçavant homme qui vive. Secondement que jamais

40 aucun ne penetra en sa matiere plus avant, ny en esplucha plus particu-
lierement les mambres et suites. Et n'arriva plus exactement et plainement, à la fin qu'il s'estoit proposé à sa besoingne. Pour la parfaire,
je n'ay besoing d'y apporter que la fidelité: Celle-là y est, la plus
sincere et pure qui se trouve. Je dy vray, non pas tout mon saoul:
45 mais autant que je l'ose dire: et l'ose un peu plus en vieillissant: car
il me semble que la coustume concede à cet aage, plus de liberté de
bavasser, et d'indiscretion à parler de soy. »

ON A CASUAL first reading, this passage, which opens one of Montaigne's most famous essays, may seem an unorganized collection of observations on movement, or autobiography, or art, or sincerity. Yet it is soon apparent that here, as so often, Montaigne's thought takes antithetical forms – he places side by side opposites of one kind or another. There are, of course, several sorts of antitheses – neither *a* nor *z* but the golden mean; or *a* is really the same thing as *z* – something he often asserts and of which this text presents an example (*constance* equals *branle*). Here the most common sort is the form: not *a* but *z*; the argument is built on a series of mutually exclusive opposites. Isolating the terms of these oppositions will help grasp the passage's meaning and unity; they centre on four matters. The text opens with a distinction between 'former l'homme' and 'réciter l'homme', between shaping or educating man, and describing or stating. Montaigne soon goes on to contrast stability and change – there is no stability, everything changes. He then introduces a third opposition, that of the 'vie basse' and the 'vie de riche estoffe', the essential life of a man presumably without distinction as opposed to the life of those who merit respect as poets or jurists. The final antithesis contrasts works done with science and art to those done by chance (*fortune*, *sort*), without art; his, he asserts, is in the latter category.

However, these antitheses are all concerned with one basic opposition, for rather than delimiting his concepts Montaigne extends their meaning to include multiple associations. Stability includes *être* (perhaps best translated by essence) and consistency; change implies *passage* and self-contradiction. This mobility of the world justifies the mobility of his self-portrait, which leads to the final restatement of the antithesis in the contrast between *essayer* and *résoudre*. *Résoudre* means to resolve into fixed, durable components, *essayer* to take soundings which accurately reveal what is only a temporary state of affairs. This antithesis is clearly linked with the first one; there is no point in trying to form man if man is unstable, changing, if he has only existence and no essence. You can only 'recite' him, reveal his various states.

The third antithesis, between the *vie sans lustre* and the life of those who merit respect for their accomplishments, is the most apt to be misunderstood, and the line 'chaque homme porte la forme entière de l'humaine condition' has been too often quoted out of context.

Montaigne is not claiming that all men are the same; indeed, later in this essay he says just the contrary, suggesting that each individual has 'une forme sienne'. He is rather distinguishing between what is exterior or acquired – our accomplishments or specialities – and what is interior or fundamental, found in each of us, that basic nature with which, properly, moral philosophy deals. The exterior is fixed, superficial, whereas man's fundamental nature is fluid, changing, a matter of daily, intimate details. Thus he prepares and justifies the final antithesis which distinguishes between works written with *science*, *art* and *façon* and those which are natural, conducted by fate or fortune (an earlier text gives *fortune* for *sort*). The world of science or art is that of the grammarian or poet, which attempts to form man, to define his essence, whereas the world of nature or fortune implies sincerity, change, *réciter l'homme*.

So, rather than four sets of antitheses we have two antithetical groups. On the one hand: *être*, consistency, acquired public attributes, *art*, *science*, *former*, *résoudre*. On the other: *passage*, inconsistency, fundamental private nature, lack of art, chance, *réciter*, *essayer*. What is superficial, unchanging and constructed is contrasted to what is deep, changing and unconstructed, with Montaigne opting for the latter. Further simplification of the opposition would betray his thought, but it is a basic and prevalent one which orchestrates not only this passage but the whole of this essay and a good many others as well.

The final part of the passage abandons this antithetical mode to make what seems a straightforward statement. 'At least,' Montaigne concludes, 'I know my subject better than anyone else does and have gone further into it, gotten closer to my goal than have others.' The pessimism born of the *branle* is replaced by a positive assertion about the success of his autobiographical effort. His fidelity (sincerity), he proclaims, is as pure as can be found. A final sentence places restrictions on how much he dares say but the selection ends on a self-confident note of victory. All things may be in constant flux, including the self, but nonetheless within that flux Montaigne manages to seize his object, himself, in its complexity. The victory is a significant one, for all moral philosophy can be derived from the study of this *moi* which the world has hitherto neglected in its concern with the exterior and extraneous. He is proud to be the first to have studied so penetratingly the significant, the *être universel*; he has reached the goal he set for himself. We seem to have a clear case of Renaissance optimism with this sense of being a sort of Columbus discovering the new world of the self-in-flux and thus making a contribution to human consciousness. Montaigne optimistically feels that the self, despite its flux, can be penetrated, known and depicted. He shows none of the anguished Romantic doubts about the validity of self-knowledge, just as he rejects the medieval use of introspection as a means of becoming aware of our sinfulness and God's glory; for him, self-knowledge is a source of ethical lessons. The whole effort is a novel one, a possible one, and a worthwhile one.

Given this emphasis upon the self, it is not surprising that the first person pronoun and its possessive adjective occur forty times in the passage. Montaigne indeed practices *égotisme*, the grammatical abuse of the first person singular. But he cannot be accused of *égoïsme*, or self-admiration and self-satisfaction, for if some of the first-person sentences evoke the importance of the self, others attack the self. The proud assertions here, as elsewhere, are the obverse of a critical analysis of mankind and the human condition, of an often derogatory portrait of that one subject Montaigne can and does know, Montaigne himself. Here these attacks against the self and the world centre on certain themes. The first is the *branle*, the omnipresent movement and change. Montaigne does not always look on this change as good; a conservative man in politics and religion, he regrets it. And, because of the *branle*, there are sharp limits to the kinds of self-knowledge man can possess. Man's *être* or essence is unknowable, he can never *assurer* his object, never pin it down, and he will of necessity be self-contradictory, claim one thing one day and its opposite the next.

However, the mobility of the self is presented as of the nature of things; Montaigne accepts it and does his best by it. Another kind of self-criticism is more personal – the notion that Montaigne's own life is without importance, *basse* and *sans lustre*. In line 22, this is only a preparation for the affirmation that even such a low life can be the object of study and the basis for wisdom, but the attack against the self in line 2 and in line 33 seems less a part of the argument than a direct expression of a deprecatory attitude. Montaigne is 'un particulier bien mal formé', and if he had it to do over again, he would be different; but, alas, it is too late, his nature is 'foiblette', weak. The text contains other criticisms of Montaigne. In line 28 he asserts that others feel that he talks too much about himself; in line 36 he admits that his 'fantaisies' are constructed without science or art. Finally in line 44 he claims that even if his fidelity and sincerity are as great as possible, there are still limits on what he says: 'Je dy vray, non pas tout mon saoul: mais autant que je l'ose dire.'

Admittedly, these attacks are not offered in a tragic tone, nor even in a highly serious one. They have nothing to do with the Christian tradition of self-abasement. They suggest resignation rather than regret, and indeed have humorous overtones. But Montaigne does not share Cellini's energetic, optimistic vaunting of the self. Seemingly whatever he gives to man, he then takes away. I recount myself, but that self is of little worth and the recounting is artless. I am totally sincere, but there are certain things I dare not say. Then he sometimes gives back part of what he has taken away: I do dare say more and more as I grow older. Behind the antitheses there is an ambiguous attitude toward self and toward mankind, where affirmation goes hand in hand with denigration. In a remarkable study on Montaigne, Hugo Friedrich has demonstrated how this dialectic between attacks on man and exaltation of man resolves itself in the synthesis of the *moi*; but our passage begins with that *moi*. To measure to what extent this text is affirmative, to what extent negative, we shall have to look at its tone, its style. There we must ask for whom the text is written – for Montaigne himself or for a larger public? And if the latter, what was his purpose, to amuse or to convince? Is the passage well organized and effectively expressed, or is it caught on the horns of dilemma? And is its tone tragic, serious or comic? Only when these questions are answered can the meaning of the text be accurately assessed.

Montaigne clearly wrote the text with the desire to convince an audience. This is already evident in the opposition of the first sentence between 'les autres' and 'je', as it is in his justification in line 22 ('c'est tout un' means 'peu importe'). In line 28 there is a *captatio benevolentiae* where he raises a possible objection and immediately answers it by a counter-objection. The questions of lines 29–35 are again not questions he is asking himself, but ones which might be asked by a possible public. And the notion, in line 45, of what he does or does not dare say presupposes the idea of a public which might be shocked. People often speak of Montaigne's scepticism; one could also speak of his dogmatism. He is absolutely sure here of the importance of the *branle*, just as he is sure of the validity and accuracy of his autobiographical effort, and his style reveals someone determined to persuade. There are, for instance, several superlatives in the passage; he is 'le plus sçavant homme qui vive' in his subject matter. There are also several negatives with comparative: 'jamais aucun ne penetra en sa matiere plus avant', etc. He often doubles or intensifies his negatives; he prefers 'ne point' to 'ne pas' (ll. 4, 20); 'n'est que' to 'est' (l. 5), or generalizes by using 'tout': 'toute la philosophie morale', or by other words: 'chaque homme', 'la forme entière', 'universel'. Other devices emphasize that the statement he is making completely covers all possibilities: line 14, 'non de fortune seulement, mais aussi d'intention,' or line 16, 'soit que . . . soit que'. He also has a predilection for the adverbial intensifier 'bien' (ll. 2, 3, 18, 33).

Another kind of verbal dogmatism is the accumulation of adjectives or nouns. There are many examples: 'mon âme est tousjours en apprentissage, et en espreuve', 'une vie basse et sans lustre', or 'sans science et sans art'. He often uses a series of verbs or terms to illustrate his points, and these series are organized with science and art. In lines 11–13, he goes from the general 'aage en autre' to the shorter 'sept en sept ans', then to 'jour en jour' and finally 'minute en minute'; the temporal unit becomes smaller and smaller. In line 9, the progression is more purely esthetic. After 'trouble', a mild word, comes the more violent and precise 'chancelant' which adds a visual image; the metaphor is then reinforced with 'd'une yvresse naturelle' which is again visual and concrete, evoking the drunkard's lack of self-control. The series in line 6 is also artfully arranged. 'Terre' comes first, as the shortest, most general term. The 'rochers du Caucase' add an exotic touch – big mountains, solid as granite, but moving. The pyramids have the quality of being ancient artifacts, the major signs of man's effort to conquer time and achieve stability. Montaigne adds an observation which serves to generalize still further and to make matters even more concrete; the *branle* is one of both all matter – the movement of the spheres – and of the particular masses of matter – mountains and pyramids wear away. The order in which the items are placed is not haphazard; they build to a convincing crescendo.

The stylistic device whose recurrence in the passage is most striking is the repetition of certain words or syntactic forms. Montaigne did not indulge in Flaubert's exterminating hunt for recurring words; rather, he used repetition frequently and wilfully. In our brief passage there are fourteen instances, the most striking being the four occurrences of 'branloire, branle' and the very constructed repetition of line 28. Sometimes, as with lines 28, 11, 16–18, the repetition serves to underline an antithesis. In other instances, it strengthens the link between two thoughts and makes a transition explicit. Such is the case of 'forment . . . forme' in line 1, whereby what seems a disconnected statement is linked with the opening idea. Again, in lines 22–4, 'vie . . . vie . . . vie' serves to set up the antithesis of the second sentence and to link the two. The most effective use is in line 37, 'jamais homme', line 40, 'jamais aucun', where repetition ties together a rather lengthy development. In this last instance, and in lines 30–1, the repetition makes us think of an oratorical style. Rather than seeking synonyms, Montaigne emphasizes a central idea by repeating one term. He also repeats in order to mark how, in a series, items grow in importance and in intensity. Such is the case with the repetition of 'nature' in line 33 and even more of 'plus avant, plus particulièrement, plus exactement et plainement' in line 40. Montaigne's thought reaches out to grasp all the implications of an idea; far from being a comfortable compromiser, he often pursues his ideas to their utmost consequences. Repetition then serves not only to unite and emphasize his thought, but also to aid that thought to seek its fullest development without losing continuity or structure.

Our passage was first published in 1588, but Montaigne continued to correct, rewrite and add to the *Essais* until his death. The text here is based on the famous 'exemplaire de Bordeaux', his own corrected copy, as typographically reproduced in the Imprimerie nationale edition (1920–31), accepting Montaigne's corrections and additions and yet keeping his own punctuation, which other modern editions do not follow. These changes raise problems about the evolution of Montaigne's thought, irrelevant here though it is noteworthy that many of the additions are personal or autobiographical in character. But we must ask whether these additions destroy the unity of the *Essais*, making them rambling and disconnected, or whether they offer further proof of his desire to convince by writing in a well-organized, effective manner – in short, whether the essays are a pot-pourri of Montaigne's meditations, or on the contrary possess unity and structure. The additions in our text, at least, far from destroying the unity of the passage contribute to it.

For instance, in lines 25–29 Montaigne adds two sentences which he worked over extensively. The addition explains what he means by 'forme entiere de l'humaine condition', the 'estre universel' as opposed to the particular partial form of grammarian or poet. The examples chosen of this 'partial' form also prepare the following discussion of books written with science and art as contrasted to his artless study. The second sentence is central to the whole meaning of the section, offering a justification for his autobiographical effort. Without this addition, the transition, from 'humaine condition' to 'Mais est-ce raison' is unduly abrupt. Again, in line 35 there is a brief change or addition. The first text reads 'bastir des livres sans science'; on the manuscript, Montaigne added '. . . ou de philosopher sans Aristote' before arriving at the final 'sans science et sans art'. Here again, the last version is surely the best. 'Art', repeated in the following sentence, prepares a transition; and the suppression of the reference to Aristotle gets rid of an irrelevant matter.

The changes made on the manuscript, though usually less important, generally also show the search for a better style or a more precise expression of his thought. For instance, line 20 at first read 'prendre pied et forme'; we might regret the suppression because of its link with the first sentence of the essay, but 'forme' occurs in line 24 in a different sense, and without the suppression the two phrases might have seemed contradictory. The complicated revisions of lines 25–29 avoid on the one hand unduly extensive enumeration; 'architectes, médecins, légistes' are replaced by 'estrangiere'. The change 'mon estre simplement' > 'mon estre universel' serves to establish a link with 'la forme entiere de l'humaine condition'. It is usually easy to understand why Montaigne made his changes; they serve to define more precisely what he is saying, to amplify or underline his thesis, or to create transitions, to unify the flow of his thought.

In our passage, there is only one instance of one of the most noted traits of his composition, the citation of or reference to classical authors. Several explanations have been offered for these quotations: the genesis of the *Essais*, which began as a common-place book; the Renaissance respect for classical wisdom and learning; the role of books in provoking Montaigne's thought. The Demades of line 19 can be traced to one of his favourite sources, Plutarch – in this instance the Life of Demosthenes. Demades was a sort of Talleyrand who claimed that if he had indeed contradicted himself several times as the state of affairs changed, he had never contradicted the public weal. Evidently, what Demades said is not exactly what Montaigne is saying, and the context has changed from a matter of politics to a matter of autobiography. Today Demades is unknown, but he was probably not generally known in Montaigne's time either; the reference neither elucidates Montaigne's idea nor makes it more easily comprehensible. Nor was Montaigne's thought here in any sense provoked by a reading of Plutarch. All the reference does is to provide a sort of footnote guarantee of the validity of what he is saying. As such, it is yet another device used to convince the reader, which is often the end to which he puts his erudition.

Montaigne's choice of vocabulary and use of imagery and metaphorical language also serve to make the passage persuasively convincing. One need only look at his verbs to see how he draws from a rich, picturesque and effective stock: *façonner, fourvoyer, branler, assurer, accommoder, saisir, prendre pied, s'essayer, se résoudre, produire, bâtir pénétrer, éplucher, bavasser.* Some are rare, some are common but have their sense emphasized by the context. Most of them are verbs of motion or suggest intense activity. Surely a link exists between the high expressivity of the verb in Montaigne and his preoccupation with *branle*; he naturally saw the world in motion, and such mobility is easily expressed by verbs. Again here, the sedentary solitary in his tower has perhaps been a misleading image: Montaigne's consciousness was preoccupied with change, motion, involvement, and not with solitude and solidity.

His language is also highly metaphoric, full of imagery and concrete expressions. He is sparing of similes, of *comme* or *ainsi que*; instead, his metaphors serve as the natural way of expressing himself. It is at times even hard to tell what is a metaphor and what is simply a colourful way of saying something. Several instances from this passage reveal much about his style and about his imagination and psychology. 'Mon objet va trouble et chancelant, d'une yvresse naturelle.' The object here is his self, an abstract concept; the metaphors render it visual and concrete, as they suggest activity and motion. With 'yvresse', a popular and even comic note is added. Line 20, 'Si mon ame pouvait prendre pied', again takes the invisible and makes it graphic and active – the motion of an object is evoked. As does line 21, 'mon âme en apprentissage et en espreuve', where the concrete terms are once more derived from lived, popular experience. Line 24, 'Une vie de plus riche estoffe', is almost an out worn metaphor, but here again Montaigne introduces an element from day-to-day existence, cloth, which is concrete and which 'visualizes'. The most extended metaphor comes in line 34, 'Est-ce pas faire une muraille sans pierre, ou chose semblable, que de bastir des livres sans science et sans art?' By the comparison, the act of writing is turned into something concrete and energetic. The metaphor of the wall is extended and the term 'bastir' applied to the writing of a book; also Montaigne, as often, invites the reader to imagine further metaphors by 'ou chose semblable', which suggests a series of images he chose to suppress while writing. The highly metaphorical passage, lines 40–1, 'penetra en sa matiere plus avant, ny en esplucha plus part-iculierement les mambres et suites', again uses concrete language and forces us to feel the activity, and, with 'esplucher', a kitchen term, it once again introduces a popular, common note. All these phrases, in short, add a concrete element, give substance to what was abstract and intellectual. They are often designedly visual and force us to see something as well as think about it; often they introduce or underline an element of activity or motion which would otherwise be absent or unnoticed. Many of them significantly also make reference to something from the realm of popular, day-by-day experience. Much more can be, and to an extent has been done with Montaigne's imagery – particularly by Albert Thibaudet and Floyd Gray. There are many images, like that of lines 40–1, which emphasize penetra-tion from exterior to interior; some have a favourable, some an unfavourable connotation. Others, like that of line 20, centre on the problem of stability versus mobility. In such instances the imagery leads to very central aspects of Montaigne's thought. However, an 'explication de texte' cannot lend itself to any such psychoanalysis of imagery, where Montaigne still awaits the kind of exhaustive treat-ment François Germain, for instance, has given Alfred de Vigny, for in such a study one must utilize all the author's works.

Montaigne's non-metaphorical language also frequently resorts to popular terms or to folk dicta. 'Mes-huy' in line 3 comes from the spoken language and has since disappeared in French. The diminutive 'foiblette' in line 33 is popular and also, to an extent, derogatory. In line 12 he specifies that the term 'de sept ans en sept ans' is a folk way of speaking. 'Tout mon saoul' is also from a low level of language, and 'bavasser' for 'bavarder' again belongs to the spoken tongue. At times, Montaigne's vocabulary is as inventively vulgar as that of Rabelais.

Why does he resort to this popular vocabulary and this realist imagery? Historically, there is a certain novelty in his doing so. There is already a novelty in his writing in the vernacular rather than in Latin, and he goes even further, using not the refined French Calvin and others had established as an instrument for the serious discussion of religious, philosophical and political matters but a quite different language including elements from the lowest level of discourse. In part he does so because of his very project of identifying philosophical considerations with individual, lived experience; as the sententiae of the commonplace book were enriched with autobiographical commentary, the language of the sententia became mixed with the language of everyday life. This helps us understand his opposition to works written with 'science' and 'art', his preference for a natural style which captures the rich fulness of life. The popular language and image drawn from everyday life certainly also serve the artistic purpose of rendering what he has to say more concrete; they make his style more vivid, easier to read and more persuasive.

These expressions also free the *Essais* from pomposity and on occasion even give them a comic tone. No stylistic trait is more difficult to analyse than humour; it is often hard to tell when a written text is meant to be comic, when it is serious, and whether the comic is sarcastic, gentle, wholesome or what. The difficulties are increased in a text whose language is as different from ours as is Montaigne's sixteenth-century French, where the full connotations of words are often lost to us. Perhaps for this reason critics have neglected how much Montaigne seeks comic effects, how often he wants to make us laugh, or smile, or at least take what he is saying *cum grano salis*. In a recent study, Floyd Gray has convincingly suggested how widespread that humour is.

This passage is not written with excessive high seriousness and humorous overtones are clearly present. Certain of the popular expressions – 'd'une yvresse naturelle', 'bavasser', 'tout mon saoul' introduce an earthy tone; if they make Montaigne's language more vivid they also demand a reaction of light amusement. The same is true of the second sentence, 'mes-huy c'est fait', which is not a grievous lament over the way he has been 'bien mal formé', nor even mature resignation, but an amused 'But now, it's done!' The matter discussed is serious, but the manner is light and deft. What, for instance, is the tone of lines 37–8, where he maintains that at least one thing can be said in favour of his writing an autobiography, that he knows his subject better than anyone else does! This self-evident tautology in its way contains what is for Montaigne an important truth (man can finally only know himself) but at the same time is so expressed that we certainly ought to be amused. Those complex verbal forms, almost precious in their organization, such as lines 28–9, are surely meant to be partly comic in their effect. The highly constructed phrase contrasts so much with Montaigne's usual casual style that we suspect he is striking a pose to make us smile, while still saying something he considers meaningful. However, this presence of the comic does not deprive the passage of its importance. The comic in literature may serve a great variety of ends – to satirize, to destroy seriousness, to make the unpleasant palatable. Here Montaigne primarily wants to put the reader in a relaxed mood where he will accept the rather disquieting things Montaigne has to say; it is in an effort to communicate effectively that he chooses this casual, conversational, humorous style.

Space does not permit a discussion here of the complete essay, which is often cited as typical of Montaigne's disorganized, rambling composition. An essay on repentance which begins with a discussion of change and a justification for self-study and autobiography! However, it is easy to see that these two notions are central to the whole essay. The *branle* reappears in the theme that the definition of vice changes from age to age, from society to society, and in the thesis that the weakening of our appetites in old age does not justify changing our attitude about, say, voluptuousness. The idea that the self is knowable and should be studied is even more central to the essay, with its argument that our valet knows us better than the general public, that we know ourselves better than does our valet, and that judgment and evaluation of the self, and hence repentance, can only stem from our perception of the 'patron' within us. Finally, the important distinction between apparent and essential vices is prepared by the distinction made here between art and nature. W. G. Moore and, later, Ephraim Baraz have shown the essential unity and organic structure of *De l'expérience*, as Etiemble has done for *Des coches*. The task with *Du repentir* would be an easy one. When Montaigne seems disorganized and chaotic, it is probably because we have not grasped the structures of his thought. Nor can we discuss at length the importance of this text for the whole of the *Essais*. Its centrality is evident when we remember Montaigne's role in the tradition of autobiography, whose basic justifications are given here. The *branle* and the sense of change underlie that sense of cultural and historical relativity which more than anything else makes Montaigne a figure of moral grandeur. Finally, his scepticism, or more properly his loss of that enthusiasm for reason, science and art so characteristic of an earlier generation of the Renaissance, is also present here. But many another equally rich passage could be found; one of the results of the complex texture of Montaigne's organization is that ideas and themes recur in new clusters throughout his work.

If Montaigne here expresses an astounding awareness of the temporal dimension of all existence as manifested in the phenomena of change, he also immediately applies this temporality to the problems of self-awareness and self-knowledge. Partly to suggest that, given change in time, only a contact with the immediate self is possible, that there is no other form of knowledge. Partly to conclude that the self also changes, that it possesses duration and not essence; and that its acquired appearances are unimportant and insignificant. Only the flux of its own personal being can be known. This whole complex of ideas is based on a largely critical analysis of the world and of man – if we take permanence and stability to be fundamental human desires. Even the pyramids, that image of timelessness so utilized by embalmers and insurance companies, suffer from change. But Montaigne goes beyond his scepticism to derive from this very change the conditions under which self-knowledge is possible, and to suggest that from such self-knowledge a moral philosophy can be derived.

It would be better to speak of wisdom, of *sagesse*, rather than of philosophy, but Montaigne's wisdom is clearly something of which he is convinced and which he expresses with conviction. The passage is carefully organized and composed in a style which wishes to persuade. But the organization does not attempt to convince by simplifying and clarifying its logical structure; though Montaigne can suppress the irrelevant, he generally tries to grasp all the implications of the relevant, to pursue his thought to its fullest consequences. Reacting against the *divisio* of scholasticism, preferring, as Maurice Croll pointed out, the Senecan amble to the constructed Ciceronian phrase, he does not have that kind of *clarté française* we have been taught to expect. He is in the tradition of Alain, not that of Condillac. In part, this is because he teaches wisdom rather than philosophy, in part because he has a global view of man's existence. For these same reasons, and especially because he sees man as plunged in history, his style is highly metaphorical and realist. He abandons the sort of language traditionally used for philosophical or moral discourse (Latin, or at least a Latinized, formal French) and writes in a relaxed manner, with a free sentence structure, where his thought flows rather than being broken up, and where he refers to details of his daily life and introduces popular terms from the spoken language. The tone is so light as to be at times comic. Given his convictions and his purposes, the choice of this style is easily understandable. The very historicity of man plunges him into daily reality and indeed makes of that reality the most significant aspect of his existence. The basic sceptical suppositions rule out a certain kind of pretentious language and organization. But his style not only reflects his ideas; it also serves to convince, on the level of wisdom on which he thought conviction possible and meaningful. In all this, in both his basic assumptions and his manner of writing, he seems quite modern. Only his belief that 'la fidélité simple et pure' was possible, indeed easily obtainable, separates him from the twentieth century; later explorations of the problem of self-knowledge have made us aware that sincerity is not a virtue so easily come by.

NOTE

1 It is perhaps brazen to explicate a text already superbly analysed by Eric Auerbach (*Mimesis*, 1953, p. 285–311). However, a comparison of approach and method may be enlightening for the student, and while I in no sense disagree with Auerbach's theses, the present analysis does not share his historical perspective. Other critical works referred to here are: Ephraim Baraz, 'Sur la structure d'un essai de Montaigne', in *Bibliothèque d'humanisme et de renaissance*, XXIII (1961), 265–81; Maurice Croll, 'Attic Prose: Lipsius, Montaigne, Bacon' in *Schelling Anniversary Papers*, 1923, which lays the groundwork for all fruitful investigations of Montaigne's style; Floyd Gray, *Le Style de Montaigne*, 1958; Hugo Friedrich, *Montaigne*, 1949; W. G. Moore, 'Montaigne's notion of experience' in *The French mind, Studies in honour of G. Rudler*, 1952, and A. Thibaudet, *Montaigne*, 1963.

*Source*
Michel de Montaigne (1533–92): *Essais*, III, 2; from the corrected Bordeaux copy as reproduced in the Imprimerie Nationale edition (1920–31) vol. III, pp. 13–14.

I.D. McFarlane

# D'AUBIGNÉ
*Les Tragiques : Vengeances*

O bien-heureux Abel, de qui premier[1] au cœur
Cette vierge[2] esprouva sa premiere douleur!
De Caïn fugitif & d'Abel je veux dire
Que le premier bourreau & le premier martyre,
5 Le premier sang versé on peut voir en eux deux:
L'estat des agneaux doux, des loups outrecuideux.[3]
En eux deux on peut voir (beau portrait de l'Eglise)
Comme l'ire & le feu des ennemis s'attise
De bien fort peu de bois & s'augmente beaucoup.
10 Satan fit ce que fait en ce siecle le loup
Qui querelle l'agneau beuvant à la rivière,
Luy au haut vers la source & l'agneau plus arrière.
L'Antechrist & ses loups reprochent que leur eau
Se trouble au contreflot[4] par l'innocent agneau;
15 La source des grandeurs & des biens de la terre
Decoule de leurs chefs, & la paix & la guerre
Balancent à leur gré dans leurs impures mains:
Et toutefois alors que les loups inhumains
Veulent couvrir de sang le beau sein de la terre,
20 Les pretextes communs de leur injuste guerre
Sont nos autels sans fard, sans feinte, sans couleurs.[5]
Que Dieu aime d'enhaut l'offerte[6] de nos cœurs,
Cela leur croist la soif du sang de l'innocence.
    Ainsi Abel offroit en pure conscience
25 Sacrifices à Dieu, Caïn offroit aussi:
L'un offroit un cœur doux, l'autre un cœur endurci,
L'un fut au gré de Dieu, l'autre non agreable.
Caïn grinça les dents, palit, espouvantable,
Il massacra son frere, & de cet agneau doux
30 Il fit un sacrifice à son amer courroux.
Le sang fuit de son front, & honteux se retire
Sentant son frere sang que l'aveugle main tire;
Mais, quand le coup fut fait, sa premiere pasleur
Au prix de[7] la seconde estoit vive couleur:
35 Ses cheveux vers le ciel hérissés en furie,
Le grincement de dents en sa bouche flestrie,
L'œil sourcillant de peur descouvroit son ennuy.[8]

Il avoit peur de tout, tout avoit peur de luy:
Car le ciel s'affeubloit du manteau d'une nue
40 Si tost que le transi au ciel tournoit la veuë;
S'il fuyoit au desert, les rochers & les bois
Effrayés abbayoyent au son de ses abois.
Sa mort ne peut[9] avoir de mort pour recompense,
L'enfer n'eut point de morts à[10] punir cette offense,
45 Mais autant que de jours il sentit de trespas:
Vif il ne vescut point, mort il ne mourut pas.
Il fuit d'effroi transi, troublé, tremblant et blesme,
Il fuit de tout le monde, il s'enfuit de soy-mesme.
Les lieux plus[11] asseurés luy estoient des hazards,
50 Les fueilles, les rameaux & les fleurs des poignards,
Les plumes de son lict des esguilles piquantes,
Ses habits plus[11] aisez des tenailles serrantes,
Son eau jus de ciguë, & son pain des poisons;
Ses mains le menaçoyent de fines[12] trahisons:
55 Tout[13] image de mort, & le pis de sa rage
C'est qu'il cerche la mort & n'en voit que l'image.
De quelqu'autre Caïn il craignoit la fureur,
Il fut sans compagnon & non pas sans frayeur,
Il possedoit le monde et non une asseurance,
60 Il estoit seul par tout, hors mis[14] sa conscience:
Et fut marqué au front afin qu'en s'enfuyant
Aucun n'osast tuer ses maux en le tuant.

1 *for the first time* 2 *the Church* 3 *overweening, arrogant*
4 *upstream* 5 *here synonymous with* fard *and* feinte
6 *Mod Fr.* offrande 7 *compared with* 8 *grievous anguish*
9 *past historic* 10 = pour 11 *superlative* 12 *cunning, crafty*
13 *note absence of* estoit 14 *except*

BEGUN IN the middle 1570s, that is during the Religious Wars, and published in 1616, the *Tragiques* express in epic form a vision of the renewal of faith after centuries of suffering and wrongheadedness, and the emergence of God's plan to restore the world to its original state of grace and purity. D'Aubigné creates the fabric of his poem with materials drawn from the history of Christianity, but with special reference to the troubles of his own times, which he also described in abundant detail in his *Histoire universelle*. We are shown, on a vast scale, the battle down the centuries between Good and Evil. In the foreground is developed the struggle between Protestant and Catholic forces in sixteenth-century France, but this conflict is always accompanied by the harmonics of earlier times; thus, parallels are drawn between the tyrants of the Renaissance and the Rome of Nero and the degenerate Emperors. Then the Huguenot poet introduces glimpses of the battle as it is carried into his own mind, and these personal, lyric references contribute powerfully to the tone of the poem as a whole. But even more important are the correspondences established between the *monde cassé* of d'Aubigné's times and Biblical history; throughout the seven books the events of this world are lit up by memories of the Old Testament and the New, and in particular the Apocalyptic texts. The forging of these allegorical links helps to show the events of the Religious wars not only as the consequence of Evil emerging in the early days of history, but as a stage in the working out of the Divine Plan.

The passage selected is thus of great significance in the pattern of the epic. The story of Cain and Abel occurs in *Genesis*, IV, and it is told in sober tones; what is notable in *Les Tragiques* is that d'Aubigné, in describing the origin of Evil, gives this episode pride of place, and ignores the story of the Fall, and furthermore develops the narrative far beyond what is given us in the Old Testament. Indeed what he is doing is to make the relationship between Abel and Cain assume special meaning for the whole of *Les Tragiques*; in this episode we have as it were the symbol of the present state of the world (ll. 4–5).

The first part of the passage (ll. 1–23) is an amplification of this theme. Very rapidly, the identity of Abel is transmuted symbolically, so that the poet thinks of him as the lamb, the symbol of innocence and martyrdom; he does not emerge as a person in the way that Cain, the wolf, does. At the same time, Abel and Cain are drawn as a symbol of the relations between the true Church and the false (Anti-

christ) down the centuries. The picture of the lamb drinking peace-
fully at the river is contrasted with that of the wolf refusing it the
right to live, and this antithesis also symbolizes the refusal of the
present Catholic church, with its thirst after wealth and honours, to
let the Huguenots live simply and offer prayers on their own unadorned and austere altars (ll. 15 ff). Though the development of
this theme is considerable here, d'Aubigné is bringing into sharper
focus a *motif* which underpins the whole structure of the poem. Much
space is devoted to the contrast between the martyrs of the true faith
and the monsters who have perverted justice and ruined humanity;
and indeed the theme of Nature that has ceased to be natural (the
world is out of joint, as contemporary Shakespeare observed) is a
main part of the fabric. Here, the poet is stressing the result of that
dis-grace, the war launched by the wolves upon the lambs. The wolf
has become the symbol of all that is *desnaturé*; he is mentioned in
connection with Catherine de Médicis, the Pope, the Emperors who
persecuted the faithful:

Ces tyrans sont les loups, car le loup, quand il entre
Dans le parc des brebis, ne suce de leur ventre
Que le sang par un trou, & quitte tout le corps
Laissant bien le troupeau, mais un troupeau de morts.
(*Misères*, 1, ll. 601–4)

The wolf is thus also the symbol of the man who attacks his neighbour, the tyrant who destroys his people; he is too a manifestation of
Satan (l. 10). In isolating this passage for commentary, one cannot
help reducing its contextual force. The theme, it is true, is developed
vigorously in these lines, with recurrent antithesis, insistent repetition, cogent comparisons and analogies, rhetorical amplification (e.g.
l. 21) and above all dramatic presentation; but the full impact of the
passage depends on the fact that the wolf has already been associated
with certain historical figures who will come to mind when the
reader reaches this passage. In *Les Tragiques* many effects derive from
the elaborate network of reference built up from book to book and
from certain *leitmotive* such as the one under discussion.

D'Aubigné is much given to the repetition of key-words, and here
not only does the pair *agneau/loup* recur time and again, but the two
words are often given companion epithets: thus the *agneau* is regularly
*doux* or *innocent*, whereas the *loup* is described as *inhumain* or *outrecuideux*, and closely linked with Satan or Antichrist. On one occasion,

the poet sharpens the contrast by bringing the two together in a single line (l. 6); and the result of these devices is to obscure the identities of the brothers under the symbolic meanings they have acquired in d'Aubigné's reading of history. In this passage, moreover, the basic theme *agneau/loup* is enriched by two other themes which are highly important in the economy of the work and are brought together in line 19: 'Veulent couvrir de sang le beau sein de la terre.' The theme of blood recurs throughout, as one would expect in a poem which tells of violence in past and present. A full analysis would be out of place here, but the symbol is in essence ambivalent: it stands for violence, destruction, inhumanity, the action of Cain and his spiritual descendants, but at the same time it represents purification – the blood of the martyrs. Though d'Aubigné naturally stresses a black-and-white antithesis between Catholics and Huguenots, his categories go well beyond so bald a simplification; for in a sense all are fallen, and the sacrifice of the martyrs is a cardinal part of God's pattern. And so blood is a sign both of violence and of redemption. The other theme is that of Nature, particularly as Mother Earth, a symbol very much in evidence in *Misères* where humanity turns against Nature and where the symbol is extended to include *France désolée*. Nature and the lamb are also brought together under the sign of pastoral innocence, and d'Aubigné's reading of the Scriptures has played its part: truth and virtue are to be found in the valleys of Nature rather than in the cities of the plain, and here too perhaps d'Aubigné's own remorse at the courtier's life he led in youth adds further colour to the anti-aulic tones so prominent in the earlier books of *Les Tragiques*.

The first section of the passage, then, is a rhetorical development of the symbolism of Cain and Abel for d'Aubigné's vision of history; in the second section we meet another aspect of the poet's style, when he describes Cain's fate after the murder of his brother. After the few opening lines which, with their contrast between the brothers sacrificing to God, afford a natural transition from the previous section, d'Aubigné shows Cain fleeing in vain from the wrath of God, condemned to fear, estrangement, everlasting restlessness and denied even the mercy of death. For d'Aubigné the state of grace is one of peace, *repos*, as is beautifully portrayed in the closing lines of the epic; movement, a characteristic of this world, is the evidence of impurity and dis-grace. The concept is not new – it is, for instance, a key-idea in mystical thought – but d'Aubigné confers on it great poetic force. His imagination is apt to see things in movement, and this is one reason why a sense of drama emerges so clearly from a reading of *Les Tragiques*. Cain is first described in this passage as *fugitif* (l. 3), and the second section is really a development of this epithet. We are given an admirable impression of restlessness and displacement, in all senses of the word: Cain is ex-centric, he cannot find his place in the scheme of things. As always in d'Aubigné, the narrative is never divorced from the symbolic; even in the scene of Cain's flight, the words used to express attempted escape, despair, guilt, bring us back to the main themes of the whole work, indeed one of d'Aubigné's qualities is his imaginative grasp of cosmic pattern. He may have claimed that his poem was not rigidly conceived in tidy order *à la française*, but his imagination gives a sense of coherence and inter-reference on the grand scale not found very often in French literature – in Balzac, Hugo, Claudel perhaps. All these authors have developed with peculiar intensity the ability to create 'l'hymne des relations de tout avec tout' (Mallarmé) and to portray movement and vitality – very often in characters for whom they have, at ethical level, an un-ambiguous disapproval.

Cain gnashes his teeth – here the Biblical phrase is remembered – he becomes pale with terror, his eye is proof of his discomfiture; d'Aubigné picks out the physical details capable of denoting fear, which is the binding theme of his flight. The sense of movement is however not presented only by reference to Cain's own actions and gestures; it is injected into the details of the portrait (*vers le ciel hérissés*, l. 35), and like certain mid-nineteenth century authors, the poet may prefer the abstract noun to the accompanying participle to bring out action the more vigorously: instead of *les dents grinçantes* we have *le grincement des dents* (l. 36). Movement is also suggested by enumeration, a constant feature of the writing: a good example is afforded in line 47, where the tempo is reinforced by dense alliteration. And indeed d'Aubigné goes further: in his desire to dramatize to maximum effect, he personifies the elements of Nature around Cain in their reactions to the murder: the sky hides itself behind a cloud, the rocks and the woods bark at his approach; everything is affected in movement by the presence of the criminal. One must be careful not to read present-day habits into sixteenth-century tense-usage, but d'Aubigné does once or twice introduce the graphic present here to intensify the immediacy of the action.

Though the theme of flight is doubtless uppermost, it does not stand in isolation, and the poet uses a number of words to describe Cain which, in the text of *Les Tragiques*, have taken on a moral significance. Though, as we saw, *grinça* has Biblical resonance, *palit* (l. 28) is a different matter; indeed all the words of that root (*pâle, pâleur, pâlir*) have acquired special meaning, a meaning which is made clear in the following lines: Cain's blood 'fuit de son front', and this flight of blood from the face is a further symbol of fear, of crime, of Antichrist, and time and again we shall come upon the enemies of God described in terms of pallor. Another cognate epithet is *transi*, which denotes the ebbing of vitality; Cotgrave, as ever, defines this word admirably: 'Fallen into a trance, or sowne; whose heart, sense or vitall spirits faile him; astonied, amazed, appalled, half dead'). D'Aubigné uses the term twice in this passage, in lines 40 and 47, and in the second case *transi* rubs shoulders with *blesme*.

Cain's crime is portrayed in another manner. We have seen that for d'Aubigné, the murder of Abel was responsible for turning the natural order upside down, and much of *Les Tragiques* is a series of variations on the theme of Nature having ceased to be herself. Here the point is made explicit in two ways. On the one hand, Cain is seen to interpret Nature, in terms of its opposite: hence the series of examples beginning at line 49, where security becomes danger, Nature the enemy, food poison, and so forth. And on the other, going beyond Cain's view of things, the poet shows us the topsy-turvy state of Nature, which has become a contradiction in terms, by extensive use of paradox to describe the consequences of Cain's action: 'Vif il ne vescut point, mort il ne mourut pas' (l. 46). Of minor importance here, though often stressed elsewhere, is the theme that an action often provokes a counter-action, of the type 'catcher-caught'; here Cain is shown fearing the appearance of a second Cain to do to him what he has done to Abel (l. 57). The action by 'come-back' is also the result of Nature's degradation.

This passage gives us an idea of the pleasure d'Aubigné takes in the handling of words; we are presented with a wide-ranging vocabulary in a series of rich rhetorical patterns. It is not surprising that d'Aubigné was a passionate admirer of Rabelais whom he describes in his *Faeneste* as an 'auteur excellent'. Like Rabelais he sees phenomena in terms of action, like him too he allows his sentence to generate its spontaneous vitality, revealed in a proliferating vocabulary. But other influences have left their mark: one of the most important is of course the Bible, though stylistically the passage under discussion is less coloured than some by scriptural echo and syntax. Another formative element is d'Aubigné's classical background, and perhaps especially in the field of rhetoric, on whose figures and tropes he has drawn extensively. In this passage, certain figures and habits predominate, partly because of the nature of the themes. For this reason, we can expect some use of antithesis: *Les Tragiques* are in great measure built on an antithesis, and here we have on the one hand the contrast between the two brothers, and on the other hand the antithesis between Cain before and after the crime, so that Nature is seen by him in contradictory terms.

Even more prominent, however, is repetition. In d'Aubigné words recur with impressive frequency, indeed sometimes to the point of indiscriminate excess; and here, for instance, one may feel that the repetition of the rhymes *guerre/terre* (ll. 15–16 and 19–20) within so short an interval is either careless or not obviously meaningful. Generally speaking, though, d'Aubigné's predilection for repetition fits in well in a context where the protagonist is obsessed with terror. The figure is used in two main ways: first, certain key-words are used systematically. Of these the chief is *fuit* (accompanied by *s'enfuir*): referring initially to the blood draining from Cain's face, it then describes his attempts to liberate himself from the consequences of his crime. Others, such as *pale, transi, peur,* have already been noted; but the repetition may take on different forms. Sometimes, the words recur at certain intervals, like *leitmotive*; but d'Aubigné may also use a word twice within a single line (as in l. 43), and repetition of the word or the same root may be found in a context of paradox, but in line 46 paradox is not a mere rhetorical device, it is the stylistic correlative of Nature at odds with herself, and, not surprisingly, it is employed at regular intervals throughout the poem. This is also true of chiasmus, as in line 38, where the figure serves quite simply to show the reciprocity of effect in the context, and *forme* and *fond* blend very happily.

In the second place, repetition appears in the form of the clause or sentence, and this may involve some form of enumeration. Here d'Aubigné is very fond of the ternary list, as in line 21, where the synonyms are strengthened by the syntactical mould in which they are set. Cain's obsession is expressed by the repetition of the same *mot-outil* at the beginning of certain triads (e.g. ll. 47–8, 52–4, 58–60); but a similar effect may be achieved by a longer series of enumeration (as in ll. 49 ff). D'Aubigné also uses repetition to reinforce antithesis as in lines 26–7, and in line 46 to underline paradox. On occasion, repetition is further stressed by alliteration (l. 47), and it may also be found in conjunction with chiasmus (l. 48). In all this, we see efforts by the poet to ring changes on a basic device which needs such variations to avoid the accusation of monotony or aridity.

One or two other features of d'Aubigné's rhetoric are pressed into service here; the most prominent perhaps is zeugma which is used as part of the enumerative process to describe Cain's misery (ll. 58 ff). Zeugma depends for its impact on the use of the same verb to govern two objects at different levels of meaning, literal and abstract; it has in recent times lost some of its status, but for classical rhetoricians it was considered particularly suitable in contexts of high emotion, and it is significant that d'Aubigné should use zeugma, together with antithesis, repetition, enumeration and paradox, to describe an episode which is one of the king-pins of the whole poem. Zeugma achieves some of its effect by its concision, and in d'Aubigné we shall find a judicious movement between amplification and reduction, as we do in other masters of rhetoric such as Corneille. One particular device working for concision is *conjunctio*, in which one verb does service for two clauses (ll. 26–7, and in a series of clauses ll. 49 ff.); this is a form of ellipse, of which more marked examples occur in lines 4–5 and 55. In all this, one must set against the evident predominance of certain figures and devices, an awareness of the need to vary style and movement as well as the sense of the thematic relevance of the style to the subject-matter.

Problems of rhetorical period and rhythm are intimately connected with d'Aubigné's mastery of the alexandrine, and this passage brings out very clearly his ability to handle rhythm and melodic line. Given the antithetic nature of the Abel-Cain theme, and also d'Aubigné's liking for chiasmus and repetition, it would be surprising if he did not introduce some lines in which each hemistich stood out boldly (e.g. ll. 26–7, 46); but, quite apart from the usually successful way in which he distributes his stresses in each single line, he achieves marked variety in the couplet. He may produce a sequence of 6 + 6

(ll. 58 ff), but he makes judicious use of the pattern 6 + 18, and
particularly in lines 55–6 and 61–2 where a series is brought to a
round, satisfying conclusion. The opposite pattern 18 + 6 is strikingly used to contrast the sacrifice of the two brothers (ll. 24–5):
Abel is allowed three quarters of the couplet and his loving sacrifice
is set against Cain's arid little contribution. In other words, d'Aubigné's mastery of the alexandrine is very fine, but its effects must be
studied with his handling of the vocabulary and rhetorical tempo
and mass; an impressive example of this is line 55 where the elliptic
syntax harmonizes with the structure of the line to allow *Tout* exceptional stress.

In this passage, we have seen some of the main elements, thematic,
stylistic and imaginative which characterize d'Aubigné's masterpiece.
Certain aspects, inevitably, are absent or at least penumbral: the
satiric poet might be suspected from d'Aubigné's vigorous portrait
of Cain in flight, but the lyric capable of the mystic vision at the end
of *Jugement* has no place here. Nor do we have much opportunity of
seeing d'Aubigné's handling of imagery: here what we have is image
transformed into symbol, and when the world is apprehended imagic-
ally, it expresses the distortion of Cain's criminal mind. Only occasionally does the poet insert the daring detail that takes on imagic
value in its own right: the striking *frere sang* (l. 32) with its syntactic
violence, the *abois* (l. 42) which liken Cain to an animal at bay. But
we have seen enough to class d'Aubigné among those rare French
writers whose vision is on the cosmic scale; he sees life as a dramatic
process in movement resulting from a break with Primitive Harmony,
his imagination grasps the pattern of and relations between phenomena
and there is a close correspondence between his awareness of
things in terms of vitality and the expression of that vision in dynamic
language. So robust an imagination tends to see things in black and
white, in antithesis, to portray reality by what Zola termed *grossisse-
ment* so that the universe it creates always seems larger than life. There
is of course loss as well as profit: so volcanic a vision and so dedicated
an attitude may result in some loss of control, lapses of taste, a
weakening of tension, as for instance in line 9; but at his best, his
exuberant imagination, his sense of structure, his richness of language combine to create poetry of a very high order. And historically,
d'Aubigné was fortunate to have at his disposal the poetic vehicle
which his master Ronsard had brought to maturity – the alexandrine.

*For further reading, see the following critical works:*
Buffum, Imbrie, *Agrippa d'Aubigné's Les Tragiques: a study of the Baroque style in poetry*, Yale Romanic Studies: second series, I. New Haven, Yale University Press, 1951.
Sauerwein, Henry A., jnr, *Agrippa d'Aubigné's Les Tragiques: a study in structure and poetic method*, Baltimore, The Johns Hopkins Press, 1953.
Weber, Henri, *La Création poétique au XVIe siècle en France*, vol. II, pp. 601–733, Paris, Nizet, 1956.

*Source*
Agrippa d'Aubigné (1562–1630): *Les Tragiques, Vengeances,* Bk. VI, ll. 155–216; ed. A. Garnier and J. Plattard, Société des Textes Français Modernes, 4 vols., Paris, 1932–3.

H. *Gaston Hall*

---

*M O L I È R E*
*Dom Juan:* 'la scène du Pauvre'

*Dom Juan, Sganarelle, Un Pauvre*

*Sganarelle.* Enseigne-nous un peu le chemin qui mène à la ville.

*Le Pauvre.* Vous n'avez qu'à suivre cette route, Messieurs, et tournez à main droite quand vous serez au bout de la forêt; mais je vous donne avis que vous devez vous tenir sur vos gardes, et que depuis
5 quelque temps il y a des voleurs ici autour.

*Dom Juan.* Je te suis obligé, mon ami, et je te rends grâces de tout mon cœur.

*Le Pauvre.* Si vous voulez me secourir, Monsieur, de quelque aumône?

10 *Dom Juan.* Ah! ah! ton avis est intéressé, à ce que je vois.

*Le Pauvre.* Je suis un pauvre homme, Monsieur, retiré tout seul dans ce bois depuis plus de dix ans, et je ne manquerai pas de prier le Ciel qu'il vous donne toute sorte de biens.

*Dom Juan.* Eh! prie le Ciel qu'il te donne un habit, sans te mettre en
15 peine des affaires des autres.

*Sganarelle.* Vous ne connaissez pas Monsieur, bon homme; il ne croit qu'en deux et deux sont quatre, et en quatre et quatre sont huit.

*Dom Juan.* Quelle est ton occupation parmi ces arbres?

*Le Pauvre.* De prier le Ciel tout le jour pour la prospérité des gens de
20 bien qui me donnent quelque chose.

*Dom Juan.* Il ne se peut donc pas que tu ne sois bien à ton aise?

*Le Pauvre.* Hélas! Monsieur, je suis dans la plus grande nécessité du monde.

*Dom Juan.* Tu te moques: un homme qui prie le Ciel tout le jour ne
25 peut pas manquer d'être bien dans ses affaires.

*Le Pauvre.* Je vous assure, Monsieur, que le plus souvent je n'ai pas un morceau de pain à mettre sous les dents.

*Dom Juan.* Voilà qui est étrange, et tu es bien mal reconnu de tes soins. Ah! ah! je m'en vais te donner un louis d'or tout à l'heure,
30 pourvu que tu veuilles jurer.

*Le Pauvre.* Ah! Monsieur, voudriez-vous que je commisse un tel péché?

*Dom Juan.* Tu n'as qu'à voir si tu veux gagner un louis d'or ou non: en voici un que je te donne, si tu jures. Tiens. Il faut jurer.

35 *Le Pauvre.* Monsieur. . . .

*Dom Juan.* A moins de cela, tu ne l'auras pas.

*Sganarelle.* Va, va, jure un peu; il n'y a pas de mal.

*Dom Juan.* Prends, le voilà, prends, te dis-je; mais jure donc.

*Le Pauvre.* Non, Monsieur, j'aime mieux mourir de faim.

40 *Dom Juan.* Va, va, je te le donne pour l'amour de l'humanité. Mais que vois-je là? Un homme attaqué par trois autres! La partie est trop inégale, et je ne dois pas souffrir cette lâcheté.

LA SCÈNE DU PAUVRE is one of the most comic, but also perhaps one of the most misunderstood, scenes in Molière. Suppressed in provincial performances following the withdrawal of *Dom Juan* from the stage of the Palais-Royal in Paris after an initial highly successful run of fifteen performances (February 15th to March 20th, 1665), the scene was mutilated in early French editions and replaced by an anodyne seduction scene in Thomas Corneille's verse version of *Le Festin de Pierre* (1677) which took the place of Molière's prose comedy in the repertory of the Comédie-Française until 1847. No one doubts that the 'scène du Pauvre' was bold and controversial in its own time; but its original outlines and its art are best understood in the light of the relevant theatrical, social and political circumstances in which Molière chose to create a scene related to the tragicomic material of the Don Juan legend but with no real source there and evidently scandalous to some of his contemporaries.[1]

CONTEXT. Warned at the end of Act II that he is being pursued by twelve horsemen (including Dom Carlos, to whose aid he rushes at the end of this scene), Dom Juan abandoned his dalliance with the peasant girls and fled with Sganarelle to the nearby woods, where they lost their way: whence Sganarelle's request for direction in the first line of our passage, which is the second scene of Act III. While Molière's use of stage time and space is imaginative (and the scene-shifting machinery at his disposal dispenses with any need to observe the strictest 'unity of place'), it seems likely (as M.R. Pintard has recently argued) that the action of Act III should be assumed to take place on the afternoon of the day begun in Act I, with Act IV following later the same evening and Act V on the evening of the following day.[2] The allusion in Act II to the horsemen and the discovery later in Act III of the tomb of the Commandeur indicate that (in contrast with earlier versions of the Don Juan legend, in which different parts of the action take place at widely separated times and places) Dom Juan and Sganarelle have not wandered further than classical verisimilitude would allow in the few hours assumed to separate the different acts.

Like Dom Juan's exit at the end of the scene to fight the brigands off-stage – an exit which dispenses with 'extras' while observing the *bienséances* limiting violence on stage – the relation of this scene to the rest of the action in a relative unity of time and place reflects Molière's adaption to fashionable contemporary French dramatic theory and practice of a legend which reached him from Spain by way of Italian comedy and French tragicomedy. Unlike the Spanish original, Tirso de Molina's *El Burlador de Sevilla* (if that play, which Molière seems not to have known, was the original), *Dom Juan* is not concerned with the theological questions of whether repentance *in extremis* or attrition without contrition is futile. For Molière's Dom Juan never repents. Such a perspective, partly restored by Thomas Corneille in *Le Festin de Pierre*, had been largely lost in Molière's immediate sources: Cicognini's *burlesque Il Convitato di pietra*, an anonymous *commedia dell'arte* scenario of around 1658, and two five-act French tragicomedies in verse, both entitled *Le Festin de Pierre*, one by Dorimond (1659) and the other by Villiers (1660). By contrast, even in the 'scène du Pauvre' where faith is an issue, Molière's *Dom Juan* is conceived more in a social than a religious frame of reference.

The meeting of Dom Juan and Sganarelle with Un Pauvre fits into a series of encounters which comprise the essential action of the comedy. It is a further 'coup de pinceau' in the portrait of a rake so comically sketched by Sganarelle in the first scene of the play [ll. 77–9]*: not a stage in a 'rake's progress', not a development of character, but an illustration the hyperbolism of which can surprise even while fulfilling the comic expectations aroused in the exposition.

The relation of the 'scène du Pauvre' to the rest of the action is best understood by analogy with the *comédie-ballet*, a genre invented by Molière through the fusion of comedy (including elements of satire, *commedia dell'arte* and farce) with the *ballet de cour*, an aristocratic and partly amateur form of *divertissement* quite distinct from modern professional ballet. In Molière's time the *ballet de cour* was characterized by a succession of *tableaux* in which verse was declaimed by the dancers. Such *tableaux* or 'turns' were normally related to a central subject or theme, but not necessarily to each other, as in *Le Ballet des Incompatibles* danced by Molière's troupe at Montpellier for the Prince de Conti. In *Les Fâcheux* (1661), Molière's first *comédie-ballet*, Eraste ('amoureux d'Orphise') is repeatedly interrupted en route to a rendezvous by a succession of importunate bores, the 'fâcheux' of the title. Now *fâcheux* does not necessarily mean *raseur*. A 'fâcheux' may well be a bore less by nature than by circumstance (e.g., another's

* All references in square brackets are to the Blackwell 1958 text. All other linear references are to the extract in this volume.

MOLIÈRE

haste); he may also of course importune a greater bore than himself. It is a question of point of view. The structure of *Dom Juan* as recast by Molière to include episodes like the 'scène du Pauvre' reflects not only the temporal structure of the *comédie-ballet* generally by its use of loosely connected scenes and possible re-use of actors in different minor roles, but also the spatial structure of *Les Fâcheux* in particular insofar as it assembles on stage a succession of incompatible or contrasting characters.

It is no accident that this encounter follows hard upon the discussion of faith in the preceding scene, to which Sganarelle alludes in lines 16 ff., and but shortly precedes the first of the miracles, the Statue's nod later in the act. It is also worth remarking that Dom Juan is never present, in this scene or elsewhere in the play, without Sganarelle. But the specific interpretation urged upon the analogy of *Les Fâcheux* is that, by asking alms of Dom Juan, who rejects any sort of obligation to other people, Le Pauvre becomes for him – like Done Elvire in Act I, Pierrot in Act II, scene 3, and the successive entries in Act IV (M. Dimanche, Dom Louis, Done Elvire again) – very much a 'fâcheux'. Nor is it difficult, in the social conditions Molière knew, to conceive of a beggar in such a role, as the section on 'Background' should make clear.

DÉCOR. Producers have of course staged this scene in various ways. But the recently discovered 'Marché de décors pour *Dom Juan*' dated December 3rd, 1664, provides a notion of the perspective set originally used in this part of Act III:

Plus une forest consistant en trois chassis de chaque costé dont le premier sera de dix-huit pieds et les autres en diminuant [an illusionist device to suggest perspective], et un chassis fermant sur lequel sera peint une maniere de temple entouré de verdure.[3]

Like some of Sganarelle's examples in the *burlesque* debate on medical and religious beliefs in the preceding scene e.g., 'ces arbres-là, ces rochers' [l. 951], the references to the 'forêt' and to 'ce bois' by Le Pauvre and to 'ces arbres' by Dom Juan (ll. 3, 12, 18) are intelligible in terms of this set and invite appropriate gestures. The scene-shifting machinery used in the original performances doubtless did not bring the folding flat depicting the Commandeur's tomb into view before scene five of this act, when Dom Juan exclaims: 'Mais quel est le superbe édifice que je vois entre ces arbres?' [ll. 1219–20].

There was no particular novelty in either perspective set or use of machinery; both had been used in January 1641 for the inaugural performance (of Desmarets' *Mirame*) on that very stage, then the Grande Salle de Spectacle du Palais-Cardinal, and repeatedly thereafter, especially for *ballets de cour* and operas in which the 'merveilleux' or supernatural played an important part (as in this play). Nor is the forest setting of the scene unusual, since it was frequent in seventeenth-century tragicomedy, pastoral, and comedy, including *Le Médecin malgré lui* in which another Sganarelle appears as a woodcutter later disguised again as a doctor. Although in the latter part of the seventeenth century there was a tendency for French writers to prefer parks and formal gardens to wild nature, forests still covered most of France. Even in the Paris region (which the peasants' dialect in Act II and certain details of this scene suggest more readily than the nominal setting in Sicily), what Saint-Simon calls 'l'immense plain pied d'une forêt toute joignante'[4] at Saint-Germain and other forests like those at Saint-Léger, Montmorency, Compiègne, and Fontainebleau – far larger than at present – were almost contiguous. Among the millions who found shelter in the real forests of Molière's France were both brigands like those who (after a warning from Le Pauvre in ll. 3–5) appear off-stage at the close of this scene and men like Le Pauvre himself.

The presence of an illusionist *décor* made a poetic evocation of the forest unnecessary.

COSTUMES. To a spectator, one of the most obvious facts about this scene is the disguise of two of the three actors, Dom Juan and Sganarelle. They have not simply exchanged outfits as proposed at the end of Act II (a detail of the legend): Molière effects instead a *coup de théâtre* at the beginning of Act III by allowing Dom Juan to appear 'en habit de campagne' and Sganarelle 'en médecin'. The latter traditionally wears a long black gown and a high conical peaked black hat, the 'attirail ridicule' mocked in the preceding scene by Dom Juan, who cannot imagine where it might have been dug up [ll. 864–5], and which owes more to comic fantasy than to observation.[5] Disguise is of course a common feature, on either side of the Channel, in seventeenth-century theatre; and its use here may be, as Professor Jean Rousset argues, a baroque feature of the play (quoted by Howarth, ed. cit., p. 87). But, in contrast with the disguises and mistaken identities in *El Burlador de Sevilla* and versions of the legend which Molière adapted, in our play it is primarily a comic one. Granted that the hero's disguise as a pilgrim in the tragicomedies of Dorimond and Villiers may have suggested the 'scène du Pauvre' and the following encounter with Dom Carlos, those authors use the episode to depict him as odious, since it is by means of the disguise that he hypocritically disarms (and in Villiers' play treacherously murders) his pursuer. Like Dom Juan's teasing and his disconcerting rescue of his pursuer, Sganarelle's 'attirail ridicule' surely helps to situate this scene in a different register.

As far as the Don Juan legend is concerned, Sganarelle's disguise originates with Molière. In Molière's theatre, it looks back to an early farce, *Le Médecin volant*, and heralds a line of doctor comedies: *L'Amour médecin, Le Médecin malgré lui, Monsieur de Pourceaugnac, Le Malade imaginaire*. To this scene, it brings an atmosphere of farce, a theatrical fantasy which even after the medical satire of the preceding scene has ended continues to distance comically the whole of the action and all three characters. Dom Juan's disguise enhances the irony of Sganarelle's rejoinder: 'Vous ne connaissez pas Monsieur, bon homme . . .' (l. 16); and disguise heightens the incongruity of Sganarelle's panic at the end of the scene.

Dom Juan's taunt in line 14 is most meaningful if his suggestion to pray for a suit implies that Le Pauvre is in rags, a costume whose possible significance is discussed in the following section.

BACKGROUND. The France of Molière's time counted more paupers than Parisians. Professor Lough quotes an observation by a doctor at the not very large town of Blois, who in 1662 could write: 'Depuis trente-deux ans . . . je n'ai rien vu qui approche de la désolation . . . non seulement à Blois où il y a quatre mille pauvres . . . mais dans toute la campagne.'[6] In such circumstances compassion is a possible and very proper reaction. But, incessantly set upon by beggars, travellers could also find their requests for money more importunate than piteous, as indeed a tourist may do today in parts of India where mendicity is common. Such appears to have been the reaction of Malherbe, of whom Racan and Tallemant des Réaux tell the following story:

> Quand les pauvres lui disaient qu'ils priaient Dieu pour lui, il
> leur répondait 'qu'il ne croyait pas qu'ils eussent grand crédit

auprès de Dieu, vu le pitoyable état où il les laissait, et qu'il eût mieux aimé que M. de Luynes [the prime minister] ou M. le Surintendant [des Finances] lui eût fait cette promesse (quoted by Howarth, ed. cit., p. 90).

Perhaps dramatizing this anecdote, Molière allows his Dom Juan to exploit the same paradox, which depends upon the assumption of a just and omnipotent God.

But Le Pauvre in *Dom Juan* is not simply a pauper. In the so-called 'non-cartonné' copies of the first edition (Paris, 1682) he had a name, *Francisque*; and in the first performances his costume may well have suggested the habit of the Franciscans, to whom the name seems to allude. The text in any case makes it clear that Le Pauvre is not indigent against his will, say through poor health or unemployment. Two *répliques* (ll. 11–12 and 19–20) make it absolutely clear that his retreat from society more than ten years earlier had been deliberate and that his poverty has a definite religious significance. Le Pauvre is unmistakably a hermit and a mendicant.

This is a fact of special significance. In 1664, Colbert had initiated measures to reduce the privileges of the monastic and mendicant orders in reaction to what he considered the 'trop grand nombre de prêtres, moines et religieuses'.[7] Such a reform encountered vigorous opposition, not only from the Compagnie du Saint-Sacrement, but from other devout people who felt that it threatened the ancient Christian ideals of monasticism and solitary retreat. In 1665 the nuns of Port-Royal were, for other reasons, under pressure from the Crown; and the so-called solitaries of Port-Royal (who had translated among other things the *Vies des Saints Pères des déserts*) were in hiding. In such a context, Dom Juan's patronizing taunt to Le Pauvre, '. . . tu es bien mal reconnu de tes soins' (ll. 28–9), must – however galling to some – have seemed topical comedy to others. And the scene may reflect commitment to Colbert's policy.[8]

Like the whole question of Molière's religious views, the nature of Dom Juan's *libertinage* is much debated; and doubtless part of the appeal of Dom Juan lies in a certain enigmatic quality that probably arises from a deliberate intention on the part of the author to create an ambiguous character. But while admitting that some of Dom Juan's lines [e.g. ll. 196 ff., and 1847 ff.] can be cited as evidence to the contrary, the arithmetical faith to which Sganarelle alludes in lines 16–17 may best be taken as dramatic shorthand confirming the atheism implied by Sganarelle in the exposition. The equation used by Dom Juan in the preceding scene (repeated here by Sganarelle) is associated with the name of Maurice de Nassau (d. 1625), the Prince of Orange who, according to Guez de Balzac and Tallemant des Réaux, advised his deathbed confessor 'que 2 et 2 font 4, et 4 et 4 font 8' (quoted by Howarth, ed. cit., p. 89), a by no means isolated attitude in the seventeenth century. Although the concept and term *atheism* can represent a variety of disbeliefs, to express Dom Juan's attitude one may prefer the vaguer term *libertinage*, which can mean free thought or nothing more than loose morals. But the associations surrounding Dom Juan's equation, the tone of this and other scenes, and the final absence of any repentance suggest, not a character conscious of deliberate sin (a *libertin* in the moral sense), but one characterized without religious belief (a *libertin* in the intellectual sense, an atheist like Maurice de Nassau). Indeed, both Dorimond's *Le Festin de Pierre* (1659) and Rosimond's *Le Nouveau Festin de Pierre* (1670) are sub-titled *l'Athée Foudroyé*.

Specifically, Dom Juan is characterized with reference to what as early as 1630 the author of the most widely disseminated treatise on manners in seventeenth-century France, Nicolas Faret, had referred to in *L'Honnête Homme* as the 'nouvelle et orgueilleuse secte d'esprits forts', whose lack of faith deprives them, *ipso facto*, of *honnêteté*, since in his view it is only through blindness and pride that they

> osent bien porter leur impiété jusques à nier une chose que les oiseaux publient, que les choses les plus insensibles prouvent, que toute la Nature confesse, et devant qui les Anges tremblent, et les Démons ployent les genoux.[9]

The difference is that in the preceding scene of *Dom Juan*, it is not so much the *esprit fort* as the superstitious Sganarelle whose understanding had seemed 'petit et aveugle' and whose reasoning had appeared 'grossier et ridicule'. *Inde irae*.[10]

In the 'scène du Pauvre' Dom Juan also departs in other recognizable ways from the *honnêteté* generally characteristic of Molière's more romantic roles, especially his faithful lovers. If Dom Juan possesses the noble birth which Faret considers so advantageous to the *honnête homme* (p. 9), his behaviour turns it to his own disadvantage, as Dom Louis suggests in Act iv. Although in his rescue of Dom Carlos he displays the courage expected of the *honnête homme* – whose chief professional activity was war – that act and the resulting *quiproquo* must be considered in the context of the dramatic action as a whole; and one recalls Faret's reflection that prowess of itself is no adequate guarantee of *honnêteté*, since 'ceux qui joignent la malice à la valeur, sont ordinairement redoutés et haïs comme des bêtes farouches . . .' (p. 14). Above all Dom Juan departs from *honnêteté* in the 'scène du Pauvre' through excessive *raillerie*. Like the inconstant lover, the *Railleur* is a seventeenth-century commonplace – in life and in the theatre – as exemplified notably by Mareschal's *L'Inconstance d'Hylas* (1635) and *Le Railleur* (1638). By his gibes, Dom Juan no doubt exposes himself as well as the hermit to ridicule, inasmuch as the *honnête homme* does not tease the unfortunate who, mocked, might attract more sympathy than a *railleur*.[11]

In the context of the action – if one can anticipate the section on interpretation – both *railleur* and *raillé* in this scene are held at a comic distance; both are treated in a manner certainly less farcical than Sganarelle, who distances the action from life, but none the less comic because it allows a certain amount of sympathy for all three of the contrasting attitudes dramatized in carefully differentiated styles: the transcendent, rather naïve faith of Le Pauvre (the ambiguity of whose prayers for the *prosperity* of others is brought out by Dom Juan); Dom Juan's callow mockery and implied denial of transcendency (introduced by Sganarelle's partial repetition out of context of the equation from their earlier conversation, a frequent comic device in Molière, as in [ll. 313 ff.] of this play); and Sganarelle's own ridiculous mixture of faith and superstition inconsistently held and specifically belied in line 37, a peripety which in the context of the scene can satisfactorily be taken only as comically grotesque.

As the temptation of Le Pauvre is a focal point of the scene, it is important that the bribe offered by Dom Juan to induce him to blaspheme, a *louis d'or*, was a great deal of money: twenty *livres*, worth (if one can hazard a guess) no less than thirty pounds sterling in December 1967. By way of contrast, Pierrot's wager in Act II, scene I, consists of thirty-four coins, any one of which a pauper might have expected as an offering; and the total amount, clearly an important sum for Pierrot, is only ten *sous*, a fortieth of a *louis d'or*. M. Dimanche's visit in Act IV suggests that Dom Juan's gesture with the coin is an act of prodigality; but to any pauper (and to the theatre public) the offer of a *louis d'or* must have been startling.

On the other hand, the purely secular risks of blasphemy were considerable, not through the survival of medieval attitudes, but because new statutes were introduced in Molière's adolescence. Except for brief periods in the reigns of Saint-Louis and François Ier, blasphemy had not been punishable in France by physical mutilation until 1636, when an edict by Louis xiii condemned

> les blasphémateurs de Dieu, de la Vierge et des Saints jusqu'à la quatrième fois inclusivement à des amendes redoublées; pour la cinquième, à être mis au pilori; pour la sixième, à avoir la lèvre de dessus coupée; pour la septième, à perdre la lèvre de dessous; et, pour la huitième, à avoir la langue arrachée (quoted by Allier, p. 215).

Renewed, and verified by Parlement, in 1639, this edict was one of the first confirmed by Louis xiv upon assuming his majority in 1651; and the penalties were reconfirmed by Parlement in 1655.

Ten years later, in 1665, the provisions of the edict were not an idle threat. Actual sentences had been harsher than the penalties provided. For nearly forty years the powerful clandestine Compagnie du Saint-Sacrement – doubtless the 'parti dévot' or 'cabale des dévots' to which Dom Juan refers in his ironic praise of hypocrisy in Act v, scene 2 – had made it its business to seek out and destroy heresy and impiety of all kinds. A pamphlet published in 1655 discloses that the Compagnie was especially concerned about blasphemers (thought to attract plague, flood, famine, etc.) and sought to make examples of them 'dans toutes les occasions' and 'avec beaucoup de ferveur' (Allier, p. 215). Such zeal went not unrewarded: a pamphlet of 1661 reveals that as early as March, 1655, one Claude Poulain was, for blasphemy,

> condamné à être tiré de la prison de Senlis à jour de marché et conduit nu en chemise, la torche au poing, la corde au col, attachée sur une claie au cul d'un tombereau, au devant de la principale église de Senlis, et là faire amende honorable, puis être conduit au marché pour y être pendu et étranglé, son corps et son procès brûlés et réduits en cendres, et les cendres jetées au vent . . . (Allier, p. 217).

Similar sentences were passed on a number of others in the later 1650s; and in June, 1661, a certain Jean le Vert, was convicted of blasphemy and

> condamné à faire amende honorable, à avoir la lèvre de dessus et celle de dessous fendues, à être rompu vif, son corps brûlé et ses cendres jetées au vent (ibid.).

No wonder that, as one reads in Rochemont's *Observations sur une comédie intitulée 'Le Festin de Pierre'* (1665) reprinted with various editions of the play, 'cet art de jurer de bonne grâce, qui passait pour un agrément du discours dans la bouche d'une jeunesse étourdie, n'est plus en usage. . . .'[12] Clearly it was unwise as well as unholy to swear in the wrong company.

The Compagnie du Saint-Sacrement, which Mazarin had very nearly succeeded in dissolving before his death in 1661, had a final burst of activity between the spring of 1664 (when it was active in forcing the withdrawal of *Tartuffe*) and some time after the first run of *Dom Juan*. On January 17th, 1665, just a month before the latter opened, the Compagnie met at the home of the marquis de Laval to discuss ways of obtaining further confirmation of the penalties against blasphemy, penalties duly confirmed by an edict eventually promulgated in September 1666. The new edict also provided heavy fines for witnesses to blasphemy convicted of failing to denounce it, and attractive rewards for those witnesses who did (Allier, p. 418).

If an edict of September 1666 is too late to have influenced Molière in writing the 'scène du Pauvre' – and we do not know whether he had got wind of the specific plans of the 'cabale' – , its provisions reflect an atmosphere of espionnage and denunciation to which Dom Juan alludes in Act v, scene 2:

> Je ferai le vengeur des intérêts du Ciel, et, sous ce prétexte commode, je pousserai mes ennemis, je les accuserai d'impiété, et saurai déchaîner contre eux des zélés indiscrets. . . [ll. 1746–9].

Is it really too far-fetched to propose that in the 'scène du Pauvre' the disguised Dom Juan may have been intended to evoke just such 'zélés indiscrets'? It is true that Dom Juan's 'provocative proposition' offers, as Professor Howarth points out, a parallel with the known behaviour of the Chevalier de Roquelaure, a libertine imprisoned for impiety in the late 1640s at the instigation of Saint Vincent de Paul: 'hearing a poor man blaspheme in public, he rewarded him and offered to pay him more if he would blaspheme more outrageously' (ed. cit., p. 90). But in the altered context of the 1660s might not Dom Juan's offer have evoked, for some of the first public at least, not only rakes like Roquelaure, but the informers who piously denounced him? Desmarets (the author of *Mirame*) had recently got the confidence of a religious fanatic, Simon Morin, and then denounced his impiety. Morin was tried and publicly burned in Paris in March 1663.

INTERPRETATION. As the preceding sections imply, the interpretation of this scene cannot be separated either from questions of staging or from the background of the play. There can be little doubt, however, that whatever comedy the scene contains plays upon some of the major anxieties of Molière's time. But if a range of possible implications can be suggested in terms of contemporary preoccupations, and certain interpretations definitely excluded as anachronistic, detailed analysis of the scene and of the *characters* who appear in it depends very much upon interpretation of their *roles*. And on a number of crucial points a student is as free to decide for himself as any critic or producer of the play.

One neglected fact has a considerable importance. If Le Pauvre exits at line 40, followed by Dom Juan after his last speech, the only character present throughout the scene is Sganarelle, the role originally played by Molière himself. This analysis has assumed that Sganarelle is no less a participant in the action than either of the other two characters; and clearly he dominates the end of the scene – which continues until Dom Juan returns with Dom Carlos – when he has the opportunity to mime panic as he hides in full view of the audience (a spectacular use of the conventional *liaison des scènes*). But there are suggestions, particularly in Rochemont's *Observations*, that Sganarelle's participation earlier in the scene should not be limited to his outlandish disguise and three *répliques*. Rochemont complains of Molière's 'grimaces' and 'gestes' as an actor in the role of Sganarelle, whose exhortation to Le Pauvre to swear a little can be read in the light of Rochemont's complaint that Molière

> rend la majesté de Dieu le jouet d'un maître et d'un valet de théâtre, d'un athée qui s'en rit, et d'un valet, plus impie que son maître, *qui en fait rire les autres* (our italics).

No less than the farcical disguise discussed above, the broadly comic mime associated with Molière's acting must have ensured that the whole scene was initially played in a comic register.

The extent to which Dom Juan may also be conceived as a comic character, obviously in a different style, depends upon an actor's reading of the role.[13] I have argued that – like so many of Molière's title roles – Dom Juan is clearly not an *honnête homme*, that his callow attitude in this scene is inspired in part by the traditional comic role of the *railleur*, and that it offers certain analogies with the *marquis ridicules* presented by Scarron and Molière in a number of comedies.[14] Much depends, of course, upon the manner in which Dom Juan thrusts the *louis d'or* upon Le Pauvre at line 34 ('Tiens'), teases with it at line 36, and thrusts it forward again two lines later ('Prends, le voilà, prends, te dis-je'). Nor can Dom Juan's style be separated from the response of Le Pauvre. Should the latter turn his back upon Dom Juan at line 39? And does Dom Juan hand the coin to him at line 40, or throw it after him? The scene is more comic if, after protesting 'j'aime mieux mourir de faim', Le Pauvre has to pick up the money from the stage floor. But Dom Juan could be made more ridiculous if, breaking with tradition, Le Pauvre does not accept the gift at all.

Silence in the theatre is also important, like rests in music. How long a pause should there be between lines 40 and 41? And to what extent should the surprise mimed by Dom Juan in exclaiming 'Mais que vois-je là?' reflect genuine astonishment? Should the line be taken instead merely as a pretext for breaking off an unsatisfactory conversation? It cannot be the latter if Le Pauvre has already exited. . . . On the other hand, it seems likely that Dom Juan's celebrated phrase 'je te le donne pour l'amour de l'humanité' (l. 40) spoken to – or perhaps after – Le Pauvre has, for the speaker, no humanitarian connotations. Phrased in antithesis to the conventional 'pour l'amour de Dieu', it implies that the money is offered, not in recognition of any religious (or humanitarian) obligation, but to flout the hermit's faith.

There is a further caution. The scene is delicately balanced, so that (as in any dramatic encounter) the interpretation of one character influences all the rest. Too little dignity in Le Pauvre, too much coarseness in Dom Juan, too much farcical by-play from Sganarelle, diminishes the symbolic value of the confrontation; too much dignity in Le Pauvre, a hard or brittle Dom Juan, an inert Sganarelle, can dissipate the comic.

CONCLUSION. The argument for a comic interpretation of this scene rests in the main upon a concept of the play's structure, its social background, current political activity, Molière's characteristic use of distorted repetition, and what we know from contemporary documents about his own style of acting in the role of Sganarelle, strongly influenced by the grotesque mime of farce and *commedia dell'arte*. But it also involves his adaptation of legendary material – the French tragicomedies in particular – in which the prototypes of Dom Juan in similar circumstances were cast as cowardly, treacherous and unredeemedly odious. Molière chose instead, by a process not without analogy with travesty or *burlesque*, to depict a character whose mockery and too narrow sympathies – for he not only taunts Le Pauvre, but betrays members of the opposite sex (Done Elvire, the peasant girls), of other classes and conditions (Pierrot, M. Dimanche), of another generation (Dom Louis), assisting only a man of his own age and condition whom he had already offended (Dom Carlos) – proclaim his lack of *honnêteté*.

As the 'scène du Pauvre' fits into a series of Dom Juan's encounters with 'fâcheux', it is more structurally related to the play as a whole than sometimes allowed; and by bringing together in this scene three 'incompatibles', Molière succeeds in illustrating not only their mutual incomprehension and failure to communicate across different orders of thought, but also the comic incongruity latent in the inner 'contrariété' or self-contradiction of each of the characters individually. The scene may also fit into another structure of the play: episodes alluding to matters which the recently revived Compagnie du Saint-Sacrement found particularly objectionable, such as Sganarelle's praise of tobacco (doubtless snuff) and Done Elvire's broken vows in Act I, Pierrot's wager in Act II, and the duel arranged (by 'direction of intention') in Act V. This structure would be especially relevant if there is an allusion in this scene to the 'zélés indiscrets' openly satirized in Act V, and also if it reflects Colbert's efforts to 'diminuer doucement et insensiblement les moines de l'un et l'autre sexe' (quoted by Allier, pp. 415–16). We now know, in any case, that the structure of *Dom Juan* is not slap-dash. The play was not put together in great haste, as once assumed. The 'Marché de décors' shows that in early December, 1664, fully ten weeks before the opening, Molière was in substantial possession of his subject.

Beyond such considerations, the 'scène du Pauvre' is a crucial episode in a play where the heavenly perspective is always present – as in baroque tragicomedies and religious paintings – from Sganarelle's first allusion to 'le courroux du Ciel' in the exposition to the miraculous dénouement. And this is true – though the implications are obviously different – even if (as seems likely) the miracles are parodied, a point on which, as upon Dom Juan's atheism, contemporary opinion is divided.[15] Yet the tone of the 'scène du Pauvre' is so different from that of providential tragicomedy that Dom Juan's taunts focus comically, rather than compassionately, the ambiguity of an ascetic ethic by which an indigent hermit can offer prayers for the prosperity of those who give him money. In particular, the taunt '. . . tu es bien mal reconnu de tes soins' rephrases thematic material already introduced in Act II, scene 3, when Sganarelle receives a clout intended for Pierrot, whom he has tried to protect, along with the jibe: 'Te voilà payé de ta charité' [l. 716] – a jibe that might have been made a little earlier to Pierrot, who had rescued Dom Juan, as later on to Dom Louis or Done Elvire, all of whom are hurt in their efforts to help Dom Juan. Louis xiv is said to have countered objections to the role of Dom Juan on the grounds 'qu'il n'est pas récompensé'.[16] Perhaps the most significant thing about the 'scène du Pauvre' is that, unless Dom Juan's *louis d'or* is looked upon as providential, Le Pauvre is not rewarded – not normally rewarded – either. The comic peripety of Sganarelle's incitement to blasphemy after extolling faith (l. 37) suggests, moreover, that there is no necessary connection between religious conviction and conduct – an interpretation shocking in the context of much seventeenth-century thought, but by no means incompatible with the 'prétexte commode' of the 'zélés indiscrets' of Act v or the line of Molière's characters who unconsciously exploit religious faith in order to crush others and gratify themselves: Gorgibus in *Sganarelle*, Arnolphe in *L'Ecole des Femmes*, Orgon in *Tartuffe*. Independently of possible satire of mendicants, *esprits forts*, cowardly valets, and/or zealots (for plays mean different things to different points of view), the *lazzi* of this scene do not diminish its significance by being comic. On the contrary, as so often in Molière, they focus its furthest implications. His *burlesque* of tragicomic material amounts to more than a travesty of theatrical tradition, and the total meaning of the scene is greater than the sum of its parts. On such important issues as the working of providence and the relation of faith to morals Molière discards the common assumptions of the tragicomic genre to offer new insights which together imply – by a denial of the opposites comically debunked – a world in which providence, asceticism, and superstition are less important than *honnêteté* – the recognition of man's social responsibilities. That today many of us have a different conception of social responsibilities is another matter.

NOTES

1 It is common practice to preserve the spelling *Dom Juan* when referring to Molière's character and play, while using the English form *Don* to refer to the legend, to which one can find a convenient introduction in R. Grimsley, 'The Don Juan Legend', in *Modern Languages*, XLI (1960) 135–41.

2 René Pintard, 'Temps et lieux dans le *Dom Juan* de Molière', in *Studi in onore di Italo Siciliano*, Florence, Olschki, 1966, vol. II, pp. 997–1006. It would be proper to acknowledge here also a general debt in this commentary to the well-known books on Molière by R. Fernandez, W. G. Moore, D. Romano, M. Descotes, and J. Guicharnaud.

3 M. Jurgens and E. Maxfield-Miller, *Cent ans de recherches sur Molière*, Paris, Imprimerie Nationale, 1963, p. 399. Spelling in other seventeenth-century quotations, as in the text of the passage itself, is modernized.

4 Saint-Simon, *Mémoires*, ed. G. Truc, vol. IV, Paris, Gallimard (Bibliothèque de la Pléiade), 1953, p. 1005.

5 The theatrical fantasy is based on the doctor's black assembly gown and may involve satire of provincial practice. Except at official gatherings (and perhaps in the provinces?), writes François Millepierre, '. . . à la ville, (le médecin) s'habille à peu près comme tout le monde, selon la mode, avec discrétion cependant, sans y mettre de fantaisie outrée' (*La Vie quotidienne des médecins au temps de Molière*, Paris, Hachette, 1964, pp. 40–1).

6 Quoted in John Lough, *An Introduction to Seventeenth-Century France*, London, Longmans, 1966 (first publ., 1954), p. 21.

7 Raoul Allier, *La Cabale des dévots*, 1627–66, Paris, Colin, 1902, p. 416.

8 It is as well to remember, however, that in the generation preceding the Revocation of the Edict of Nantes in 1685, it was Government policy in France to buy consciences (the conversion of Huguenots). As an illustration of the word *pistole* in his *Dictionnaire*, Littré cites from the correspondence of Colbert the observation that 'le nombre de ceux qui se convertissent ici (à Rochefort) est très-grand, et il est arrivé fort souvent de rendre catholiques des familles entières pour une pistole' – just half the amount which Dom Juan offers to Le Pauvre.

9 Faret, *L'Honnête Homme, ou l'art de plaire à la Cour*, Paris, Nicolas et Jean de la Coste, 1639 (first publ., 1630), p. 56. Faret uses these phrases with reference to the *esprit fort*, p. 56.

10 Comic treatment of religious questions in this play offended not only those who considered the theatre as a whole a wicked waste of time and those who thought playwrights should not touch upon any religious subject, but also those who, while accepting the theatre in principle and even religious themes reverently handled, objected to their comic presentation.

11 'Il observera particulièrement de n'attaquer jamais de ses brocards . . . les misérables. . . . Pource que l'inclination naturelle qu'ont presque tous

les hommes à se laisser toucher de pitié des pressantes calamités dont ils voient ces malheureuses gens affligés, empêche qu'on ne puisse rire d'eux . . .' (p. 173). My argument is that Molière's polyvalent satire liberates the spectator from the anxiety diagnosed by Faret.

12 Molière, *Œuvres*, ed. Despois and Mesnard, Paris, Hachette (Grands Ecrivains de la France), 1873–93, vol. v, p. 231.

13 Dom Juan was created by La Grange, who often played 'jeune premier' roles. The case for a comic Dom Juan is argued by R. Laufer, 'Le Comique du personnage de Dom Juan', in *Modern Language Review*, LVIII (1963), 15–20.

14 Molière remarks in the first scene of *L'Impromptu de Versailles*: 'Le marquis aujourd'hui est le plaisant de la comédie . . . dans toutes nos pièces de maintenant il faut toujours un marquis ridicule qui divertisse la compagnie.'

15 Rochemont complains that Dom Juan's punishment is only 'un foudre imaginaire et aussi ridicule que celui de Jupiter . . . et qui, bien loin de donner de la crainte aux hommes, ne pouvait pas chasser une mouche ni faire peur à une souris', a point not satisfactorily answered in the *Réponse aux Observations* (Molière, *Œuvres*, ed. cit., pp. 227, 234, etc.).

16 Louis xiv, quoted ibid., vol. v, p. 246.

### Source

Jean-Baptiste Molière (1622–73): *Dom Juan, ou le Festin de Pierre*, Act III, sc. 2, ed. W. D. Howarth, Oxford, Blackwell, 1958, pp. 35–6, ll. 983–1028.

R. C. Knight

RACINE

Iphigénie, Act iv, scene 4, ll. 1174–1220

                                        Mon père,
Cessez de vous troubler, vous n'êtes point trahi.
Quand vous commanderez, vous serez obéi.
Ma vie est votre bien. Vous voulez le reprendre ;
5 Vos ordres sans détour pouvaient se faire entendre.
D'un œil aussi content, d'un cœur aussi soumis,
Que j'acceptais l'époux que vous m'aviez promis,
Je saurai, s'il le faut, victime obéissante,
Tendre au fer de Calchas une tête innocente,
10 Et, respectant le coup par vous-même ordonné,
Vous rendre tout le sang que vous m'avez donné.
    Si pourtant ce respect, si cette obéissance
Paraît digne à vos yeux d'une autre récompense,
Si d'une mère en pleurs vous plaignez les ennuis,
15 J'ose vous dire ici qu'en l'état où je suis,
Peut-être assez d'honneurs environnaient ma vie
Pour ne pas souhaiter qu'elle me fût ravie,
Ni qu'en me l'arrachant, un sévère destin
Si près de ma naissance en eût marqué la fin.
20 Fille d'Agamemnon, c'est moi qui, la première,
Seigneur, vous appelai de ce doux nom de père.
C'est moi qui, si longtemps le plaisir de vos yeux,
Vous ai fait de ce nom remercier les Dieux,
Et pour qui, tant de fois prodiguant vos caresses,
25 Vous n'avez point du sang dédaigné les faiblesses.
Hélas ! avec plaisir je me faisais conter
Tous les noms des pays que vous allez dompter ;
Et déjà, d'Ilion présageant la conquête,
D'un triomphe si beau je préparais la fête.
30 Je ne m'attendais pas que, pour le commencer,
Mon sang fût le premier que vous dussiez verser.
    Non que la peur du coup dont je suis menacée
Me fasse rappeler votre bonté passée.
Ne craignez rien. Mon cœur, de votre honneur jaloux,
35 Ne fera point rougir un père tel que vous ;
Et, si je n'avais eu que ma vie à défendre,
J'aurais su renfermer un souvenir si tendre.
Mais à mon triste sort, vous le savez, Seigneur,
Une mère, un amant, attachaient leur bonheur.

40 Un roi digne de vous a cru voir la journée
Qui devait éclairer notre illustre hyménée.
Déjà, sûr de mon cœur à sa flamme promis,
Il s'estimait heureux; vous me l'aviez permis.
Il sait votre dessein, jugez de ses alarmes.
45 Ma mère est devant vous, et vous voyez ses larmes.
Pardonnez aux efforts que je viens de tenter
Pour prévenir les pleurs que je leur vais coûter.

CONTEXT. These are lines 1174–1220 (Act IV, sc. 4) of *Iphigénie* (1675), the most successful initially and the least appreciated today of Racine's major plays. Iphigénie addresses her father Agamemnon, who under pressure from his fellow leaders has decided to obey the oracle demanding her death, and has brought her to Aulis on the pretext of a marriage with Achille, to whom she is betrothed.

Agamemnon is commander of the Greek confederation formed to fight Troy (or 'Ilion', l. 28). They are becalmed at their point of departure from Greece, and Calchas the soothsayer has announced that Iphigénie must be sacrificed to the gods before a wind will rise. (Racine appears to make Calchas also a sacrificing priest, which he is not in the Greek poets.) Iphigénie and her mother have learnt the truth just before she is to be taken to the altar.

SOURCES. Racine is for the first time in his career working over a play on the same subject by Euripides (which had not been the case with *La Thébaïde* or *Andromaque*). Comparison of the two treatments is complicated by the existence of an intermediate source which he never mentioned, Rotrou's *Iphigénie*, a tragicomedy of 1644; this text, last published in 1820, is hard to obtain. It is of interest however to know that in both these plays Achilles had advised mother and daughter to appeal to Agamemnon before he himself tried to defend them by force: whereas Racine's Achille, more of a *héros de roman*, has had to be restrained, largely by Iphigénie herself, and persuaded to let them plead first. This gives the heroine an additional motive – to avoid a scandalous and dangerous clash (cf. l. 44 here, and *Iph.* ll. 1063–4:

> Je sais jusqu'où s'emporte un amant irrité;
> Et mon père est jaloux de son autorité.)

Racine has also improved the sequence of events: in his two predecessors it is the mother who first addresses Agamemnon with a torrent of violent reproaches, leaving him little disposed to hear the girl's appeal.

ANALYSIS. In Euripides, Iphigenia has brought her infant brother in her arms to touch her father's heart; she weeps, kneels and frankly begs for life. In Rotrou she is resentful, contemptuous of Agamemnon's betrayal, and stiffened by a Cornelian sense of the demands of *la gloire*. (Rotrou – and Racine – remembered Aristotle's condemnation of the sudden shift in Euripides' Iphigenia, from fear of death to her final mood of heroic self-immolation; v. *Poetics* chap. 15.)

Racine's Iphigénie has lost this hardness – the Cornelian vogue is over – but is less spontaneous than Euripides'. She begins in haste: her father has just realized the situation, and begun to vent his wrath on his messenger: 'Ah! malheureux Arcas, tu m'as trahi'. She reassures him, and deftly inserts into her protestations of obedience all the pleas likely to touch his emotions.

| | | |
|---|---|---|
| I A | 1–2 | You need not fear (nor dissemble, she adds, 5)[1] |
| | 3 | I shall obey; my life is yours to take; |
| | 6 | as readily as when I accepted Achille, |
| | 8 | I will die. |
| B | 12 | But if you pity me |
| | 14 | and my mother |
| | 15 | let me remind you |
| | 16 | of my position |
| | 19 | and of my youth, which make it bitter to die; |
| | 21 | of your love for me from childhood; |
| | 26 | of the irony by which I shall not enjoy your hoped-for triumph. |
| II A | 32 | Not that I am faltering: |
| | 34 | I will not shame you, |
| | 36 | and I would not have pleaded |
| B | 38 | But for, 39, my mother, and my betrothed |
| | 40 | who is worthy of you, |
| | 41 | expects to marry me today, |
| | 42 | (and knows I love him!) |
| | 44 | He is anxious (understatement!), |
| | 46 | my mother is weeping. |
| *Conclusion* | | |
| | 47 | Forgive me for doing this on their account. |

MATTER. Iphigénie says, on the face of it, that she knows her duty and will do it. This may seem today over-prim or over-heroic according to one's view: but not only was it demanded by *bienséance* of a seventeenth-century princess (in fiction at least), it was the only way to calm Agamemnon and obtain a hearing. In any case we see that each assertion of obedience (IA, ll. 1 ff., IIA, ll. 32 ff.) is followed by *pourtant* (l. 12) or *mais* (l. 38). This is a device common in Cornelian tirades, common in Racine,[2] and possibly common in real life, at times when etiquette forbade a direct contradiction or refusal. The important parts of the reply are therefore the restrained appeal to paternal affection (IB, ll. 15 ff.) and the reminder in ll. 38 ff. (IIB). But under the surface there is something else: while in IA, she speaks of submission, the most telling expressions are veiled reproaches, intended to sting her father's conscience: line 5 (with *sans détour* stressed at the caesura) recalls his deceit with studied understatement: line 7, a broken promise; line 9, her innocence (the word has all the stress of a quatrain-ending); line 10, his responsibility.

The hints cease in IB, which is introduced with deprecatory signs of hesitation – *si pourtant* (l. 12), *j'ose vous dire* (l. 15), *peut-être* (l. 16). Never in this section is Agamemnon indicated as the author of her death – from lines 15 to 19 all the turns are impersonal. After *ordonné* (l. 10) we must wait for a direct, and bitter, allusion until line 31.

IIA returns to the tactic of hints (the first appeal has failed): *votre bonté passée* (l. 33), the almost insolent (and strongly stressed) *Ne craignez rien* (l. 34); *un père tel que vous* (l. 35) is the most cruelly equivocal of them all.

IIB carries a just-submerged warning. First, for *bienséance*, her mother's grief is mentioned (l. 39) (if Clytemnestra is given very little prominence, it may be because she is to speak later herself); her own disappointed love is mentioned, ostensibly in excuse: *vous me l'aviez permis* (l. 43, cf. l. 7), where the enigmatic *l'* must mean 'to let Achille know that I returned his love'. But Achille gets all the space: the important theme is Achille's disappointment and his *alarmes* (l. 44) – or, to speak plainly, his furious anger which she has been holding back (*Iph.* III, vi, vii, cf. I, i, 97 ff.).

The conclusion (ll. 46–7) is formally an apology, containing a justification which is really the recapitulation of the plea which Iphigénie wishes to leave in the forefront, since it does not concern her own fate nor threaten Agamemnon's pride: *les pleurs que je leur vais coûter*. Except in lines 16–19 she has preferred to make her plea through the feelings of others – her mother (lines 14, 39, 45), her father (ll. 20 ff.), her lover (ll. 39 ff.). This avoids the appearance of disobedience or cowardice.

This is the 'réponse terrible . . . , d'une grande cruauté tragique' in which Péguy declares that 'il n'y a pas un mot qui ne mette l'adversaire, (le père), dans son tort. . . . Les victimes de Racine sont elles-mêmes plus cruelles que les bourreaux de Corneille.' For 'les cornéliens ne se blessent jamais, même et surtout quand ils se tuent'.[3]

It would be no defence to say that Racine thought he had made his heroine so perfect that his public could not bear to see her die (v. Preface); the implication is that Racine imparted this cruelty to his characters in spite of himself. But Péguy has forgotten the spitefulness of some of Corneille's women, though he claims to know the plays so well. And he might have remembered that Iphigénie is the victim of considerably greater cruelty; might have remembered too the total impression of the girl that the tragedy gives us – the pure affection of her first greeting to her father (ii, ii), her quick amends to Eriphile (iii, iv), the absence of all recrimination when she learns her father's designs, and her defence of that father against her own defenders (iii, vii, 1059 ff., and iv, ii). True, she uses words that will shock and shame (yet always with *bienséance*): but Péguy has forgotten what she knows will follow if they fail – unseemly violence between two men she loves, and no doubt the death of one of them. If she seeks to 'wound' and is less than candid, that is the only reason and this is the only occasion.

The protestations that mask her appeals are nevertheless sincere – she proves it by her acts later; *le devoir* still speaks in a Cornelian voice to Racine's virtuous characters.

Is her plea too studied? She has had time to rehearse it – and this would be in the manner of the time[4] – though she could not have foreseen her actual cue. But then, this perfect mastery of language is what all dramatists (of the seventeenth century at least) try to give their characters; a matter not of *vraisemblance* but of convention. Actors make their points perfectly in tragedy, as they sing in tune in opera. This intelligence, this art and poetry, together with the opposite characteristic of (relative) spontaneity in other scenes, are what give life to the rather copybook virtues Iphigénie displays.

Social and moral conventions of the times are apparent too (how could it be otherwise?). Instead of saying like Euripides' Iphigenia, 'Do not kill me untimely – it is sweet to see the light', she talks of the *honneurs* (l. 16) she enjoyed; but is not this the demure way to refer to her imminent marriage (to a prince, son of a goddess)? Honour will be the motive of her sacrifice; but unlike heroes of Corneille or some of Racine's, she means her father's honour (l. 34).

In having no scruples over war and conquest (ll. 26 ff.) she is, we must admit, only too typical of her time.

Racine was in no doubt, nor were his contemporaries,[5] that the appealing figure of Iphigénie was the central point of interest in his tragedy – so appealing, that he would not let her sacrifice be consummated. Whether thereby the tragedy as such is marred; whether there are not weaknesses in the suspense-plot and the happy ending, in the scapegoat role of Eriphile, or in the role of Agamemnon, who, moving as he is in his evasions and remorse, never reaches the purgation of decision or even death – or for that matter whether the action ascribed to the gods is not morally and rationally a stumbling-block: these are important questions for critics of the play, but they must not detain us in the examination of this passage, where they do not directly arise.

It is relevant however to point out that the theme of the will of Heaven is conspicuous by its absence in Iphigénie's speech. Once she has resigned herself to die she does – not very often – use this argument (ll. 1494, 1545, 1642, 1658): while she is pleading for life, she can only ignore it, since it admits of no answer.

Many other normal elements of a *plaidoyer* are absent from this one. No *captatio benevolentiae*, no flattery, or no more (l. 35) than is *bienséant* from a daughter to a monarch; no recourse to commonplaces, which might look pedantic or intellectual; no overt pathos, no dwelling on the horror of her doom.

MANNER. In the matter of expression also, we shall find the speech notably lacking in the normal ornaments of rhetoric. An emotional plea calls for the figures of apostrophe (and here we have three bare vocatives, lines 1, 21, 38), exclamation (there is one *hélas*, l. 26) and question (there are none): we may contrast Clytemnestre's outburst almost immediately following (*Iph.*, ll. 1249 ff.).

Epithets are few and lack-lustre; there is no paradox or oxymoron, no antithesis, only a few 'patterns' of symmetry or repetition which shape, without heightening, the language (ll. 6; 12, 14; 20–25; 44, 45).

Images, based on metaphor or metonymy, though few and inconspicuous, seem to be the principal means of colouring the style and touching the imagination:

*votre bien . . . reprendre* (l. 4) is barely noticeable;

*vous rendre . . . le sang . . . donné* (l. 11) plays – with some effect – on two senses of *sang*, a word which reappears as a pure metonymy (l. 25) and with (ironical) allusion to a festival sacrifice (l. 31); *tendre au fer . . . une tête* (l. 9), *almost* literal, exists largely for the value of the epithet *innocente*, stressed at the end of the couplet; Lines 16, 19, 37, 39 call for no special comment.

Characteristic metonymies (*œil, cœur, bras*) and abstractions (*ordres, coup, respect, ennuis, caresses, faiblesses*), and the 'distancing' indefinite article (*une tête, une mère, un père, un amant, un roi*: but *mon sang* 31, *ma mère*, l. 45) are offset by an unusual abundance of personal pronouns – Agamemnon's acts and (ll. 23–5) feelings receive at least as much prominence as Iphigénie's. But this element of directness and emotion is *estompé* in its turn by ever-recurring periphrasis, veiling the ideas which must not be nakedly expressed – those of death and killing. The only two verbs that come anywhere near to painting real physical action (*tendre . . . une tête*, l. 9; *verser mon sang*, l. 31) belong to this order of metonymies.

*Fille d'Agamemnon* (l. 20), so pregnant with meaning, is not metonymy, but a characteristically Racinian use of an apposition preceding the statement (with a proper noun chosen as being more pointed than a possessive) – and the statement almost forms an anacoluthon,[6] for, stripped of periphrasis, it says simply 'c'est moi qui suis votre fille'. A means of repeating a strong point? or a case where poetic utterance becomes impatient of the bonds of prosaic meaning?

This sentence shows the *bienséances* ruling matters of vocabulary too. Rotrou wrote early enough in the century to be able to follow Euripides literally: his Iphigénie is the first, she says,

Qui vous ait appelé de ce doux nom de père,
Qui vous ait fait caresse, et qui sur vos genoux
Vous ait servi longtemps d'un passe-temps si doux (v, iii).

In Racine's tragic lexicon knees exist only to be fallen on, or fallen at and clasped. But his muted version has charm in its setting. The equilibrium between dignity and naturalness is caught by the virtual double negative *point dédaigné*, which echoes an equally pregnant understatement: *ne pas souhaiter qu'elle me fût ravie* (l. 17). These are special cases of the soft-pedalling or avoidance of obvious pathos which is such a feature of this passage.

For it is not quite a characteristic piece of Racinian dramatic poetry (if there is such a thing); like the father-daughter situation, it is unique in Racine. It is played *en sourdine*, and is perhaps the more beautiful for that.

Any ear attuned to Racine can hear the melody here, though for all but phonologists it is hard to track down. It depends firstly, of course, on avoidance of cacophony and of consonant-clusters, occasionally on alliteration or assonance (v, f, ll. 4–5; i, ll. 6–9), but mostly on discreet patterns of vowel- or consonant-repetition (s, u, p, l. 21) and of vowel-modulation (of which an unusually conspicuous example is l. 6: ɛ̃-œ | o-i-ɔ̃-ɑ̃ ∥ ɛ̃-œ | o-i-u-i|. A non-French critic will do well to pursue this path no further (though I am told it helps to be a reader of Welsh *cynghanedd*).

The extreme fluidity of the rhythm, on the other hand, is more easily perceived. Behind most dramatic alexandrines of the seventeenth century – not so far behind, in much of Corneille – lies the quatrain framework (the quatrain is the smallest unit that can be interpolated or cut out, because of alternation of rhymes; it tends therefore to contain one unit of thought developed in two or three parallel ways): here it has almost dissolved away. Successive movements swell out into groupings which break the conventional limit, though the ends of couplets and quatrains still demand a pause of some kind; then they subside to allow another wave to form. But always the sense justifies the form, and the form helps us to read more deeply into the sense.[7] The vocative 'Mon père' *en contre-rejet* interrupts Agamemnon's outburst (at one of the less common and more impressive positions in the line); it prefaces three lines, each symmetrically divided – paratactic statements, reasonable, sedate and soothing. A line of one sentence, drawing the conclusion (l. 5), completes a kind of quatrain. Next, in the profession of readiness to die, a two-line protasis is answered by a two-line apodosis (ll. 6–9), but this (in case it seems insufficient or incredible?) is followed up by a restatement, emphasizing new aspects, in another couplet; so this group has spread into six lines. Another protasis of *précautions oratoires* seems insufficient to the speaker in the same way, so she adds a third line (l. 14), containing her strongest plea – her mother's tears. But now the quatrain no longer has room for the apodosis; its fourth line (l. 15) brings in only the introductory *J'ose vous dire* and dares to end on a couple of *chevilles de remplissage* (*ici, en l'état où je suis*). *What* she ventures to say has a quatrain to itself (ll. 16–19), which, if it were alone, could be quoted as typical of the familiar kind, with the second couplet taking up and developing on a larger scale an expression occupying only the last quarter of the first (*qu'elle me fût ravie, Ni que* . . .). Another anxious reduplication prolongs the next statement too (beginning *Fille d'Agamemnon*) into a six-line group. In the next again, lines 30–31 go so closely with the preceding four that the same is true once more.

Now (l. 32) Iphigénie appears to revoke her plea for mercy – four lines, with an emphatic *coupe* in the third: but the sense runs on, with a *si* (l. 36) introducing the *mais* to follow (l. 38). The movement subsides now, with two quatrains, the second with lines of strongly-marked symmetry; a couplet concludes.

The passage, then, reflects and responds to its particular context in these various ways – the ironic 'cruelty' of the insinuations; the restraint, or constraint, evinced by vocabulary and diction and by the self-contradictions of the plan; the spontaneous and sincere emotions that sing in the verse; the hesitations, and the reduplications of arguments, which are betrayed by the rhythm; all these are present together. Their complexity is that of the situation, which an inexperienced girl has to find the intellectual and spiritual resources to face alone.

NOTES

1 'Your orders could have been given (*pouvaient = auraient pu*) without any subterfuge.'
2 Cf. *Horace*, I, i, 27, 52, 79, etc.; *Iph.* v, iii, 1619 ff.; and P. France, *Racine's Rhetoric*, Oxford, 1965, p. 221 and n².
3 *Victor-Marie, comte Hugo*, in *Œuvres complètes*, Paris, NRF, t. IV, 1916, pp. 422–3, 428.
4 Cf. Othon's *Effort de mémoire*, *Othon*, II, i, 399 ff.
5 *Iph.*, pref.; cf. Boileau, *Ep.* VII, 3 ff.
6 I owe this remark to Professor P. J. Wexler (see next note).
7 Many of the comments that follow were inspired by a letter from my friend Professor P. J. Wexler.

*Source*
Jean Racine (1639–99): *Iphigénie*, Act IV, sc. 4, ll. 1174–1220, in *Œuvres*, t. III, ed. P. Mesnard (Les Grands Écrivains de la France), Paris, 1885.

*A. J. Steele*

# LA FONTAINE
## Le Fermier, le Chien et le Renard

*Le Fermier, le Chien, et le Renard*

Le loup et le renard sont d'étranges voisins:
Je ne bâtirai point autour de leur demeure.
  Ce dernier guettait à toute heure
Les poules d'un fermier; et quoique des plus fins,
5  Il n'avait pu donner d'atteinte à la volaille.
D'une part l'appétit, de l'autre le danger,
N'étaient pas au compère un embarras léger.
  'Hé quoi! dit-il, cette canaille
  Se moque impunément de moi?
10  Je vais, je viens, je me travaille,
J'imagine cent tours; le rustre en paix chez soi
Vous fait argent de tout, convertit en monnoie
Ses chapons, sa poulaille; il en a même au croc:
Et moi maître passé, quand j'attrape un vieux coq,
15  Je suis au comble de la joie!
Pourquoi sire Jupin m'a-t-il donc appelé
Au métier de renard? Je jure les puissances
De l'Olympe et du Styx, il en sera parlé.'
  Roulant en son cœur ces vengeances,
20 Il choisit une nuit libérale en pavots:
Chacun était plongé dans un profond repos;
Le maître du logis, les valets, le chien même,
Poules, poulets, chapons, tout dormait. Le fermier,
  Laissant ouvert son poulailler,
25  Commit une sottise extrême.
Le voleur tourne tant qu'il entre au lieu guetté,
Le dépeuple, remplit de meurtres la cité;
  Les marques de sa cruauté
Parurent avec l'aube: on vit un étalage
30  De corps sanglants, et de carnage.
  Peu s'en fallut que le soleil
Ne rebroussât d'horreur vers le manoir liquide.
  Tel, et d'un spectacle pareil,
Apollon irrité contre le fier Atride
35 Joncha son camp de morts: on vit presque détruit
L'ost des Grecs, et ce fut l'ouvrage d'une nuit.
  Tel encore autour de sa tente

Ajax, à l'âme impatiente,
De moutons et de boucs fit un vaste débris,
Croyant tuer entre eux son concurrent Ulysse,
Et les auteurs de l'injustice
Par qui l'autre emporta le prix.
Le renard, autre Ajax, aux volailles funeste,
Emporte ce qu'il peut, laisse étendu le reste.
Le maître ne trouva de recours qu'à crier
Contre ses gens, son chien, c'est l'ordinaire usage.
'Ah! maudit animal, qui n'es bon qu'à noyer,
Que n'avertissais-tu dès l'abord du carnage?
— Que ne l'évitiez-vous? C'eût été plus tôt fait.
Si vous, maître et fermier, à qui touche le fait,
Dormez sans avoir soin que la porte soit close,
Voulez-vous que moi, chien, qui n'ai rien à la chose,
Sans aucun intérêt je perde le repos?'
Ce chien parlait très à propos.
Son raisonnement pouvait être
Fort bon dans la bouche d'un maître;
Mais n'étant que d'un simple chien,
On trouva qu'il ne valait rien.
On vous sangla le pauvre drille.
Toi donc, qui que tu sois, ô père de famille
(Et je ne t'ai jamais envié cet honneur),
T'attendre aux yeux d'autrui, quand tu dors, c'est erreur.
Couche-toi le dernier, et vois fermer ta porte.
Que si quelque affaire t'importe,
Ne la fais point par procureur.

INTRODUCTION. A first cursory reading of this *Fable*[1] shows that it is basically the narration in *vers irréguliers* of a very simple incident, the killing by the Fox of the Farmer's poultry, and the punishing of the Dog, who is blamed for allowing this to happen; from which the equally simple lesson is drawn that it is better to look after one's own affairs than to rely on others. The object of our analysis must be to see how and to what effect La Fontaine has used this meagre *datum*.

I. Many of the *Fables* open directly with the narration of the tale. In this case, however, we have in lines 1–2 a very brief preliminary reflection, which rouses the reader's expectancy by calling for proof or illustration. The two lines are formally incomplete, since they do not rhyme, and this necessitates the *enchaînement* with the narrative that follows.

These prefatory lines usher us at once into the imaginary world of the *Fables*, where men and beasts live together as good or bad neighbours, in which animal and human are interchangeable and in fine indistinguishable from each other. The conventions of the genre are thus discreetly recalled at the outset, and the reader duly prepared for the sort of story that is to come.

Finally, in these opening lines, through the use of the first person and the confession of his own attitude in the matter, the poet strikes a note of conversational familiarity. Here he is, as it were in person, talking to us with informal ease. If we have grasped these lines aright, we shall regard ourselves less as readers than as listeners.

II. The narrative extends from line 3 to line 59, and on inspection falls into three parts. In the first (ll. 3–18) the situation is expounded and the crisis prepared; the second (ll. 19–44) recounts the slaughter of the fowls; the third (ll. 45–59) deals with the sequel. We must examine each of these in turn.

(i) Lines 3–18. In this section, linked grammatically and formally with the prefatory lines, we are shown the predicament of the Fox (ll. 3–7) and its psychological repercussion. La Fontaine wastes no words in describing the Fox's distress from without; he suggests it rather in the eloquent litotes of line 7, followed at once by the speech in which the Fox gives vent to his baffled rage. At the same time the potential pathos of the situation is checked by the use of the familiar word *compère*[2] – we are in the presence of a figure well known to us for what he is and who will be up to his tricks again: the tone is that of the patronizing, but almost affectionate reproach that a magistrate may address to an old lag.

The exploding emotion of the Fox's speech is marked by the switch to octosyllabic lines (though here again the rhyme maintains the link with what goes before). Injured pride is the dominant feeling expressed, resentment at being made to look a fool in the eyes of such a scurvy knave (the word *canaille* probably referring to the Farmer rather than to the poultry). The stress at the end of the line is happily used to bring out the arrogance of *moi* and to underline the contrast with the contemptible *canaille*.

In the lines following, a further effect of contrast is evident between the desperate and fruitless efforts of the Fox, well suggested by the force of the verb *je me travaille*,[3] by the alliteration and breathless rhythm of lines 10–11, and on the other hand the ease and regularity, again expressed in the rhythm of the verse, with which the clodhopper[4] of a farmer contentedly piles up his profits. The insolence of his prosperity and the indignation of the Fox are further stressed by the 'ethic dative' *vous* in line 12.[5] What makes the Fox's cup of bitterness overflow is that the Farmer is well enough off to have poultry in the larder for his own consumption – *il en a même au croc*. (The detail is a striking one, and certainly reflects La Fontaine's knowledge of the realities of rural life at a time when the peasantry were still far from enjoying 'la poule au pot le dimanche', as Henri iv had hoped that one day they would be able to do.)

Contrary then to natural justice, the oafish lout is living in luxury, while the Fox must count himself more than happy if he can get hold of a *vieux coq* – the Fox who by contrast is *des plus fins* (l. 4) and who now describes himself as a *maître passé* – a master craftsman; but the phrase also carries the hint that he is, as we might say, a slick operator. The Fox is tempted at first to yield to a mood of lassitude and despair (ll. 16–17); as people will do, he girds at his destiny, deplores, so to speak, *la condition vulpine*, and shifts the responsibility for his failure to the powers that be and that have denied him a fair chance in life. La Fontaine is exploiting the comic incongruities involved in his imaginary world, at once animal and human – presided over, not exactly by Jupiter, but by *sire Jupin*.[6]

The Fox's weakness is only momentary: he at once recovers his spirit and swears a great oath of vengeance. The supernatural

LA FONTAINE

dimension has already been opened up by the reference to Jupin, burlesque though it be. Here, the familiarity of *il en sera parlé* preserves the burlesque nuance; and the enormity of the oath, engaging the Powers above and below, is a rodomontade in the best fustian tradition. Nevertheless the tone has darkened, and epic resonances have been awakened which lift us to a different stylistic level and prepare us for what follows. It is a reflection of the skill with which La Fontaine has inveigled us into sympathy with his text and calculated its various pressures upon us, that while we relish the burlesque contrast involved, we are at the same time more than half ready to accept the epic element at its face value.

(ii) Lines 19–44. Once again the transition is reflected in the pattern of the rhyme: line 19 which opens a new section of the narrative also concludes a *quatrain à rimes croisées*. It is, besides, a highly evocative line, the effect of which derives from the interplay of sound and sense. Coming where it does, it is laden with the burden of the preceding account of the Fox's mental state, the tragic potential of which is amplified with the always rich and suggestive word *cœur*; *roulant* conveys at once the fevered activity of his thought and its obsessional nature, and in this context enhances by its sombre tone the sense of brooding menace. A menace as yet undetermined and so all the more fearful, as is brought out by the unusual plural *ces vengeances*.[7]

It is under stress, then, of pent-up emotion that the Fox undertakes his revenge one particularly drowsy night – the phrase *libérale en pavots* reminding us discreetly of the burlesque character of the episode by the slightly comical twist it gives to the image of Night the strewer of poppies. Lines 21–3, by their alliterations and cadences, vividly evoke the sleeping farmstead: besides the play of the [o] and [u] vowels, a factor contributing to the effect is certainly the combination of the slow tempo called for by the sense, with the smooth *enchaînement* of part to part over the caesuras and verse-ends. This slumberous flow is checked, however, on the word *dormait*, at a most unusual place in the alexandrine.[8] The effect of the isolated subject *Le Fermier* at the end of the verse is to introduce a sudden disquiet, an alarmed expectancy. What can have happened? What is going to happen? And the poet uses the opportunity to slip in the information about the Farmer's carelessness in forgetting to lock up his poultry-house. The excitement generated by this new element in the situation is reflected by the temporary switch to octosyllabic verse.

The following two lines are in the 'historic present' for the sake of vividness. The action is presented in two phases – the watchful prowling of the Fox around the enclosure, then the kill, lightning-swift. Three consecutive rhymes – a most unusual device – force this central event of the poem sharply on our attention. The first verb of line 27 expresses both the swiftness and the scale of the massacre; the second clause serves as a gloss to drive home the full horror implied in the first, and at the same time unobtrusively transforms the farm-yard into a city taken in war and sacked, thereby setting the action quite explicitly now on the mock-epic level.

In line 29 the reversion to the past historic tense is the more apt in that it covers the time-lag between the massacre and discovery the next morning of the havoc wrought by the Fox's *cruauté* – a word that still carries something of its etymological meaning and might be rendered here by 'bloodthirstiness'.[9] It has been no ordinary depre-dation, limited to the satisfaction of the Fox's immediate needs, but an excess of furious passion. Anything less would of course have been out of keeping with what we have learned earlier about the Fox's psychological condition; conversely, this is now seen to be more than gratuitous fancy – the whole amounts to a demonstration of the distortion of behaviour under the stress of emotion.

La Fontaine may seem, at this peak point of his poem, to be indulg-ing in literary fun; and so indeed he is – but his fun is very close to *humour noir*. Though the archaic word *manoir*[10] underlines the sham-heroic quality of lines 31–2, the undertone is sinister, for we are here referred to one of the most horrific deeds of vengeance to be found in classical legend, the banquet at which Atreus served Thyestes the flesh of his own children.[11]

There follow two epic similes, each formally introduced in the classical manner by *Tel* . . .; for the time being we might easily for-get the natural level of our topic and allow ourselves to be coaxed into the epic mood. The first simile is based on the account, in the first book of the Iliad, of Apollo's revenge on Agamemnon (*le fier Atride*). The laconic eloquence of *Joncha son camp de morts* echoes the savagery of line 27. In Homer, as critics have pointed out, Apollo's revenge is by no means *l'ouvrage d'une nuit*; but we shall be foolish if we allow such pedantry to stand in the way of the imaginative associations and emotional responses with which La Fontaine intends to enrich his poem at this point.[12]

The second simile, based on the story told in the opening scenes of Sophocles's *Ajax*, is particularly apt in content and function. On the death of Achilles, Ajax and Ulysses contended for his arms, which were awarded to the latter. Wild with jealousy, Ajax sought to kill his rival and those responsible for the award. Athena, however, intervened and put Ajax out of his senses, so that he mistook a herd of sheep and goats for his quarry, slew most of them, and dragged the remainder off home to subject them to a yet crueller death. The virtue of the comparison for La Fontaine's purpose here is therefore two-fold, consisting first in the analogy of Ajax's frenzy with the fury of the Fox, and secondly in that the victims in each case are farm animals. Thus the poet is able to bring us back as smoothly as one could wish from the heights of Homeric legend to the poultry-yard. *Le renard, autre Ajax . . .* – the deftness of the stroke could not be bettered; and the comparison is allowed to run on, after this precise identification, to the end of line 44, in terms fully supported by the Sophoclean text. It is with heroic echoes ringing in our ears that we are ready to attend once more to the tale.

(iii) Lines 45 – 59. In this case there is no rhyme-link with the preceding section, which ends firmly on a *distique*. Although the narrative continuity is of course unbroken, we find ourselves now on a quite different rhetorical level, and furthermore we are looking at things now from a different angle – namely the Farmer's. Unable to alter the hard facts of the situation, suddenly and completely deprived of that minimum control over circumstance indispensable for normal human behaviour, he turns to vent his ineffectual wrath on those whom he can still subject to his will – *ses gens, son chien*. The dry parenthesis, *c'est l'ordinaire usage*, is a personal comment addressed directly to the audience, and makes it easy to imagine the poet reading his *Fable* in some *salon*.

He is content with a mere hint about the Farmer's abuse of his servants, and takes up, economically, only the point that matters in the context of the *Fable*, namely the fate of the Dog. In the earlier part of the poem the excess of the Fox's rage lies at the source of the action, and indeed of the mock-heroic inflation of the style; here, although without the heroics, we find the counterpart in the irrational anger of the Farmer. He at once tries to throw the blame on the Dog.

The question put in line 48 is clearly of the sort intended to elicit not information, but an admission of guilt, and so to afford a colourable pretext for punishment. The Dog, however, takes the question at its face value, and answers it, with every justification, by a retort *ad hominem*. He could at most have raised the alarm, after the slaughter had started; but the Farmer, if he had been attending to his business, could have prevented it happening at all. He follows this unanswerable argument with another which is both *a contrario* and *a fortiori* (ll. 50–3).

After a longish run of alexandrines, the change of metre at line 54 is very noticeable, and marks a change in the mode of narration. The dialogue between the Farmer and the Dog has been directly reported, but in lines 54–9 the poet steps into the foreground, weaving his comment into the tale, and so the narration is now set at a remove from the events narrated. Correspondingly, the figures of the protagonists recede into the distance and become blurred. The shift of focus is accurately reflected in the use of the impersonal, colourless pronoun *on*. The poet is winding up his tale, detaching himself and his audience from it.

The Dog gives a rational answer to an ostensibly rational question: he is about to learn, however, that the power of reason to persuade depends on the state of feeling of the person addressed and on his relation to the speaker. What is still more significant is the pretence put up by the Farmer of listening to reason and acting from reason. The Dog is allowed to have his say; and in line 58 the choice of words is such (*trouver* – consider, find, conclude; and *valait*) as to suggest a due weighing up of *pro* and *contra*. Above all, the very question put by the Farmer in lines 47–8 shows that he is trying to *justify* the violence he is about to commit; and as he has the Dog in his power already, this means that it is really his own conscience he is attempting to set at rest.[13] In line 59 the 'ethic dative' again heightens the effect by associating the audience with the action. The context, however, imparts a different value to it from what we found in line 12. The passage is written, ironically, from the Farmer's point of view; and the *vous* implies the listener's participation in the satisfaction the Farmer derives from inflicting a richly deserved thrashing. Note, however, that besides the obvious irony, La Fontaine corrects the false perspective by focussing our sympathies once again on the victim (*le pauvre drille*).

III. The fabulist has finished his tale. According to the conventions of the genre he proceeds to 'draw the moral'. Instead, however, of planting a maxim and leaving it at that, he takes the listener directly to task – any, that is, who happens to be a *père de famille* – a *pater familias*, the master of a household. La Fontaine shakes a cautionary finger at him – the *donc* is magisterial – and takes leave of him with solemn exhortation.

Although the advice given is no doubt sound in terms of ordinary prudence, such a 'lesson' certainly strikes us as being disappointingly superficial. Perhaps, then, this concluding section of the poem is not so straightforward as it seems. Its content is certainly thrown into a curious light by the disarming and quite unexpected personal interjection in line 61. This wry comment, possible only in the graceful informality of a *salon* recitation, deflates the solemnity of the injunction and raises a doubt as to its significance. It is as though we were being invited to beware of the obvious; and indeed, alerted in this way, we may well form the impression that the last six lines are merely a flourish, a well-bred, deprecatory gesture of the *honnête homme* smiling at heavy-handed moralizing; that the formal 'moral' of this *Fable* is a kind of parody pointing us back indirectly to the real import of the text, namely the insight it affords into the heart of man and the springs of human conduct.

CONCLUSION. Now that we have analyzed closely the make-up of the text, we are ready to read it once more as a whole, and with greatly increased understanding. Grasping it now both in its complexity and in its unity, we should be able to say something about its general characteristics.

We have found throughout a very subtle calculation of effect, and great economy of means. This sureness of control is all the more admirable in that the poem, besides being written in the dangerously flexible medium of *vers irréguliers*, is highly diversified in content and tone.

The texture of the poem is determined mainly by two stylistic variables, the interplay of which confers on the text a complex ambivalency. One of these is the relation between the poem and the audience. The poem is at one and the same time the story itself and the poet telling the story – it mingles the three grammatical persons. The audience is directly addressed at the beginning and the end, occasionally in the body of the text (l. 46), and also, it could be argued, through the 'ethic datives'. The status of the poem is thus highly ambiguous: we are at once in the real world, listening to the poet, and in the fictional world through which he is guiding us – the frontier between the two has become uncertain. Paradoxically, however, the effect of this is to ensure that while the 'suspension of our disbelief for the time being' is achieved with the greatest possible ease, we remain always aware that it is indeed a fiction, a *fabula* that we are attending to; and besides following the tale we are in a position to appreciate at the same time the telling of it. This is of course particularly appropriate in a poem intended for recital in a *salon* as a form of polite entertainment.

The other stylistic variable in the poem is its rhetorical level, which moves between the familiar and the epic, and so allows La Fontaine to exploit – but always in subservience to his purpose – the humour of the burlesque. Are we in a farm-yard or on the windy plains of Troy? We are switched to and fro from the one to the other, and here too the line of demarcation becomes uncertain. We should have to answer that we are in both of these places, and for that reason in neither. As he does elsewhere with other elements of the literary traditions he had inherited, La Fontaine is *playing* here with the burlesque, and thoroughly enjoying his mastery over the resources at his disposal. By the exercise of irony, he is freeing us at once from heroic illusion and from burlesque insolence, while still permitting us to relish their peculiar qualities. Here they become means to a higher end, the illustration of a facet of human nature, and La Fontaine uses them in such a way that the burden of his *Fable* – the distortion of thought and behaviour through passion – is disengaged from association with any particular level or section of mankind, to be invested instead with classical universality.

NOTES
1 First published in *Fables choisies mises en vers*, tome IV, 1679. Standard modern edition: *Œuvres complètes*, ed. H. Régnier, Grands Ecrivains de la France, 1883–93; Régnier indicates a possible source for this fable in Nevelet's *Mythologia aesopica*, the *de Patrefamilias succensente Cani ob gallinas raptas* of Abstemius.
2 Cf. Furetière, *Dictionnaire* (1684): 'la plupart des Bourgeois se nomment compère' – much as the nobility (adds Littré) call each other *cousin*.

Furetière also glosses the phrase *c'est un compère* as 'c'est un homme fin, habile, et intelligent en son métier'. Cf. also the expression *c'est un rusé compère*.

3 *se travailler* is equivalent to *se tourmenter*, just as *travaux* may mean *tortures*. Cf. English *travail*.

4 Richelet, *Dictionnaire* (1680) defines *rustre* as 'grossier, paysan, lourdaud'.

5 The so-called ethic dative is essentially an appeal to the common sense and sympathy of the audience. The Fox expects all reasonable people to share his sense of outrage. The expression may be understood as referring secondarily to the overt self-satisfaction of the Farmer.

6 This familiar diminutive of *Jupiter* belongs to the language of seventeenth century burlesque.

7 This might be regarded as a latinism. Régnier refers to Virgil, *Aeneid*, I, 50 – *Talia flammato secum Dea corde volutans*. The plural use of words like *ira* is common in Latin poetry.

8 The seventeenth-century listener would sense that the line was incomplete at this point, since, like other practitioners of *vers irréguliers*, only on the rarest occasions does the poet use *vers impairs* in his Fables, and then only short ones.

9 The word *carnage* is happily chosen, because of its secondary meanings: the prey of carnivorous animals, the killing of game, etc. Furetière gives 'corps morts, charognes'.

10 The Académie in its *Dictionnaire* (1694) declares that *manoir*, apart from its legal (feudal) meaning, survives only in the poetic phrase *le sombre manoir* (the underworld). It is precisely because it is a piece of obsolescent poetic diction that it lends itself to burlesque usage. Richelet calls it a 'mot burlesque'.

11 The sun's turning back in its course is a detail of the story that may have been known to La Fontaine and his public either as a piece of traditional classical learning, or from a number of sources, e.g. Seneca's play *Thyestes*, Ovid, *Tristia* ii and *Ars amatoria* i, etc.

12 Line 33. The use of *de* here is strange. It must be taken as equivalent to *donnant*. See remarks on *de* in Cayrou, *Le français classique*, and Haase, *La Syntaxe française au XVIIe siècle*.
   Line 36. *ost* is quite common in the sixteenth century in the sense of 'army' or 'camp'. Furetière describes it as a 'vieux mot', and La Fontaine is clearly using it to lend a certain quaintness to his otherwise rather overpowering simile.

13 This cardinal point is also made in certain other *Fables* – in *Les Animaux malades de la peste*, and with exemplary clarity and simplicity in *Le Loup et l'Agneau*.

*Source*
Jean de La Fontaine (1621–95): *Fables*, Livre XI, 3; in *Fables, Contes et Nouvelles*, pp. 266–7, Bibliothèque de la Pléiade, ed. R. Groos and J. Schiffrin, Paris, 1954.

*H.T. Barnwell*

# MME DE LA FAYETTE
## Extract from *La Princesse de Clèves*

« Il parut alors une beauté à la cour, qui attira les yeux de tout le monde, et l'on doit croire que c'était une beauté parfaite, puisqu'elle donna de l'admiration dans un lieu où l'on était si accoutumé à voir de belles personnes. Elle était de la même maison que le vidame de
5 Chartres et une des plus grandes héritières de France. Son père était mort jeune, et l'avait laissée sous la conduite de Mme de Chartres, sa femme, dont le bien, la vertu et le mérite étaient extraordinaires. Après avoir perdu son mari, elle avait passé plusieurs années sans revenir à la cour. Pendant cette absence, elle avait donné ses soins à
10 l'éducation de sa fille; mais elle ne travailla pas seulement à cultiver son esprit et sa beauté, elle songea aussi à lui donner de la vertu et à la lui rendre aimable. La plupart des mères s'imaginent qu'il suffit de ne parler jamais de galanterie devant les jeunes personnes pour les en éloigner. Mme de Chartres avait une opinion opposée; elle faisait
15 souvent à sa fille des peintures de l'amour; elle lui montrait ce qu'il a d'agréable pour la persuader plus aisément sur ce qu'elle lui en apprenait de dangereux; elle lui contait le peu de sincérité des hommes, leurs tromperies et leur infidélité, les malheurs domestiques où plongent les engagements; et elle lui faisait voir, d'un autre côté, quelle
20 tranquillité suivait la vie d'une honnête femme, et combien la vertu donnait d'éclat et d'élévation à une personne qui avait de la beauté et de la naissance; mais elle lui faisait voir aussi combien il était difficile de conserver cette vertu, que par une extrême défiance de soi-même et par un grand soin de s'attacher à ce qui seul peut faire le bonheur
25 d'une femme, qui est d'aimer son mari et d'en être aimée.

Cette héritière était alors un des grands partis qu'il y eût en France; et quoiqu'elle fût dans une extrême jeunesse, l'on avait déjà proposé plusieurs mariages. Mme de Chartres, qui était extrêmement glorieuse, ne trouvait presque rien digne de sa fille; la voyant dans sa
30 seizième année, elle voulut la mener à la cour. Lorsqu'elle arriva, le vidame alla au-devant d'elle; il fut surpris de la grande beauté de Mlle de Chartres, et il en fut surpris avec raison. La blancheur de son teint et ses cheveux blonds lui donnaient un éclat que l'on n'a jamais vu qu'à elle; tous ses traits étaient réguliers, et son visage et sa
35 personne étaient pleins de grâce et de charmes. »

CONTEXT. This passage is taken from Part I of *La Princesse de Clèves*. It occurs immediately after the author's completion of her introductory sketch of the court of Henri II, in the course of which several of the major characters of the novel have been presented to the reader (notably the Prince de Clèves and the Duc de Nemours). As reference to Emile Magne's notes will show, the picture of the court painted by Mme de La Fayette is far from realistic or faithful to history: it is contrived in such a way as to place the emphasis on the atmosphere of intrigue and on the importance of love-affairs, largely irregular. In particular, the passage under review follows hard upon the suggestion of a possible marriage of the Duc de Nemours with Elizabeth, who had just succeeded Mary Tudor as Queen of England. This connexion between marriage and diplomacy is further emphasized by the allusions to the proposed marriages to be arranged under the terms of the peace treaty between France and Spain. The arrival of the heroine of the novel at the French court coincides in fact with the return of the King from the peace negotiations; furthermore, Mme de La Fayette rounds off her introductory survey of the court as she began it – with a direct reference to the King himself. But perhaps one of the most important aspects of the court, as described by Mme de La Fayette, is its atmosphere of agitated emotional life, accentuated by the sense of intrigue and spying peculiar to a small society closed in on itself.

THEME AND STRUCTURE. The passage clearly concerns the arrival of Mlle de Chartres (the future Princesse de Clèves) at court, and serves to introduce her to the reader as she appeared at that time to the courtiers. This introduction advances by well-defined stages:

I (a). From 'Il parut alors . . .' to '. . . sans revenir à la cour'.
These lines constitute the introduction proper of Mlle de Chartres to the court and to the reader. They give some indication of the impact she made on the court and of her antecedents.
(b) From 'Pendant cette absence . . .' to '. . . et d'en être aimée'.
The theme of the heroine's antecedents is here elaborated in terms of her education and of the relationship which existed between her mother and herself.
II (a) From 'Cette héritière . . .' to 'elle voulut la mener à la cour'.
We are now shown that the reason for Mme de Chartres's bring-

ing her daughter to court is her hope of finding a suitable match for her.

(b) From 'Lorsqu'elle arriva . . .' to '. . . pleins de grâce et de charmes'.

The author takes us back to the first lines of this passage by indicating the visual impact made by her heroine on her kinsman, the Vidame de Chartres.

DETAILED ANALYSIS. The detailed analysis of the passage will follow the lines of development indicated, and will lead to conclusions concerning the intrinsic characteristics of the passage under review and its importance and significance in the novel as a whole.

1 (a). The first sentence is immediately striking (and a contrast) after the account of diplomatic negotiations and public affairs. It opens with the vivid, concrete expression: 'Il parut alors', and it is noticeable that the emphasis is placed at once upon sight and appearance. The same emphasis is maintained throughout the sentence in two series of expressions, one indicating what was seen (*beauté, beauté parfaite, belles personnes*) and its physical attractiveness, the other the act of seeing (*attira les yeux, voir*). The effect produced by the appearance of the heroine is universal (*tout le monde*) and one of astonishment (*admiration*: the Academy Dictionary defines *admirer* thus: 'considérer avec surprise, avec étonnement une chose qui est extraordinaire en quelque manière que ce soit.') Only perfection of beauty (*une beauté parfaite*) could so astound the court (*où l'on était si accoutumé . . .*). It is vital that we should note the way and the terms in which the heroine is introduced, for it is her physical beauty which will bring men to her feet. Yet this is here expressed in abstract terms, and it is clear that Mme de La Fayette is much more concerned with the reactions of the beholders than with her heroine's beauty itself. It is noticeable, too, that no attempt is made to describe Mlle de Chartres (but of this there will be more to say later), and that she remains anonymous and, as yet, not even a person (*beauté*, as opposed to the *belles personnes* already known at court). This anonymity is of course exactly fitting, since the newcomer was unknown and the initial visual impression immediate and, on account of the astonishment it produced, unanalysed. Another point is that it is at once made clear that the heroine is an exceptional person even in what Mme de La Fayette has already described as a distinguished court

('Jamais cour n'a eu tant de belles personnes et d'hommes admirablement bien faits . . .', etc.). Finally, it is noteworthy that the essential fact of the heroine's beauty is given the prominence of the co-ordinate main clauses, and the effect produced (attraction of sight, followed by astonishment) indicated in the subordinate clauses – a strictly logical arrangement.

In the second sentence, the word *beauté* loses its partly abstract quality to become *elle*, the heroine, the *person*. She remains anonymous, however, and is now introduced (doubtless following the pattern of enquirers' questions and the answers given) through her family relationship to the Vidame de Chartres and through her wealth. The Vidame is already known to the reader as coming of an ancient and respected aristocratic family, and as a man of distinction in war and love as well as in generosity, courage and good looks. The heroine's connexion with him therefore gives her at once a certain distinction: this, together with her wealth and beauty, will naturally cause her to be much sought after.

After indicating something of Mlle de Chartres's attractiveness, physical and social, the author moves back in time, as though in answer to further enquiries, to provide information about her circumstances and upbringing. Attention is drawn particularly to two features of the situation: first, that after the death of her father the heroine was brought up by her mother (and it is only through her that father and daughter are named); and second, that the mother is at this stage the dominating personality – she is not anonymous, her qualities are extraordinary (and we must take the word in its most literal sense, especially since it seems to be linked to the exceptional beauty of the daughter), and, unlike most young widows of her rank, she did not return to court immediately the conventional period of mourning for her husband was ended. (The phrase, *sans revenir à la cour*, suggests deliberate avoidance of more usual practice.) The dominating status of Mme de Chartres is also suggested in the word *conduite* – she is made *responsible* for controlling and directing her daughter's development, and is put in a position of authority. It is Mme de Chartres's moral qualities that are picked out in the three almost synonymous words: *le bien* (in the context this could only mean moral goodness: see Furetière's dictionary: 'pureté de mœurs; vertu, honnetêté'), *la vertu* (virtue in the usual sense, but with particular stress on strength of character), *le mérite* (moral worth –

'assemblage de bonnes qualités' (Furetière) – but with perhaps some suggestion of intelligence, or talent, as in La Fontaine's fable, *Le rieur et les poissons*).

What emerges most clearly in this first part of our passage is the emphasis given to the exceptional nature of Mme de Chartres and her daughter: this emphasis may well help us to interpret what follows.

1 (b). The reason for Mme de Chartres's prolonged absence from court is now explained and enlarged upon. In particular, the phrase 'sous la conduite de Mme de Chartres' is developed: it is interpreted through the words *soins* and *éducation*, the first denoting a combination of effort, attention and solicitude, the second standing in contradistinction to mere instruction (cf. *cultiver* a few lines further on: see Furetière's dictionary on *éducation*: 'Soin qu'on prend de cultiver l'esprit des enfants et de les bien élever, soit pour la science, soit pour les bonnes mœurs'). Again, immediately following this simple statement, the exceptional character of Mme de Chartres is emphasized: the word *mais* indicates clearly that she is not following the conventional pattern of education for girls (making the most of their social and physical attractiveness: *esprit, beauté*). The mother has reflected (*elle songea*) on the problem of her daughter's education and, as a result, directed it towards the acquisition of *la vertu*. Mere inculcation, is, however, not enough. Mme de Chartres realizes that exhortation will not necessarily result in compliance with a particular moral code – that code must be seen to be worthy of attachment ('à la lui rendre aimable'). While the word *vertu* did, in the seventeenth century, denote moral virtue in the ordinary modern sense, it was also closely connected with the dominant idea conveyed by the Latin *virtus* and Italian *virtù*. In Richelet's dictionary we read: 'La vertu, en général, consiste dans la force et l'habitude de se déterminer toujours bien, c'est-à-dire, de ne vouloir que ce que la raison dicte, et de ne se servir de sa liberté que pour choisir le meilleur.' The stress is laid on strength of character and of purpose, on habit of mind, on choices made freely in the light of reason: this is confirmed by Furetière. Mme de Chartres herself has already been shown to possess this quality. As this paragraph develops, it becomes apparent that she is chiefly concerned to build up her daughter's powers of resistance to the kinds of temptation which will beset her at court, and to strengthen her moral fibre.

In order to achieve this aim, the mother behaves once more in an exceptional way. She is contrasted with 'la plupart des mères' who adopt the ostrich-like attitude of pretending that there is quite simply no danger. Applied to them, the verb *s'imaginer* (associated with the fantastic and chimerical) stands in marked contrast to *songer* and *opinion* (cogitation and its result) which characterize Mme de Chartres. (The suggestion of intelligence in the word *mérite* is being followed out.) The particular danger which must be resisted by Mlle de Chartres takes the form of *la galanterie*: the word has already been used to typify the activities of the courtiers. The Academy dictionary defines the word *galant* in these terms: 'se dit le plus ordinairement de celui qui fait l'amour à une femme mariée ou à une fille qu'il n'a pas dessein d'épouser.' The term is more often than not used in a pejorative sense, and it certainly has that nuance here. It is significant too, that the ostrich-like tactics adopted by most mothers are defined in terms, not of facing and resisting this particular danger, but of running away from it (*pour les en éloigner*).

Mme de Chartres, on the other hand, does not conceal the truth from her daughter, nor the attractions of love. She does not argue the matter out in terms of abstract principle or logic, but describes vividly (*peintures*), appealing to her daughter's imagination, and – though they are not actually specified in Mme de La Fayette's account – points to actual examples (see the verbs: *montrer, conter, faire voir*). Through them, Mme de Chartres seeks less to convince logically than to persuade (*persuader*). The emphasis is placed on practical conduct, not on abstract principle. The methods adopted are, however, not one-sided. The antithetical style which points the contrast between Mme de Chartres and other mothers (*une opinion opposée*) is now directed towards defining those methods. Passionate love is attractive, but dangerous; the woman who yields to it risks being deceived, while she who shuns it is assured of peace of mind as well as reputation; the attractiveness of love makes it the harder to resist, but resistance brings its own reward. The antitheses are immediately apparent in the substance of the long sentence which concludes this paragraph, but they are brought to our notice by expressions such as *d'un autre côté* and *mais . . . aussi*. The truth is presented to Mlle de Chartres negatively in the form of the dangers arising out of extra-marital attachments, and positively in the form of the contentment consequent upon absolute fidelity. The pleasures attendant upon illicit affairs serve only to accentuate the dangers (see the contrast between *agréable* and *dangereux*).

Those dangers are explicitly attached to what was regarded as the habitual waywardness and philandering of the male. His fundamental characteristic in matters of the heart is insincerity (*le peu de sincérité*) which takes the form of repeated deception (*tromperies* – according to Richelet, this means deliberate deception: *tricherie, fourberie*) and habitual infidelity (*infidélité*, defined by Richelet as a vice and form of treachery). If a woman succumbs to the temptations of *galanterie*, by seeking or accepting extra-marital attachments (*les engagements*), her domestic happiness will be destroyed. It is clear from this that the initiative in *galanterie* does not necessarily come from the man, and indeed La Bruyère (*Caractères*, III (Des Femmes), 22) characterizes the *femme galante* as the one who deliberately seeks a sentimental attachment. There seems, therefore, to be a double warning here – against yielding to amorous advances, and against making them. Again we should notice that there is no appeal to authority or to principle: love-affairs are not condemned as wrong in themselves but as productive of unhappiness. What Mme de Chartres aims at is such happiness as may be found within marriage, not a reform of morals or of society, nor some abstract sense of duty.

That happiness is immediately characterized as *tranquillité*, itself the result (*suivait*) of a woman's *honnêteté*. This very complex concept is essentially social, denoting the kind of behaviour acceptable in polite society; but, as Richelet points out, it signifies, 'à l'égard des femmes, la chasteté, la pudeur, la modestie', and so concerns moral as much as social attributes. (Cf. Furetière's definition of: *honnête femme, honnête fille*: 'Se dit proprement d'une femme et d'une fille qui sont chastes et vertueuses'). As we read on to the end of the paragraph, it becomes clear that *tranquillité* is regarded as essential to happiness for a woman (*le bonheur d'une femme*), and that *honnêteté* is equated with chastity (*aimer son mari et en être aimée*).

However, moral rectitude – even subordinated to practical considerations – is not the only incentive to this virtue. *La vertu* (and in this context our definition of the term remains important) now reappears as a source of social distinction. (In her search for such distinction, Mme de Chartres would appear to be an authentic *précieuse*.) Distinction is indicated by exceptional reputation (*éclat*: an almost visual concept, having to do with brilliant light, and the

Academy dictionary gives as its synonym *gloire, splendeur; élévation*: i.e. *raised* above the ordinary), the kind of reputation which enhances two characteristics already attributed to Mlle de Chartres herself – beauty and high birth (in the same order as at the beginning of the paragraph). Yet, however important these social considerations may seem, they are preceded by the need for tranquillity. What Mme de Chartres appears to suggest, from the juxtaposition of these two spheres – the private and the public – is that they are not necessarily in conflict, but that peace of mind and high social reputation can go hand in hand. Still, labouring under no illusions as to the power of contrary attractions, she makes sure that her daughter understands it, too.

It is this concern which leads her to issue her final warning: moral rectitude, peace of mind and social distinction cannot in themselves safeguard *la vertu*. To them must be added a condition – mistrust of oneself, and in particular of one's own *vertu* or strength of character (see Furetière: *défiance*: 'crainte d'être trompé; doute de soi-même ou des autres') – and a means – attachment to the source of a woman's happiness, love given to and by her husband. This last is the clue to 'la vie d'une *honnête femme*', as tranquillity is the key to happiness. In the last few lines of the paragraph we are led up to the aim of Mme de Chartres's ethical training, and in them – contrasting with the *tromperies, infidélité, malheurs* and *engagements* associated with *la galanterie* – each element in her system falls into place. It is, however, worthy of remark that neither Mme de Chartres nor, through her, the author adopts a dogmatic tone. Just as no appeal is made to abstract or absolute principles, so the problems of love, marriage and happiness are presented in terms of both attractions and dangers. *La vertu* is not considered as a moral imperative, but, for the sake of the tranquillity it ensures, as *aimable*. It is apposite to recall Richelet's and Furetière's insistence on reason in their definition of *la vertu*, for reason shows the dangers of extra-marital attachments as well as the satisfactions of tranquillity, and so indicates clearly the path to be followed. There is perhaps something Cartesian in the non-dogmatic tone and in the idea that reason can distinguish what is worthy of attachment and so provide a basis for sound moral conduct.

II (a). In the second paragraph of our extract, we are taken back to the opening of the first, both in subject-matter and in time. The theme of Mlle de Chartres's first appearance at court is resumed, with an indication of its cause, then with some development of the impression her beauty created.

Following the way in which her mother had prepared her for life at court, we are carried back to Mlle de Chartres as an heiress, though not now as 'une des plus grandes héritières de France', but as 'un des grands partis qu'il y eût en France'. Her mother's teachings on marriage bring us to consider the heroine as a marriageable girl, much sought after – even before her presentation at court – for her wealth. Mme de Chartres, who has so far been shown as an exceptional person, is also extremely proud (Richelet gives as synonyms for *glorieux: superbe, fier, orgueilleux*). That the word is not to be taken as a term of approbation (or even of neutrality) is suggested by the phrase: 'ne trouvait presque rien digne de sa fille'. It is, then, in the hope of finding at court a worthy match for her daughter – which she had been unable to find outside it – that she has brought her to the centre and summit of social life. (Here the importance of the King's presence becomes apparent.) And she has done so at the earliest opportunity consistent with propriety (*dans sa seizième année*).

II (b). These social considerations, which loomed so large in the life of the seventeenth century and particularly in the arrangement of marriages, may not, however, be compatible with the mutual attraction of young people stemming from quite different sources. It is this, one may suppose, which causes Mme de La Fayette to move immediately back to the impact made by the physical beauty of her heroine. The link is provided by the Vidame de Chartres who, quite naturally, being her kinsman, welcomes her to the court. He provides the social link, but it is neither the girl's social status nor her wealth which impresses him: for them he was prepared – for her beauty he was not. *Surpris*, according to Richelet and Furetière, is to be understood both as *étonné* and as *pris à l'impourvu*. The emotional shock is further suggested by the epithet in *la grande beauté*, itself more emotive and less objective and aesthetic than *une beauté parfaite* of the first paragraph. That *surpris* and *la grande beauté* are to be taken in the strongest possible sense is evident from the author's own comment (and such comments are extremely rare in this novel): 'et il en fut surpris avec raison.' Then, as if to justify her remark, Mme de La Fayette suggests some aspects of her heroine's beauty, though only in the vaguest and most general terms ('la blancheur de son teint et ses cheveux blonds'). Again, it is the effect produced which is significant – *un éclat*, on which we have already commented, can here be understood on two levels: as meaning dazzling, in the literal sense, and, when taken with 'que l'on n'a jamais vu qu'à elle', as indicative of distinction. Together with the astonishment of the Vidame, this phrase once more draws attention to the exceptional nature of the heroine. The final clauses of the paragraph link the purely physical aspects of her beauty with her manner – *sa personne, grâce* (see Furetière: 'Le bon air, la bonne mine d'une personne; ses manières d'agir, de parler, de s'habiller qui plaisent aux autres'), *charmes*, the last of these suggesting, etymologically, the irresistible and inexplicable spell cast over her admirers.

We have now returned, therefore, to the opening theme of the first paragraph of our passage, but with a hint of more specific details of the effect produced by Mlle de Chartres's first appearance and, in particular, the effect produced on one individual. We are thus prepared for the account, which follows immediately, of the impression created by the heroine on the Prince de Clèves and, later, on the Duc de Nemours.

CONCLUSIONS. The passage under review can first be seen as a unit which is self-contained. In regard to subject-matter, we are provided with an introduction to the heroine of the novel at the moment when she is introduced to the court. No attempt is made, however, to paint a comprehensive or detailed portrait of Mlle de Chartres, and indeed, as far as her character is concerned, we are left to deduce practically everything from the account given of her upbringing and education. We must assume that these were accepted and that they became part of her, since there is no suggestion of resistance to them. The unity of the passage is further ensured by its form, for it begins and ends in the same way – with emphasis on the heroine's beauty.

It is, however, striking that few details of that beauty are either explicitly provided or even suggested. Two consequences flow from this observation. One is that the author is not much concerned here with physical beauty in itself, but rather in the irresistible effect it produces on the beholder – what matters is the psychological and emotional effect of beauty. The second consequence is that the reader's imagination is left free to conjure up his own vision of beauty: Mme de La Fayette does not restrict him to her own conception of the beautiful. This technique of making suggestive generalizations, vague as they often seem, accounts in part for the universal appeal and relevance of her novel and for each reader's sense of personal involvement in it.

In the same way, no precise examples to illustrate Mme de Chartres's ethical training are actually cited in the text. We have seen, however, that it is suggested, through the vocabulary, that it was through examples that she taught. This impression is reinforced by the use of such phrases as '*quelle* tranquillité suivait la vie d'une honnête femme', '*combien* la vertu donnait d'éclat . . .', and '*combien* il était difficile . . .' Again, the reader's imagination is left free and encouraged to discover examples for himself, rather than be confined within those which might be provided by the author and which might be alien to his own experience.

Closely connected with this absence of precise details is the abstract nature of the language and the lack of direct intervention on the part of the writer. Bernard Pingaud has suggested that abstraction in language signifies an author's abstention. This does not mean so much total withdrawal (cf. Mme de La Fayette's use of demonstrative pronouns: *ce prince*, *cette héritière*, etc.) as a refusal both to shackle the reader's imagination and to judge or even suggest judgement. Paradoxically, perhaps, the author's non-involvement ensures the involvement of the reader.

At the same time, Mme de La Fayette's style makes general inferences possible and enables her in a matter of a few lines to give a comprehensive view of Mme de Chartres's teaching and, in particular, to show her turning the problems round and balancing one argument against another. While the emphasis in this passage is placed on that teaching, its juxtaposition with the references to the heroine's beauty is indicative of the moral problems with which she will be faced.

When we place our extract in its context, we can see that the education given to Mlle de Chartres is related to the kind of society described in the first few pages of the novel. It is precisely against the dangers inherent in that society that the mother seeks to arm the daughter. Yet there is something contradictory in Mme de Chartres's desire to see her daughter a dazzling social success, while at the same time urging her to abstain from following patterns of behaviour admitted and even encouraged by society. This is precisely one of the sources of subsequent conflict in the mind of the heroine.

The passage under review is followed immediately by her first encounter with her future husband. The immediacy of passionate love – for which the reader has been prepared by Mme de La Fayette's introduction of her heroine – is shown at once to be at any rate temporarily frustrated by the need to ensure social compatibility; and it is significant that, as soon as that compatibility has provided a basis for marriage, the Prince de Clèves discovers that his passion is not reciprocated and, at once, his wife meets the Duc de Nemours. Their mutual passion is immediately set at odds with the exigencies of a marriage newly contracted within a rigid social order.

It is thus not surprising that Mme de Chartres should persist in renewing her advice to her daughter right up to the time of her own death. In view of her strength of character and her single-minded pursuit of what she considers to be a proper education, it is also not surprising that she retains the trust, confidence and obedience of Mme de Clèves, as she so soon becomes. In a society in which 'personne n'était tranquille, ni indifférent', and characterized by ambition and *galanterie*, and that 'agitation sans désordre . . . qui la rendait très agréable, mais aussi très dangereuse pour une jeune personne', Mme de Chartres seeks to establish for her daughter an oasis of tranquillity founded on a marriage based itself on a sense of duty.

It is, however, made clear as the novel develops that this tranquillity is not only the ultimate good in itself (as the key to happiness). It cannot exist unless one's life is in reality what it appears to be. In the particular kind of society in which Mme de La Fayette sets her story, appearance is at variance with reality: outwardly, the appearances of fidelity in marriage are maintained; in reality, extra-marital attachments prevail. 'Si vous jugez sur les apparences ici', says Mme de Chartres to her daughter, 'vous serez souvent trompée: ce qui paraît n'est presque jamais la vérité.' In her own married life, therefore, the Princesse de Clèves is conditioned to seek tranquillity first and foremost, and therefore to ensure that appearances are not belied by reality.

Two features of the novel which have sometimes puzzled readers are thus explained. The first is the famous *aveu*, the confession made by the heroine to her husband about her (ungratified) passion for the Duc de Nemours. That confession is an attempt to undeceive the Prince de Clèves through the revelation of reality, and to avoid living with him merely on the level of a conflicting appearance. The second feature concerns the Princesse de Clèves's rejection of the Duc de Nemours after the death of her husband. Here, the other aspect of tranquillity takes its place. The heroine would not find happiness in marriage with the duke, because – remembering in particular her mother's teaching about the habitual unfaithfulness of men – her peace of mind would be constantly disturbed by suspicion, and specifically suspicion that apparent fidelity might not correspond to reality. And this means that the two aspects of tranquillity are interwoven. When we look at the closing pages of the novel, we are struck by the dominating need felt by the Princesse de Clèves for tranquillity: it is clear that this is central in her mother's teaching and has become the aim of the heroine's whole existence. 'Les raisons qu'elle avait de ne point épouser M. de Nemours lui paraissaient fortes du côté de son devoir et *insurmontables du côté de son repos*.' One is constantly reminded of Pascal: 'Tout le malheur des hommes vient d'une seule chose, qui est de ne savoir pas demeurer en repos, dans une chambre'; 'Ils ont un instinct secret qui les porte à chercher le divertissement et l'occupation au dehors . . . (cf. the agitation in Mme de La Fayette's picture of court life); et ils ont un autre instinct secret . . . qui leur fait connaître que le bonheur n'est en effet que dans le repos.'

Yet it is duty that Mme de Clèves pleads in her final rejection of the duke, and, when challenged, she has to admit that it is only 'un fantôme de devoir.' This is usually understood to mean simply that she is no longer really tied by her duty to a dead husband whom she did not love, and that she is therefore making a pretext of that duty in order to avoid marriage to a man she loves but cannot fully trust. Another, complementary, interpretation seems possible. The Princesse de Clèves lives out her mother's ethic in her own life. Is it not her duty to Mme de Chartres which would be betrayed by marriage to Nemours? Is it not that ghostly duty to a dead mother which she follows right to the end? There seem to be good grounds for thinking so, not only in her own constant acquiescence in her mother's teaching, but also in the way in which, particularly in the passage we have studied, Mme de Chartres is presented as the dominating character, and – paradoxically – in the way in which her daughter's introduction to the reader is effected very largely in an oblique manner, through that teaching.

Our extract is, seen in the light of these considerations, of crucial importance for a proper understanding of the book as a whole. It already begins to make inevitable the moral dilemma with which the heroine will be confronted and the way in which she will endeavour to resolve it. But the passage is important for more than its content. Through its emphasis on psychological and moral questions, it concentrates the reader's attention from the outset on these aspects of the narrative; through its generalizations, suggestive as they are of particularities, it invites the reader to use his imagination and by so doing to involve himself emotionally in the story; through the abstract nature of its style, it shows the author keeping her distance and refusing to make explicit judgments, and thus sets the tone for a seemingly inevitable and relentless development of the narrative in which the writer abstains from interfering – and that development is the representation of the inevitability and relentlessness of the passions within a society which permits of no escape. That is what emerges as the theme of the novel, over which, in its entirety, this introduction of the heroine casts forward its long shadow. And, seen in the context of the whole book, what seems at first sight to be a thumbnail sketch of the heroine is in fact the seedbed of the central theme of conflicting passions and duties.

*Source*
Mme de La Fayette (1634–93): *La Princesse de Clèves*, ed. E. Magne, Droz, Geneva, 1950, pp. 17–18; and in *Romans et Nouvelles*, ed. E. Magne, Garnier, Paris, 1948, pp. 247–8.

*J.H. Brumfitt*

## *VOLTAIRE*
Extract from *Candide*

« 'Messieurs, dit Cacambo, vous comptez donc manger aujourd'hui un jésuite? C'est très bien fait; rien n'est plus juste que de traiter ainsi ses ennemis. En effet le droit naturel nous enseigne à tuer notre prochain, et c'est ainsi qu'on en agit dans toute la terre. Si nous n'usons
5 pas du droit de le manger, c'est que nous avons d'ailleurs de quoi faire bonne chère; mais vous n'avez pas les mêmes ressources que nous: certainement il vaut mieux manger ses ennemis que d'abandonner aux corbeaux et aux corneilles le fruit de sa victoire. Mais, messieurs, vous ne voudriez pas manger vos amis. Vous croyez aller
10 mettre un jésuite en broche, et c'est votre défenseur, c'est l'ennemi de vos ennemis que vous allez rôtir. Pour moi, je suis né dans votre pays; monsieur que vous voyez est mon maître, et bien loin d'être jésuite, il vient de tuer un jésuite, il en porte les dépouilles; voilà le sujet de votre méprise. Pour vérifier ce que je vous dis, prenez sa
15 robe, portez-la à la première barrière du royaume de Los Padres; informez-vous si mon maître n'a pas tué un officier jésuite. Il vous faudra peu de temps; vous pourrez toujours nous manger, si vous trouvez que je vous ai menti. Mais, si je vous ai dit la vérité, vous connaissez trop les principes du droit public, les mœurs et les lois,
20 pour ne nous pas faire grâce.'
Les Oreillons trouvèrent ce discours très raisonnable; ils députèrent deux notables pour aller en diligence s'informer de la vérité; les deux députés s'acquittèrent de leur commission en gens d'esprit, et revinrent bientôt apporter de bonnes nouvelles. Les Oreillons
25 délièrent leurs deux prisonniers, leur firent toutes sortes de civilités, leur offrirent des filles, leur donnèrent des rafraîchissements, et les reconduisirent jusqu'aux confins de leurs États, en criant avec allégresse: 'Il n'est point jésuite, il n'est point jésuite!'
Candide ne se lassait point d'admirer le sujet de sa délivrance.
30 'Quel peuple! disait-il, quels hommes! quelles mœurs! si je n'avais pas eu le bonheur de donner un grand coup d'épée au travers du corps du frère de mademoiselle Cunégonde, j'étais mangé sans rémission. Mais, après tout, la pure nature est bonne, puisque ces gens-ci, au lieu de me manger, m'ont fait mille honnêtetés dès qu'ils
35 ont su que je n'étais pas jésuite.' »

VOLTAIRE has many styles of his own, not to mention his considerable gifts as a parodist. Yet it is in the vivacity and irony of his lighter prose writings, and above all of his *contes philosophiques*, that he is unsurpassed. There are many lesser works from which these qualities could be illustrated, but nowhere else have they quite that combination of brilliance and density which makes *Candide* his masterpiece. The above extract not only exemplifies this, but reveals, in addition, the complexity of the thought which often lies beneath the superficial gaiety.

We are midway through the story. Candide has two principal mentors: the Optimist Pangloss, whose teachings are constantly being belied by the facts of experience, and the Pessimist, Martin, whose world-view is far more realistic, but essentially negative. At this point in the tale, however, Pangloss is missing, presumed hanged; Martin has not yet appeared on the scene. Candide, in practical matters at any rate, is guided by his faithful and resourceful servant, Cacambo. We are also, both geographically and sociologically, at the most distant point in the parabola of Candide's journeyings. These began in the demonstrably false paradise of the dilapidated castle of Thunder-ten-Tronkh and are to end with the disillusioned hero and his small group of friends, cultivating their little garden beside the Sea of Marmora. Now, however, Candide is in the hands of primitive South-American savages, and in the next chapter he is to be transported into the utopian civilization of Eldorado. The two most extreme forms of human society are juxtaposed, and Candide faces the task of understanding them without a 'philosophical' guide at his side.

Up to this point, his efforts have not been markedly successful. Fleeing from Jesuit Paraguay, where he has just killed the brother of his beloved Cunégonde, he has come across the spectacle of two naked and 'natural' women, pursued by their simian lovers. Naively assuming them to be 'deux demoiselles de condition', he has proceeded to shoot the two apes. This has led to his and Cacambo's capture by other members of the same tribe, the Oreillons, and the latter are now dancing round the stewpot in which their captives look like coming to an untimely end.

The activities of the two 'natural' women are beyond Candide's comprehension. They were not, however, beyond Voltaire's, for it did not seem improbable to him that, in primitive times, man and beast had cohabited. In *La Philosophie de l'histoire* and elsewhere, he

VOLTAIRE

was later to speculate on the possibility that such unions had given birth to centaurs and other similar creatures which Antiquity assured him had really existed. Yet 'natural' was for him an ambivalent term. It could mean, as in this case, something that was primitive and therefore possibly different from anything within modern experience. Such, however, was not his usual standpoint. On the whole he accepted the Newtonian view that 'natura est semper sibi consona' and therefore believed that what was 'unnatural' now had always been so. It was on grounds such as these that he was later to devote many pages to indignant denials of Herodotus' affirmation that all Babylonian women had indulged in ritual prostitution. Fortunately for Candide and Cacambo, the 'natural' men who are busy preparing to feast off their captives turn out to be 'natural' in the Newtonian rather than in the primitive sense.

Candide himself, however, is in no position to appreciate this; or rather, with that psychological *raideur* which makes him one of the most genuinely puppet-like of Voltaire's characters (and they are all, in some sense, puppets), he 'jerks' abruptly from one extreme position to the other. 'Ah! que dirait maître Pangloss, s'il voyait comme la pure nature est faite', he has just bitterly exclaimed, whilst watching the Oreillons prepare for their banquet. Pangloss is primarily a caricature of the philosophical Optimism of Leibniz and Pope, neither of whom had been particularly enthusiastic about the virtues of natural man. But he has also imbibed some of the ideas of Rousseau's *Discours sur l'inégalité*, and this would appear to be one of them. Though Rousseau was far from being the inventor of the myth of the happy savage, he had contributed much to it; in particular he had argued that the progress of civilization had corrupted the fundamental goodness of human nature. Voltaire, now at the beginning of his long quarrel with Rousseau, is far from accepting such a view.

He does no more than touch on it here, but he does seem to go out of his way to give a very different picture of man at his most primitive from that drawn by Rousseau, who had asserted that the earliest man was a solitary individual. When Voltaire's savages speak, it is always in chorus; even when they go out love-making with apes or on ambassadorial missions to the Paraguayan Jesuits, they go in pairs. In his view, as he frequently insists, man has always been a social animal.

Yet the Oreillons are un-Rousseauesque, and even un-savage, in a more important way. Their primitive anthropophagous habits are incongruously linked with a remarkably 'civilized' politico-religious awareness. Their triumphant cry as they prepare their meal (a cry which is echoed towards the end of this passage) is: 'C'est un jésuite, c'est un jésuite! nous serons vengés et nous ferons bonne chère; mangeons du jésuite, mangeons du jésuite!'. The Oreillons, after all, turn out to be only mock primitives. Their primary role in the story, as so often with Voltaire's 'natural' men, is to ridicule the beliefs, conventions and religious institutions of European society. Fundamentally, they are just as 'civilized' as that society itself.

They are civilized because they obey the sentiment of justice and the voice of reason. Yet it is not to these that Candide would appeal. When Cacambo rises to the situation (as he always does) and assures his master that he can address the savages in their own language, Candide forgets his earlier disillusioned comment on 'la pure nature', and urges his servant to appeal to sentiments and beliefs which these primitives can hardly be expected to possess. 'Ne manquez pas', he says, 'de leur représenter quelle est l'inhumanité affreuse de faire cuire les hommes, et combien cela est peu chrétien.'

Wisely, Cacambo turns a deaf ear to this plea. He harangues his savage audience in very different, but far more effective terms. One may hesitate before accepting M. Roger Laufer's contention that Cacambo represents a viewpoint which can be labelled 'Opportunism' and which is later to be rejected by Candide just as are Optimism and Pessimism. Certainly, however, in both word and deed, he is a superlative opportunist. By a brilliantly constructed, though logically far from flawless argument, he forces the savages to listen to him and, in the end, to accept his point of view. Yet the interest of his harangue does not arise merely from the part it plays in the development of the story or from its effectiveness as a piece of rhetoric. It springs also from the fact that Cacambo is at times expressing Voltaire's own ideas, whilst at others he is employing a form of irony of which he himself is presumably unaware, but which corresponds to the intentions of his creator. The threads of his discourse are subtly woven into a semblance of unity and yet they are of widely differing natures.

His main argument is neither particularly subtle nor particularly Voltairian, but eminently straightforward and practical: the cannibals are preparing to eat a Jesuit, but far from being a Jesuit himself,

Candide has just killed one and is wearing the spoils – the dead man's hat and cloak. The Oreillons can ascertain the truth of this statement for themselves and, having done so, they will have sufficient sense of justice to treat their prisoners as friends, not as enemies.

However, servant though he is, Cacambo is not unskilled in the art of disputation. Among his many previous careers, he has included that of monk, and it is perhaps in theological controversy that he has learnt something of the rules and tricks of rhetorical argument. He therefore begins by addressing his audience as gentlemen and follows this with a statement calculated to arrest their attention: they are perfectly justified in eating their enemies, since natural law teaches us to kill our neighbour, and this is what we do the whole world over. These words are surprising because they appear to express a willingness to be roasted and eaten; they are also in accordance with the traditions of formal disputation, since they are in agreement, or so it appears, with the point of view of the other side.

This opening is most effective, but Cacambo is, of course, conceding too much. If the cannibals had remembered his words, they might well have greeted the news that Candide had killed a Jesuit with a laconic 'so what?' and proceeded to eat their meal all the same. Cacambo's exaggeratedly pessimistic statement about the teachings of natural law arises less from the exigencies of his argument than from those of Voltaire's own ironical purpose. If Voltaire has a dual attitude to 'nature', his attitude to 'natural law' is even more strikingly ambivalent. On the one hand he is deeply attached to the concept which had formed the subject of his own *Poème sur la loi naturelle*. All men, at whatever stage of civilization, have an innate sense of justice. There are certain basic moral principles which are universal and God-given. Particularly in his later years, this belief is to become one of the main planks of his deistic platform; it is one of the few subjects on which he is prepared to take issue with the otherwise revered Locke, who had argued that moral standards were relative and the result of education.

'Natural law', however, can and did have another meaning. Seventeenth- and eighteenth-century jurists like Grotius and Pufendorf had sought to codify its principles and in particular to lay the foundations of 'le droit public' – of an international law which would govern the relations between peoples. Basically, they were attempting something entirely laudable – to create a universal code of civilized behaviour. Yet if they were idealists, they were also pragmatists who started from society as they found it, and classical scholars who tended to venerate the customs of Antiquity. They and their disciples (who were numerous, particularly in Protestant countries) probably detested abuses such as slavery and pillage, but since these existed, they felt the need to provide some sort of theoretical justification for them. Not surprisingly this outraged the humanitarian conscience of men like Voltaire, for whom 'natural law' in this sense became, as here, the target of ironical abuse. For whilst it was a deliberate overstatement to say that natural law taught man to kill his neighbour, Voltaire felt that there were times when the natural lawyers came very near to doing so.

In these opening phrases, Cacambo is the mouthpiece of Voltaire the ironist. In what follows, he expresses, more directly, views which are Voltaire's own, as can be shown by the fact that they are closely paralleled by the argument of the article 'Anthropophages' in the *Dictionnaire philosophique*. Yet they are views which illustrate further the complexity of the thought of their creator. Voltaire believes in the universality of innate moral standards. Yet he is also a relativist who believes that customs vary with social, economic and climatic conditions. Whether or not one eats the bodies of those one has killed is a matter of custom, depending, partly at any rate, on the availability of alternative sources of food supply. For Candide, such an act is 'inhuman' and 'unchristian'; for Cacambo and Voltaire, it may be regrettable, but the real inhumanity lies in killing one's fellow-men in the first place.

It is at this point that Cacambo turns to the more practical side of his argument – to urge the tribesmen to find out for themselves that Candide has killed a Jesuit. He does so because he, like Voltaire, believes they have an innate sense of justice. Yet once again, in his method of expressing this, he ceases to be the straightforward spokesman of Voltaire's views and becomes rather a vehicle for his irony. For he ends as Candide would have had him begin, with an appeal to the abstract, civilized concepts of 'le droit public, les mœurs et les lois'. Luckily, his audience respond, for they have by now ceased to be real savages. However, the reader has probably also ceased to take the argument seriously; instead he is savouring the incongruous absurdity of the way in which these primitives are convinced by such sophisticated terminology.

From Cacambo's declamation, we pass to action. As always in *Candide*, the description of action consists of a rapid series of short phrases which give the impression of breakneck speed. Voltaire's narrative technique has been compared to the projection of a series of magic-lantern slides, but here they follow each other so quickly that only occasionally do we get a relatively clear picture such as the piquant detail of the Oreillons offering girls to the men they were on the point of eating. For the most part we have to be content with generalizations such as 'toutes sortes de civilités'. Description is cut down to a minimum; adjectives and adverbs are almost completely absent. We are, as it were, projected through a sequence of events in order to reach the triumphant and repeated cry of 'il n'est point jésuite!' with its echo of their earlier refrain and its ludicrous implication that, had they been Jesuits, it would have been perfectly in order to eat them.

Candide himself has the last word; but he is a Candide transformed. He has forgotten his doubts about 'la pure nature'; he has forgotten that at the beginning of this same chapter he was lamenting the fact that he had killed Cunégonde's brother and could see no point in prolonging his own miserable existence. Having escaped death, he is once again reconciled to the Optimistic philosophy of Pangloss. He is reconciled to the concept of the noble savage and rhapsodises in absurdly exaggerated terms over the morals of those who had all but eaten him. More important, he is reconciled to the belief that all is for the best and that everything is determined, for he proceeds to give a Panglossian, semi-logical form to an argument that is manifestly illogical: his killing of the Baron's son was for the best, since had he not killed him, he himself would have been eaten. That intervening circumstances make nonsense of this argument worries him no more than it would have done his master in a similar situation. The crowning absurdity (and here one must remember that Candide had originally gone to offer his services to the Jesuits) is that he appears to believe (as do the Oreillons) that eating Jesuits is perfectly legitimate. Here again, of course, Voltaire is speaking through his creature. Relations between the Jesuits and the *philosophes* had steadily deteriorated in recent years and Voltaire, though once a pupil of the Jesuits, now did everything in his power to make them appear ridiculous.

There is no place, in a swift-moving *conte*, for subtlety of characterization or realism of description. Nevertheless, Voltaire does succeed in giving a half-life to his characters and a certain degree of verisimilitude to his narrative. The resourcefulness and inventiveness of Cacambo are manifest here as they are throughout the story; the naivety of Candide, easily brought to doubt his mentor's philosophy, but still more easily persuaded to accept it again, is clearly seen. There is a sufficient sprinkling of local colour (Cacambo's name, the reference to 'Los Padres', the savages' offer of girls to their guests) to give an air of veracity to the story, and this is hardly surprising, for Voltaire had very recently been engaged on the study of South-American history. Yet these qualities are of secondary importance. Apart from its underlying thought, it is the humour and structure of this passage, as of *Candide* as a whole, which make it unique.

The humour is essentially that of incongruity. It is incongruous that Cacambo, pleading for his and Candide's lives, should begin by justifying cannibalism. It is incongruous that he should address the Oreillons as 'messieurs' and harangue them according to the rules of civilized rhetoric. It is incongruous that the Oreillons themselves should change their minds so completely and so rapidly. Above all, it is incongruous that Candide's doubts should so suddenly give place to lyrical enthusiasm for his former captors and that he should express his illogical ideas in such an apparently logical form.

However, this is to take examples of humour individually, and what is really unique about *Candide* is the way they are welded into a comic form which, both on a large and on a small scale, is repeated throughout the work. In a perceptive study of the structure of the work, published in 1964 in the *Australian Journal of French Studies*, M. Roger Laufer called it a 'joyau du style rococo'. If we were to take the word 'style' in a narrow sense, we might well feel like contesting this description. The style of *Candide* has none of the sustained antitheses or the careful delineation of interesting detail which characterize Montesquieu's *Lettres persanes*. It has none of the whimsical love of linguistic invention to be found in lesser writers like the Prince de Ligne, who exemplifies one aspect of the rococo in literature. In its simplicity, regularity and verbal austerity, it has much in common with the Classicism Voltaire admired, though its sentence structure has far less rigidity. However, if we look at the form of the *conte* we see far greater affinities with the practice of the rococo. There is a remarkable unity of construction, but it is never a symmetrical unity. The *conte* as a whole begins with the little community in Westphalia and ends, after Candide's wanderings throughout the world, in the little community near Constantinople, but though the two have something in common, they are profoundly different. Similarly, throughout the story, there are ideas, characters and situations which describe what may be called arabesques and end in a form reminiscent of, but often very different from, the one they originally possessed. To change the metaphor, a theme enunciated in a minor key may later appear in a major one, or *vice versa*.

Within the chapter from which this extract is taken, we may observe a remarkable number of such transformations. When it opens, Candide is despairing of life because he has killed the Baron's son; when it ends, he is delightedly affirming that he owes his own life to precisely this action. The Oreillons prepare their meal to the cry of 'mangeons du jésuite!'; when they free their prisoners, it is to the analogous but completely different shout of 'il n'est point jésuite!'. Candide, at the point of death, doubts Pangloss' theories about the noble savage; a page later, he is ecstatic in his praises of 'la pure nature'. Cacambo begins by asserting that natural law teaches us to kill our neighbours, but saves his own and Candide's skin by his final appeal to an almost identical concept. The same themes reoccur, the same phrases are re-echoed; this gives a remarkable feeling of unity to *Candide*. But they evolve and are transformed, so that when we encounter them again they seem to us at one and the same time both familiar and strange; the comic quality of *Candide* is built around these transmutations.

*Source*
François-Marie Arouet de Voltaire (1694–1778): *Candide,* chapter xvi, ed. J. H. Brumfitt, oup, 1968, pp. 95–6.

*John Weightman*

## ROUSSEAU
### Extract from *Les Confessions*

ROUSSEAU

« Un jour j'allai m'établir au fond d'une cour dans laquelle était un puits où les filles de la maison venaient souvent chercher de l'eau. Dans ce fond il y avait une petite descente qui menait à des caves par plusieurs communications. Je sondai dans l'obscurité ces allées
5 souterraines, et les trouvant longues et obscures je jugeai qu'elles ne finissaient point, et que si j'étais vu et surpris, j'y trouverais un refuge assuré. Dans cette confiance j'offrais aux filles qui venaient au puits un spectacle plus risible que séducteur; les plus sages feignirent de ne rien voir, d'autres se mirent à rire, d'autres se crurent insultées et
10 firent du bruit. Je me sauvai dans ma retraite; j'y fus suivi. J'entendis une voix d'homme sur laquelle je n'avais pas compté et qui m'allarma: je m'enfonçai dans les souterrains au risque de m'y perdre; le bruit, les voix, la voix d'homme, me suivaient toujours; j'avais compté sur l'obscurité, je vis de la lumière. Je frémis; je m'enfonçai
15 davantage; un mur m'arrêta, et ne pouvant aller plus loin il fallut attendre là ma destinée. En un moment je fus atteint et saisi par un grand homme portant une grande moustache, un grand chapeau, un grand sabre, escorté de quatre ou cinq vieilles femmes, armées chacune d'un manche à balai, parmi lesquelles j'aperçus la petite co-
20 quine qui m'avait décelé, et qui voulait sans doute me voir au visage. L'homme au sabre en me prenant par le bras me demanda rudement ce que je faisais là. On conçoit que ma réponse n'était pas prête. Je me remis, cependant, et m'évertuant dans ce moment critique je tirai de ma tête un expédient romanesque qui me réussit. Je lui dis d'un
25 ton suppliant d'avoir pitié de mon âge et de mon état; que j'étais un jeune étranger de grande naissance dont le cerveau s'était dérangé; que je m'étais échappé de la maison paternelle parce qu'on voulait m'enfermer, que j'étais perdu s'il me faisait connaître; mais que s'il voulait bien me laisser aller je pourrais peut-être un jour reconnaître
30 cette grâce. Contre toute attente, mon discours et mon air firent effet. L'homme terrible en fut touché, et après une réprimande assez courte, il me laissa doucement aller sans me questionner davantage. A l'air dont la jeune et les vieilles me virent partir, je jugeai que l'homme que j'avais tant craint m'était fort utile, et qu'avec elles
35 seules je n'en aurais pas été quitte à si bon marché. Je les entendis murmurer je ne sais quoi dont je ne me souciais guère; car pourvu que le sabre et l'homme ne s'en mêlassent pas, j'étais bien sûr, leste et vigoureux comme j'étais, de me délivrer bientôt et de leurs tricots et d'elles.

40 Quelques jours après, passant dans une rue avec un jeune abbé mon voisin, j'allai donner du nez contre l'homme au sabre. Il me reconnut, et me contrefaisant d'un ton railleur: je suis Prince, me dit-il, je suis Prince; et moi je suis un couillon; mais que son Altesse n'y revienne pas. Il n'ajouta rien de plus, et je m'esquivai en baissant
45 la tête et en le remerciant dans mon cœur de sa discrétion. J'ai jugé que ces maudites vieilles lui avaient fait honte de sa crédulité. Quoi qu'il en soit, tout Piémontais qu'il était, c'était un bon homme, et jamais je ne pense à lui sans un mouvement de reconnaissance: car l'histoire était si plaisante, que par le seul désir de faire rire tout
50 autre à sa place m'eût déshonoré. Cette aventure, sans avoir les suites que j'en pouvais craindre, ne laissa pas de me rendre sage pour longtemps. »

IN THE COMPLICATED history of the Western individual's attitude towards himself, Rousseau's *Confessions* is a vital document, still as fresh and immediate today as it was when he wrote it in the second half of the eighteenth century. Confessional literature, in either a direct or a slightly disguised form, has become so common in the modern world that we may have difficulty in remembering that it is a comparatively recent phenomenon, initiated to no small extent by Rousseau's example. There had, of course, been first-person narratives before his time. He himself was influenced by St Augustine's *Confessions* and the more revelatory passages of Montaigne's *Essais*, and the concept of personal memoirs, whether intended as a strict record of private or historical events or fictionalized so as to provide entertainment, was firmly established by the middle of the eighteenth century. Such works as the early picaresque text *Lazarillo de Tormès* (late fifteenth century), Cellini's *Memoirs* (sixteenth century) and Tristan L'Ermite's *Page disgracié* (seventeenth century) are symptomatic of the fact that the sense of individual destiny, without which it would not occur to anyone to write his own life-story, is essentially an outcome of the Renaissance and of the picaresque hero's uneasy awareness of himself as a displaced entity during the long and complex change-over from the mediaeval to the modern world. It is true that the Middle Ages, being Christian, had attached importance to the individual soul (and this respect for the soul could, later, by a process of transposition, reinforce the new sense of personal individuality), but the soul was featureless and eternal, and institutionalized confession allowed it to cleanse itself periodically, not through some inner impulse but according to the set, external rules of the Church. It was only at the Renaissance that the mind and personality inhabited by the soul came to seem of prime importance and that the individual, as we now know him, first began to appear. And it was only in the eighteenth century that the complicated and untidy truth about one individual was set down at length by the individual himself.

Rousseau was right in claiming, as he does at the beginning of the *Confessions*, that he was the first person ever to attempt such a complete and outspoken account. He was totally wrong in asserting that he would have no imitators; in contemporary European and American literature his disciples are legion, although they may never have read him. The most obvious parallel in modern France is with André Gide's *Si le grain ne meurt*, but one can also think of the writings of

JOHN WEIGHTMAN

Jean Genet, Violette Leduc, Maurice Sachs, Raymond Guérin and
Etiemble – to mention only a few names – and there are any number
of comparable English and American confessional authors, perhaps
more American than English because of the peculiar development of
the picaresque character in America in the form of the 'drop-out'.
The evolution of confessionalism raises two interesting questions
with regard to the history of sensibility: (1) if Rousseau's example
was important, and indeed unique, why was it so long in bearing
fruit, since, after its immediate imitation in Restif de la Bretonne's
*Monsieur Nicolas* at the end of the eighteenth century, there was little
or nothing of the same nature in the main body of nineteenth-
century French literature, apart from Musset's *Confession d'un enfant
du siècle*, which is pale in comparison, or Chateaubriand's *Mémoires
d'Outre-Tombe*, which is splendidly general? (2) in any case, if the
individual began to emerge at the Renaissance, why was his first,
full-length self-portrait delayed until the second half of the eighteenth
century?

To answer the second question first – the explanation probably is
that, in France at least, the period of individualistic self-expression at
the Renaissance was followed by the acceptance of neo-classical
formalism, Counter-Reformation severity, monarchical authori-
tarianism and what American sociologists have called 'outer-direct-
edness'. Descartes and Pascal still wrote as individuals and one can
guess to some extent from their writings what they were like as
persons (Pascal's *Pensées* reads rather like a great confessional work
in embryo, and his famous dictum, *le moi est haïssable*, is an exaspera-
ted expression of the Christian view of the impurity of the personality, as compared with the anonymity of the soul). But during the
hey-day of neo-classicism which followed their generation, the
personality became concealed behind such a mask of ceremonious-
ness that it is difficult, if not impossible, to imagine what Racine,
Boileau, Bossuet, Mme de La Fayette or Louis XIV really felt as
individuals. Even Mme de Sévigné, in her letters, seems to be acting
the part of the *salon* conversationalist rather than expressing her
individuality directly. Perhaps, in strongly formalistic periods, the
individual is incapable of being intimate with himself, even in solitude. Saint-Simon spent thirty years writing his memoirs in retire-
ment, yet he never departed from the same tone of dignified
remoteness in dealing with personal matters. It was only after the

breakdown of the *grand siècle* mentality and the revival, in the eighteenth century, of the spirit of Renaissance enquiry that the individual again came to think of himself as such and to put his own opinions and feelings before social decorum. The eighteenth century also saw the re-emergence all over Europe of the picaresque character, of whom Rousseau himself was a notable example, and it was only to be expected that the *pìcaro*, moving as he did from one social setting to another and thus made aware of the relative nature of behaviour patterns and moral beliefs, should ask himself who he really was, and raise the problem of the limits of personal identity and personal freedom. What Diderot and Beaumarchais expressed through the medium of the characters of Rameau's Nephew and Figaro and what the Marquis de Sade explored in his dark, rhapsodic fictions, Rousseau tackled directly in his own name, possibly because he was an almost perfect example of the displaced person. As a French-speaking Swiss, a motherless boy entrusted at an early age to foster-parents, a young *révolté* in flight from repressive authority, a wanderer in Savoy and Italy, a temporary believer in two religions and the inventor of a third, a jack-of-all-trades, a homeless exile and a paranoiac obsessive, he was ideally suited – since he also had literary genius – to make the attempt to define the modern individual. He cast his work not in the form of a humble confession murmured to a priest within the collective precincts of a Church, but in the more startling shape of an open letter to God from an individual who was convinced that the Creator should be able to stand a detailed account of his own handiwork. Rousseau's proclamation of the validity of the individual as a moral and emotional system neatly echoes Descartes' affirmation in the *Discours de la Méthode* – a century or more earlier, before the ethos of the *grand siècle* had been firmly established – of the validity of the individual as a source of intellectual judgment.

To go back now to the first question – why was the effect of Rousseau's example so long delayed? – I would suggest that the Romantic period was far from being such an era of liberation as it has sometimes been thought. It also involved a revulsion against what it considered to have been the speculative excesses of the Enlightenment, so that the major literary figures of the time, with the possible exception of Stendhal, are remarkably reactionary in some of their basic attitudes, in spite of their Romantic self-centredness. The boldness of the late eighteenth century was equated with decadence since it was thought to have led to the Revolution, and nineteenth-century literature is full of nostalgia for belief and principles of order or exotic escapism. These reactionary tendencies were naturally emphasized, after the Romantic period, through the gradual establishment of bourgeois conformism. Only in the second half of the century, when the anti-bourgeois revolt gained momentum, was there a return to something like the outspokenness of the eighteenth century. But instead of the eighteenth-century cult of reason, there was now a cult of unreason, spontaneity and instinct, which went much further than anything Rousseau had advocated, because he had always remained a vigorous rationalist in spite of his frequent denunciations of rationalism. It was, however, in the line of post-Rousseauistic development, since it implied the acceptance and expression of man's given nature. Through such figures as Rimbaud and Jarry, this new cult led into the feast of unreason of Surrealism, while at the same time the growth of psychology was spreading the idea that the true categorical imperative was not, as Kant had supposed, the inner moral law but the amoral drive of man's natural make-up – the Id – which is influenced only intermittently by the Super-Ego. We have now reached a point in sophisticated literary circles where almost everyone pays lip-service to unreason and impulse and takes it for granted that the difference between the virtuous person and the delinquent is no more than a perhaps accidental twist in the relationship between the Id and the Super-Ego. This is why contemporary culture explores violence and perversion so frankly and sympathetically and why there has been such a renewal of interest in the writings of the late eighteenth century, which now seem nearer to us than a great deal of nineteenth-century literature. The Marquis de Sade and Restif de la Bretonne have benefited from this fashionable trend much more than Rousseau, whose originality as a scandalous writer is now perhaps rather underestimated. This representative extract from the *Confessions* has been chosen to show how far he could go in self-revelation, while maintaining a literary standard rarely equalled by his contemporaries. The passage is a treatment, in the first person, of the pathological phenomenon of exhibitionism, and probably the very first ever written. Although two hundred years old and couched in a slightly archaic style, it must appear quite up-to-date to the modern reader of André Gide or Henry Miller or Norman Mailer.

Rousseau was sixteen or seventeen at the time of this incident and it took place in Turin, where he had been sent by his protectress, Mme de Warens, to be instructed in Catholicism after his flight from Calvinist Geneva. When his conversion was completed, he was turned out onto the streets with a small sum of money and left to find his own way in the world. His first regular employment had been as a lackey in the house of a certain Mme de Vercellis, who had just died. Rousseau had left her house burdened with a strong sense of guilt because, during the winding up of her affairs, he had stolen a ribbon and blamed its appropriation on an innocent maid-servant, Marion, who was dismissed without a reference. He has just finished telling this story, and while he freely admits his guilt and says he has been troubled all through his life by the fate that may have befallen Marion, he emphasizes how incomprehensible his action had been to himself. It was precisely because of his fondness for Marion that he had uttered her name when challenged about his possession of the ribbon. Then, though full of remorse, he had persisted in his untruth through embarrassment and the impossibility of finding words to explain his behaviour. Therefore, he was both guilty and not guilty, and he ends his account with the confident declaration that he has suffered so much in this world because of his misdeed that it will not be held against him in the next. This is Rousseau's normal procedure, also illustrated to a lesser degree in our extract; he describes his actions with great detachment, almost as if he personally were not involved, and then he adds various touches which help him to rehabilitate himself in his own eyes. In other words, he does not resist the temptation to use confession as a means of self-justification; what has been confessed to is somehow wiped off the slate.

It is also necessary to know, for the understanding of this passage, that Rousseau had had a decisive sexual experience as a young boy, when he was a boarder and a pupil in the house of a Calvinist minister. Corporal punishment was administered by the minister's unmarried sister, Mlle Lambercier, until she noticed one day – Rousseau does not say how, but one can easily guess – that her young charge was deriving more pleasure than pain from it. Thereafter, so Rousseau tells us, his sexual urge took the specialized form of a desire to be beaten by the beloved, a desire which he never dared admit to the few women with whom he had sexual relations. This seems plausible enough and would help to explain, for instance, the psychological

masochism and peculiar sexuality of Saint-Preux, the fictional hero of
*La Nouvelle Héloïse*, into whom Rousseau put a great deal of himself.
He claims, characteristically, that this quirk of sensibility kept him
'pure', through deflecting his imagination into day-dreams about
beatings, which prevented him from becoming amorously enter-
prising or from indulging in masturbation, a practice he was not
fully aware of until the age of nineteen. It would be a nice point to
decide whether musing about the lash is more 'pure' than masturbation or fornication; at least we can be sure that it helped to
complicate his already uneasy relationship with the external world
and encouraged him to take refuge in his imagination and so, in the
end, to write rather than to act. One modern critic, Jean Starobinski,[1]
goes further and argues that the thwarted sexuality which led to
exhibitionism has its counterpart in the thwarted urge to communicate which led to writing such outspoken confessions. This is
impossible to prove, but it seems quite likely. The most frequent
impulse mentioned by Rousseau is a compensatory urge: he imagined
the lovers in *La Nouvelle Héloïse* to make up for the absence of perfect
love in his own life; he assures us that he can best conjure up summer
in the depths of winter, and vice-versa; he wrote *Emile*, a vision of
perfect education, because he himself had had such an unsettled and
disorganized childhood and youth. At the root of many a literary
vocation there may be the feeling that direct communication with
actual individuals has failed, or is impossible, and that the only hope
left is an appeal to the great anonymous public. Similarly, the
exhibitionist is appealing to the public because, even if he exposes
himself to individuals, they are unknown to him and are chosen only
because they happen to be there and have the general characteristics
he requires. And the act itself is absolute; it is not usually meant to
lead to closer communion any more than, in publishing a book, the
average writer expects to enter into individual contact with his
readers; he is usually satisfied to know that he has readers, without
enquiring into their identity. Of course, not all exhibitionists are
artists, nor are all artists exhibitionists in any very definite sense, but
there is a psychological area where the two types can overlap, and
this area may be especially important in Rousseau's case.

He describes, then, how, during the period of idleness which followed his dismissal from the Vercellis household, he became

obsessed with sensual thoughts, which at first could find no outlet because of his ignorance and timidity. In the end his frenzy drove him to look spontaneously for shady avenues and secluded spots where he could display his buttocks to such members of the fair sex as happened to pass ('Ce qu'elles voyaient n'était pas l'objet obscène, je n'y songeais même pas, c'était l'objet ridicule'). Needless to say, he never had the nerve to wait and see if any of them would provide him with the satisfaction he was yearning for.

He selects only one episode for extended description, and this again is characteristic of his method. He does not attempt to maintain an even density of narrative; he will summarize weeks or months in a few words and then dwell at length on some momentary incident or flash of enlightenment, i.e. he has an admirable sense of the traumatic experience or the *scène à faire*. What the reader of the *Confessions* remembers is a series of set-pieces, which may not be literally true; indeed, scholars have shown that, more often than not, Rousseau's facts are to some extent inaccurate, either because his memory was at fault or because his conscience or his literary imagination was arranging the details in a more satisfactory form (cf., in particular, Jean Guéhenno's study of the *Confessions*).[2] Yet the poetic truth of the episode usually comes over with tremendous force. And what does it matter if Rousseau is telescoping together a number of experiences or rounding out his account with a little fiction? In the last resort, this is the only way to grasp the reality of living, since undifferentiated facts, however accurate, have no significance until they are moulded into aesthetic patterns. Rousseau is clearly trying to be truthful, and he is prepared to violate the conventions of decency to achieve self-definition, yet at the same time his literary instinct never ceases to operate. He does not, like some modern confessionalists, give a higgledy-piggledy recital of turpitudes and obscenities which produces a blurred impression. His telling moments, whether shameful or sublime, humorous or instructive, are fully worked out and, once read, remain unforgettable. In fact, the *Confessions* is full of *morceaux d'anthologie*: the reading sessions with his father during childhood, the first idyllic meeting with Mme de Warens, the affair of the ribbon, the ludicrous episode of the concert of his own unplayable music, his visions of the beauty of nature during his walking tours or when sleeping out of doors, his quarrel with the French ambassador in Venice, and so on. This

exhibitionist episode is perhaps not a major passage, but it is instinctively composed with an eye to the overall effect. Rousseau, introducing the passage, says with some embarrassment that his mishap
is 'comique'. It is much more than that, and even has something
sinisterly beautiful and dream-like about it. Possibly it *was* a dream
that Rousseau came to remember as a real happening, or fused with
his actual experiences. It certainly reads like a typical guilt nightmare
followed by a sensation of escape, as if his previous exhibitionist
practices had crystallized into an imaginative representation, expressive of danger and its resolution.

First of all, there is something remarkably appropriate about the contrast between the well in the middle of the courtyard (and therefore
in broad daylight) and the dark labyrinthine background from which
Rousseau is looking out and into which he intends to retreat in case
of need. It may be stretching things too far to suggest that the well is
to be appreciated as a symbolic aperture representing 'normality',
glimpsed from a distance by the outcast and pervert. The well is
certainly a meeting-point, a collective, social place, as opposed to the
lonely and vaguer area in which the exhibitionist is lurking. Interest-
ingly enough, Rousseau usually takes the well or fountain as a centre
of that innocent, primitive communion which he harks back to as
part of the lost beauty of the past or looks forward to as a future
ideal. In his *Essai sur l'origine des langues*, he makes the suggestion
that language first developed around springs or wells where young
men and women naturally congregated and made professions of love
to each other. As he puts it, in a typically eighteenth-century pastoral
conceit . . . 'du pur cristal des fontaines sortirent les premiers feux
de l'amour'.[3] Here we see him bringing his *premiers feux* inarticu-
lately to the fountain and dimly conscious of sullying its purity.

It seems contrary to common sense that he should choose as his
escape route a labyrinth of which he himself did not know the secret.
If the detail is true, it must mean either that he was in a state of
frenzy which made elementary prudence impossible or that, through
some vestige of childishness, he supposed that if he could not see
other people in the darkness of the cellars, they would not see him.
The latter interpretation is implied by the phrase: 'j'avais compté sur
l'obscurité, je vis de la lumière'. But, in either case, the flight from
daylight into dark, subterranean passages corresponds perfectly to

the psychological overtones of the situation. It conveys the impulse to recoil from awareness of guilt into the comforts of oblivion; also, the obscure, unfathomable network suggests both the physical depths of female sexuality and the ramifications of the unconscious (the escape from the consequences of sex is into a still more womb-like setting, i.e. the adolescent is hesitating between going forward into adulthood and receding into infancy). And the wall, too, may be polyvalent; it is the real wall which creates the crisis of terror and suspense in the narrative, but it could also be the imprisoning wall of childhood nightmares and the wall of inevitability or necessity formed by temperament and events. Although Rousseau was always trying to revise creation in the light of his assumptions and ideals, he had an intermittent, but surprisingly strong, feeling for necessity, which gives a backbone of realism to certain of his writings, such as *La Nouvelle Héloïse*, that would otherwise collapse into pure wish-fulfilment.

The impression that the unfortunate picaresque anti-hero has momentarily reverted to childhood is confirmed by the fact that his captors are old women carrying broomsticks (the attributes of witches and not the deliciously chastising rod or strap wielded by Mlle Lambercier) and a big man, whose first-mentioned characteristic is his big moustache, an adult male sign. The order of words is both childish and ironical: 'une grande moustache, un grand chapeau, un grand sabre'. The size of the hat is – one would have thought – immaterial, but a sudden reversion to infantilism might make the victim notice the size of the moustache and the hat before the size of the sabre. At the same time, the older Rousseau telling the story is suggesting that a poor deluded adolescent is being threatened with a comically disproportionate aggressive weapon, which is more or less of the same logical order as a large hat, i.e. a child might be just as terrified of a large hat as of a large sabre. And behind the weapon, perhaps, there is also the principle of adult sexuality, which is reacting violently against the pathetically tentative manifestation of youthful lust.

Rousseau manages to escape from fate ('ma destinée') by exercising his imagination and giving himself a different, and more exotic, identity. This is in keeping with the instinct for self-dramatization which runs all through his writings and is particularly noticeable in the *Confessions*. Indeed, one of the most remarkable features of the work is the skill with which Rousseau shows himself to be living constantly on two levels, the real and the imaginative. At any given moment, he is his 'objective' self – the runaway boy, the unhappy parasite in great houses, the idolized author, the ailing, suspicious exile – and the various people his imagination allowed him to be – the knight-errant about to marry a princess, the virtuous citizen of Geneva, a democrat of Roman austerity, the honoured friend of great lords and ladies, a simple hermit, a musician and performer of genius, a persecuted refugee and Legislator to the universe, sitting as it were on the right hand of God. He shares with General de Gaulle the distinction of being the French-speaking celebrity who refers to himself most often in the third person, but whereas the General, as befits the self-appointed incarnation of France Eternal, is always on the heights of sublimity, Rousseau has two series of *personae*: the proud and the modest or the assertive and the recessive – on the one hand, the citizen of Geneva, Mr Dudding the travelling Englishman, Saint-Preux (a name which combines the attributes of saintliness and chivalrous aristocracy and ensures that Nature's gentleman and the perfect lover is also a sort of honorary Knight-Templar), and on the other, *le promeneur solitaire*, the elusive M. Renou, and the pathetic 'Jean-Jacques'. Here, he leaps in one bound from being the homeless delinquent caught displaying his backside to the rôle of mad, tragic prince, a kind of Hamlet in Turin. These kaleidoscopic changes of personality, which are found in a less pronounced form in many other picaresque figures, are a notable symptom of Rousseau's modernity. He tells his life-story in terms of the oscillation between 'Being-for-oneself' and 'Being-for-others', and is constantly wondering about 'Being-in-itself'.

Behind the delinquent and the mythomaniac there is also a cool and cynical intelligence, capable of making all the necessary points against itself quickly and deftly and of appreciating the situation in the round. The narrator sees the kindness and the humour of the man with the sabre and the more vindictive tendencies of the women. He understands that his form of exhibitionism is literally '*preposterous*', because he not only refers to it as 'un spectacle plus risible que séducteur', but also mocks at himself by suggesting that the girl who had denounced him had joined in the chase to catch a glimpse of a less anonymous part of his anatomy ('. . . voulait sans doute me voir au visage'). It should be noted that this ironical, off-hand tone is not the one Rousseau is most famous for, nor the one he employs most often. Usually, he is lyrical, rhetorical, sonorous and vibrant. But occasionally, when he is in a more typically eighteenth-century mood or when he is embarrassed about some-thing, he may adopt this style, which is really more Voltairean than Rousseauistic. The passage of rapid narrative from 'Dans cette confiance . . .' down to '. . . me voir au visage' is not unlike an extract from one of Voltaire's *Contes*; there is the same sprightly rhythm and use of throw-away effects and sudden darker implica-tions; even the fourfold repetition of *grand* has a Voltairean ring. Similarly, in the second paragraph, the deprecatory turn of phrase in 'On conçoit que ma réponse n'était pas prête' is an example of the kind of understatement Voltaire is very fond of.

Perhaps, having decided to reveal this adolescent peccadillo, Rousseau was moved to use the Voltairean mode because the moral issue was not large enough to warrant pulling out the *vox humana* stop, as he does, for instance, when he is writing about Marion and the ribbon or about his abandonment of his five children. Strictly speaking, what he is dealing with is less a moral issue than a patho-logical symptom and so he disinfects it and makes it more palatable by handling it in this glancing, allusive style, instead of dwelling on it with earnest insistence. However, the method has a slight draw-back, which is that Rousseau does not actually discuss his behaviour; he relates it effectively and leaves the matter at that. Or rather, if anything, he displaces the centre of interest by pretending, con-sciously or unconsciously, to attach most importance to peripheral questions. In the second paragraph, he implies that the main problem was merely how to escape from the old women and their sticks ('. . . j'étais bien sûr, leste et vigoureux comme j'étais, de me délivrer bientôt et de leurs tricots et d'elles') and, in the third paragraph, that his honour depended on the story not being repeated by the man with the sabre ('tout autre à sa place m'eût déshonoré'). But, in a sense, he had already been dishonoured in the eyes of half-a-dozen women and one man, not to speak of the young abbé; some people would have been so overcome by the shame of this that they would not have given much thought to the possible extension of the knowledge of their mishap; is the dishonourable or shameful nature of an action to be judged by the number of people who know about it? Rousseau's sense of shame operates rather erratically and he does not always draw the boundaries of his honour along the lines one might expect. Even when he is being most honest, he can suddenly strike a note of dishonesty, hypocrisy or sanctimoniousness. We may say either that this was an almost inevitable consequence of his attempt to do something new (an innovator is almost always in danger of adopting an uncertain tone), or one may think that, in spite of his genius, he can display vulgarity of feeling. The passage would undoubtedly have been better if he had capped the vivid narrative with some comment which showed that he had got the whole matter firmly in perspective.

We can tell from a number of details that he is not altogether in control of his writing, or that the final draft has, accidentally, been left a little incoherent. Why, in the third paragraph, does he suggest very condescendingly that the Piedmontese are usually unkind ('Tout Piémontais qu'il était, c'était un bon homme')? In the preceding pages he makes no general remarks about the Piedmontese character, and he himself had met with more than one proof of kindness on the part of the people in the area. Had Voltaire made such an incidental gibe (in fact, this is one of Voltaire's habitual tricks), the reader would have known whether he meant it as a joke or whether there was some serious reason behind it. Also, after showing himself to be entirely in the wrong, at least according to conventional views, Rousseau applies derogatory terms to his pursuers. At the end of the first paragraph, he refers to the young girl as 'la petite coquine qui m'avait décelé', as if a girl who denounces an exhibitionist were as much to blame as the exhibitionist himself. And, in the third paragraph, he writes: 'J'ai jugé que ces maudites vieilles lui avaient fait honte de sa crédulité', as if the man with the sabre had been right to believe Rousseau, whereas the old women were wrong to see through him. In both instances the terms may be transferred epithets, merely expressive of Rousseau's irritation at being found out; but it is more likely that they indicate a slight revulsion against his own awareness of his 'guilt'. As has been pointed out above, he often confesses and then reacts to some extent against the confession.

The passage, like so many others in the *Confessions*, suggests one general comment. The basic assumption in all Rousseau's theoretical writings is that there is, or was, or may be, a natural order of things distinguished by its soundness, its beauty and its divine appropriateness. As he declares at the beginning of *Emile*: 'Tout est bien sortant des mains de l'auteur des choses, tout dégénère entre les mains de l'homme'. The whole effort of his speculative thought is directed towards the return to this divinely sanctioned naturalness. It obviously rests on a myth since, if the source of evil is in man, it could only have been put there for some reason by the Creator. Consequently, 'tout *n'est pas* bien sortant des mains de l'auteur des choses'.

Admittedly, the myth leads Rousseau to many interesting and original formulations, but the mystery is how he could believe in it while at the same time being capable, in the *Confessions*, of showing such a subtle awareness of all the strange quirks of nature. Here, for instance, he presents himself not only as an exhibitionist (straightforward exhibitionism might at a pinch be deemed 'natural'), but as an 'unnatural' exhibitionist, afflicted with a permanent masochistic fixation as a result of his experiences in childhood. He does not imply that the punishment given him by Mlle Lambercier was in any way 'wrong'; she and her brother were virtuous and fair-minded and, in any case, the beatings gave Rousseau pleasure, and pleasure is surely nature's sign that all is well. Yet from pleasure came perversion and this touching episode in which Rousseau finally dignifies his posterior with a princely fiction. He himself thus demonstrates that there is far more in nature than his philosophy of nature consciously catered for.

NOTES
1 Jean Starobinski, *Jean-Jacques Rousseau, la transparence et l'obstacle*, Plon, 1957, p. 211 *et seq.*
2 Jean Guéhenno, *Jean-Jacques, histoire d'une conscience*, 2nd ed., 2 vols. Gallimard, 1962, *passim*.
3 *Essai sur l'origine des langues*, ch. IX.

Source
Jean-Jacques Rousseau (1712–78): *Les Confessions*, Livre III, in *Œuvres complètes*, Bibliothèque de la Pléiade, 1959, t. I, pp. 89–90.

*Vivienne G. Mylne*

*BEAUMARCHAIS*
Extract from *Le Mariage de Figaro*

« Figaro: . . . Pour le coup, je quittais le monde, et vingt brasses d'eau m'en allaient séparer, lorsqu'un Dieu bienfaisant m'appelle à mon premier état. Je reprends ma trousse et mon cuir anglais; puis laissant la fumée aux sots qui s'en nourrissent, et la honte au milieu du
5 chemin, comme trop lourde à un piéton, je vais rasant de ville en ville, et je vis enfin sans souci. Un grand Seigneur passe à Séville; il me reconnaît, je le marie: et pour prix d'avoir eu par mes soins son épouse, il veut intercepter la mienne! intrigue, orage à ce sujet. Prêt à tomber dans un abîme, au moment d'épouser ma mère, mes
10 parents m'arrivent à la file. (*Il se lève en s'échauffant.*) On se débat; c'est vous, c'est lui, c'est moi, c'est toi; non, ce n'est pas nous; eh! mais qui donc? (*Il retombe assis.*) O bizarre suite d'événements! Comment cela m'est-il arrivé? Pourquoi ces choses et non pas d'autres? Qui les a fixées sur ma tête? Forcé de parcourir la route où je suis entré sans
15 le savoir, comme j'en sortirai sans le vouloir, je l'ai jonchée d'autant de fleurs que ma gaieté me l'a permis; encore je dis ma gaieté sans savoir si elle est à moi plus que le reste, ni même quel est ce *Moi* dont je m'occupe: un assemblage informe de parties inconnues; puis un chétif être imbécile; un petit animal folâtre; un jeune homme ardent
20 au plaisir, ayant tous les goûts pour jouir, faisant tous les métiers pour vivre; maître ici, valet là, selon qu'il plaît à la fortune! ambitieux par vanité, laborieux par nécessité, mais paresseux . . . avec délices! orateur selon le danger; poète par délassement; musicien par occasion; amoureux par folles bouffées; j'ai tout vu, tout fait, tout
25 usé. Puis l'illusion s'est détruite, et, trop désabusé . . . Désabusé!
. . . Désabusé! . . . Suzon, Suzon, Suzon! que tu me donnes de tourments! . . . J'entends marcher . . . on vient. Voici l'instant de la crise. »

THIS PASSAGE comes from the celebrated monologue in Act v of *Le Mariage de Figaro*, and this play in its turn is part of the Figaro trilogy consisting of *Le Barbier de Séville*, *Le Mariage* and *La Mère coupable*. Beaumarchais would have liked to see the three plays performed as a connected series. However, *La Mère coupable* is a highly sentimental *drame* with little appeal for modern audiences, and it is the two Figaro comedies which have survived.

*Le Mariage de Figaro* was completed, according to Beaumarchais, by 1778. It was accepted for production in 1781, but some of its jokes and allusions were considered offensive by the authorities and by Louis XVI in particular, so that production was delayed. After various modifications the play was given a private performance in 1783, and in April 1784 it was at last staged by the *Comédie Française*.[1] It was an immediate success.

The plot is complex and fast-moving, with two main threads. One of these is a series of obstacles which might prevent Figaro from marrying Suzanne at all. But by the end of Act III these obstacles have been surmounted, largely through the discovery that Figaro is Marceline's long-lost son, so there is nothing more to hinder the wedding-celebrations. For many comedies, including *Le Barbier de Séville*, such a situation provides the final dénouement. But in this case another problem awaits solution: will Figaro's married life be happy? This question is raised in the first scene of the play, where Suzanne reveals that the Count wishes not only to be her lover once she is married, but also to exercise the traditional *droit du seigneur* and be the first to enjoy her favours. The last two acts turn on the secret rendez-vous which Suzanne has supposedly granted the Count for this purpose. In reality, of course, it is the Countess who plans to keep the assignation, disguised as Suzanne.

When Figaro learns that the rendez-vous is to take place, he is beside himself with jealousy (IV, 14, 15). Marceline points out how unreasonable this reaction is, in view of his knowledge of Suzanne's character. Admitting that he was wrong, Figaro concludes: 'Examinons en effet avant d'accuser et d'agir.' However he uses the time between Acts IV and V to summon a crowd of minor characters. They are to lie in wait, and emerge in due course as witnesses of the Count's perfidy and Suzanne's venality. In other words, Figaro is now once again assuming that Suzanne is guilty. In terms of motivation this assumption is not adequately explained. It is however useful – one might even say necessary – for the effective development of Act V. Figaro's summoning of the vassals ensures that they are all present when the Count is humiliated.[2] They also provide the equivalent of an opera chorus for the celebrations and dancing of the *finale*. And Figaro's broodings on Suzanne's infidelity form the starting-point of his soliloquy, an interlude which makes the subsequent scenes of gaiety all the more brilliant.

In spite of Figaro's initial depression, the speech as a whole is far from gloomy. Ratermanis and Irwin, discussing Beaumarchais' comic style, analyse only those parts of the soliloquy which they consider 'subject to comic interpretation'; but this covers over two-thirds of the text, including almost the whole of the middle section where Figaro tells his life-story.[3] As for the first section, Figaro here speaks more in anger than sorrow. His reproachful attitude towards Suzanne passes quickly into criticisms of the Count, and Roger Pons entitles this section, with some justification, *un défi*.[4] It is only in the closing passage, with its moments of quasi-philosophical questioning, that Figaro seems to give way to dejection. One important factor, however, should prevent us from lending too much weight to even this apparent gloom. The pretext for the entire speech, recalled in the closing lines, is the assumption that Suzanne is prepared to be unfaithful to Figaro. But the audience knows that this assumption is unjustified. The situation is thus one of dramatic irony: the audience is aware that Figaro's plaints are unnecessary, that Suzanne *is* faithful, and that all will be made happily clear in a matter of minutes. With this knowledge in mind, how can one see Figaro as a truly sombre figure? His past sufferings were real, but he relates them with humorous verve. His present suffering is based on an illusion which will dissolve in laughter in its turn.

The satiric review of Figaro's past life takes up the longest section of the soliloquy. We are offered a recurring pattern of intelligent effort being frustrated by prejudice and oppression, or by the envy and dishonesty of others. It was in this passage, and particularly in Figaro's account of his literary efforts, that Beaumarchais' early audiences would be most aware of the allusions to contemporary French life and to the author's own career. And it was this part of the speech which underwent the most extensive adaptation, as Beaumarchais worked out effective, and politic, ways of airing some of his old grievances.[5] The more one knows of Beaumarchais' personal history, the more relevant and biting these criticisms become. On the other hand, they are presented in such a way that the general principles involved are clear to see. And since abuses such as arbitrary imprisonment and tyrannical censorship continue to be living issues, even the spectator who knows little or nothing of Beaumarchais' involvements can still share Figaro's indignation.

Our detailed consideration of the speech begins at the stage of Figaro's reminiscences where he has been reduced to poverty and despair. His last effort to gain wealth and social esteem had been to run a gambling-table, but other people's dishonesty put him out of business: 'Pour le coup je quittais le monde . . .' The general sense of the sentence is plain enough: I was on the point of drowning myself when I was prompted, instead, to return to my first trade. But the mode of expression is relatively complex and circumlocutory. Beaumarchais can, and often does, write dialogue which is quite straightforward and plain in its meanings. Some of his characters, and notably the Countess, are very rarely made to speak in allusive or periphrastic ways. Figaro, on the other hand, frequently utters remarks which convey his ideas in a picturesque but roundabout manner. Earlier in the soliloquy, for instance, he describes first his imprisonment and then his release from prison as follows: 'Je vois du fond d'un fiacre baisser pour moi le pont d'un château fort, à l'entrée duquel je laissai l'espérance et la liberté.' And: 'Las de nourrir un obscur pensionnaire, on me met un jour dans la rue.' We may notice two characteristics which these statements have in common: Beaumarchais is discussing a thorny subject, and in relating the events he uses concrete terms which can evoke a pictorial image. It is worth emphasizing that these are not similes or metaphors, but literal references to some concrete reality which was part of the experience in question. The same two characteristics can be found in his remark about drowning himself. Probably because suicide was held to be a sin, he avoids an explicit literal announcement of his decision. At the same time, the reference to twenty fathoms of water calls up a concrete aspect of the projected action. As for the mention of 'un Dieu bienfaisant', it was of course right and proper that Figaro should be recalled from his sinful intention by God, but we need not take this divine intervention too seriously. The God who is so vaguely referred to here merely enables Beaumarchais to express

Figaro's change of heart in an edifying phrase – and conceals, incidentally, the fact that the change has no motivation or explanation in human terms.

The final phrase of the sentence, 'mon premier état', raises the question of Figaro's 'biography'. In *Le Barbier de Séville* (I, 2) we learn that his first job was that of a servant in Almaviva's household, and it was the Count's recommendation which gained him a post as *garçon apothicaire* and started him on his travels. Only after his failure as a playwright did Figaro decide to make a living by 'l'utile revenu du rasoir'. Thus when Figaro, in *Le Mariage*, refers to barbering as his 'premier état', the remark is not strictly accurate. This minor discrepancy is only one of several inconsistencies between the two plays. In particular, the Figaro of *Le Barbier* is already married, since Rosine talks of sending sweets to 'la petite Figaro'. It is therefore clear that although *Le Mariage* is in some ways a sequel to *Le Barbier*, Beaumarchais is not attempting a systematic and consistent *retour des personnages*. As several critics have pointed out, the Figaro of the second play seems younger, livelier and less settled in life than the earlier Barber.[6]

The next sentence, 'Je reprends ma trousse...', is chiefly remarkable for its mixture of literal and figurative terms. The *trousse* and the *cuir anglais* are the real, tangible object he carries. (*Anglais* here suggests that leather goods were among the articles of fashion being imported from England.) And Figaro is really walking from town to town as a *piéton*. But the load he abandons as too heavy for a traveller on foot is *la honte*, while he also rejects *la fumée*. The latter must be taken in its general sense of 'something vain and futile', presumably with the implication that Figaro has ceased to care about 'the bubble reputation'. The slightly comic phrase, 'je vais rasant de ville en ville' recalls the earlier version of *Le Barbier*: 'faisant la barbe à tout le monde'. And the conclusion, 'et je vis enfin sans souci', sums up the simple idealized picture of an intelligent man who rejects ambition and the vanities of the world in order to gain peace of mind by following some humble but useful occupation. Such a withdrawal from the evils of society is among the ideals advanced by some eighteenth-century writers, and Rousseau of course even put it into practice, rather ostentatiously, during his later years. Satisfaction with such a way of life is perhaps more unexpected in the mouth of Figaro.

The main function of this brief reference to a life without worries is however to prepare us for the contrast with what follows. Once the *grand Seigneur* appears, Figaro's carefree life is over. By the calculated vagueness of '*un* grand Seigneur', Figaro may seem to imply that such trouble-making behaviour is typical of the class. In any case the whole sentence puts Almaviva in an unfavourable light. All the noble lord does, to begin with, is recognize his former servant. It is Figaro who wins the Count his bride, and the phrase 'je le marie' effectively indicates who is the real master of the situation. But his reward for this service is the Count's plan to 'intercept' Suzanne and be the first to enjoy her favours. That is, the Count shows initiative only in being ungrateful and immoral. The forceful effect of the sentence is emphasized by its rhythm. It can be envisaged as four independent sentences, combined into a single unit only by the punctuation. Of the three initial statements, each is shorter than the preceding one, so that 'je le marie' caps the decreasing sequence. After this comes a more complex construction expressing the new and complicated situation. The opening, 'Pour prix d'avoir . . .', would lead one, on first hearing, to expect that it is Figaro who will receive some reward. But there is a reversal of rôles: it is the Count who, having passively acquired his wife by Figaro's efforts, now claims the further 'prize' of possessing Suzanne. This situation is summed up by the elliptical, 'Intrigue, orage à ce sujet'.

Now comes a reminder of the dispute with Marceline and its comic conclusion. Figaro begins with a phrase in tragic style, 'Prêt à tomber dans l'abîme'. This elevated image is followed by a more familiar expression of the same notion, 'au moment d'épouser ma mère', and the emotion is further deflated – and the grammatical construction broken – by the arrival of his parents 'à la file'. The mock debate which ensues is clearly an opportunity for the actor playing Figaro to show his powers of mimicry by echoing the voices of Marceline and Bartholo in the recognition scene. The words, however, are quoted not from the relevant scene of *Le Mariage*, but from Beaumarchais' narrative of the recognition in the *Lettre modérée* which serves as a preface to *Le Barbier*.[7] As for the effect of this little snatch of dialogue, we should remember that one of Figaro's talents is acting. He is the type of man who, more often than not, is playing a rôle and seeking to impress or influence others. It is therefore quite in keeping that even when he is alone he should recreate a little scene of this kind.

This is the end of Figaro's account of his eventful career. In the passage from 'Un grand Seigneur . . .' to, 'eh! mais qui donc?' he has brought us up to date by summarizing the action of *Le Barbier* and then the main problems he has so far encountered in *Le Mariage*. The swift and vivid effect of these most recent phases of his life is heightened by the use of the so-called 'historic' present for all the verbs from the moment that 'un Dieu bienfaisant' calls him back to life.[8]

Having risen to his feet for his 'performance' of the recognition scene, Figaro now sinks down again: (*'Il retombe assis'*). Stage directions of this kind, inserted by the playwright, are an eighteenth-century innovation in French drama. Diderot was the first major theorist to stress the importance of the visual presentation of plays, as distinct from purely literary values. His own plays include directions as to grouping and movement, and indications of the kind and degree of emotion to be shown by the actors. Beaumarchais follows this practice and even describes the costumes to be worn. This procedure is part of a more general trend, which later spread to opera and instrumental music, for the creative artist to assume more responsibility for the presentation of his work, leaving less to the initiative of performers.

Figaro had introduced his reminiscences with the remark: 'Est-il rien de plus bizarre que ma destinée?' and he now closes them with the echoing comment: 'O bizarre suite d'événements!'[9] The strangeness of his career has two aspects: first, the sheer variety of his adventures; and second, the illogical or unjust consequences of all his efforts to make his mark in the world. So from merely describing his adventures, he passes on to consider problems of a wider scope. This passage deals with two main questions: what are the forces that shape the course of a man's life? And what is the nature of the 'self'? Elsewhere in the play there are remarks which help to supply Figaro's own answer to the first question. The outcome of our actions, it seems, is often due to chance:

> Le hasard a mieux fait que nous tous, ma petite: ainsi va le monde; on travaille, on projette, on arrange d'un côté; la fortune accomplit de l'autre. (IV, i)

(Later in the soliloquy Figaro is to say that he has been 'maître ici, valet là, selon qu'il plaît à la fortune'.) But although chance governs much of one's life, including the social rank to which one is born, each man can exercise his individual talents, and these may help to shape his career:

Par le sort de la naissance,
L'un est Roi, l'autre est Berger;
Le hasard fit leur distance;
L'esprit seul peut tout changer.
*Vaudeville*, 7e couplet.

In this respect, Figaro's philosophy is that of Beaumarchais, which finds its clearest expression in the *Projet de Dissertation philosophique relative au Prologue de Tarare*.[10]

The remark that leads on to Figaro's ponderings on identity is a statement about his own behaviour on the path of life: 'je l'ai jonchée d'autant de fleurs que ma gaieté me l'a permis'. This poetic and slightly précieux expression seems to suggest that Figaro has scattered flowers for others as well as for himself. But his *gaieté* is often a weapon to prick or goad others, and there is little in his life-story to suggest altruism. His gaiety is nevertheless an ingratiating quality, partly because we can admire the cheerfulness with which he usually accepts either slight setbacks or graver misfortunes, and partly because he makes us laugh at the victims of his wit. One is tempted again to identify this attitude with that of Beaumarchais, but this would be to over-simplify our author. While he certainly faced adversity with courage and managed, in the Goëzman affair for instance, to write some brilliantly funny pages about his troubles, yet these same *Mémoires* also contain passages of *sensibilité* or even *sensiblerie*. Figaro is rarely sentimental. When he is, for once, *attendri* by Marceline's joy, he does weep, but with the exclamation: 'je veux rire et pleurer en même temps'. Beaumarchais himself, and the characters in his three *drames*, come far closer to the eighteenth-century conception of *une âme sensible* than does the Figaro of *Le Mariage*. Figaro's prevailing *gaieté* thus represents only one aspect of Beaumarchais' emotional range.

On the question of the 'self', Roger Pons has pointed out that the starting-point here may well be the passage in Pascal which begins: 'Je ne sais qui m'a mis au monde, ni ce qu'est le monde, ni que moi-même,' but that Beaumarchais is raising a different problem from Pascal's. Figaro's puzzle is that of continuous and recognizable identity persisting through various stages – embryo, baby, child and youth. What is the 'self' which is harboured by such diverse forms? Figaro offers no solution to this problem. He states categorically that he does not know the nature of his own *moi*, and after three phrases covering the first stages of human development, the words 'un jeune homme' lead him into a somewhat flattering self-portrait. He may not know the essence of his underlying 'self', but he can describe in affectionate detail the characteristics of the young man he has been and still is. (This qualification of himself, now aged about thirty, as an immature 'jeune homme' is one of the more obviously flattering aspects of the portrayal.) By allowing himself to dwell on the personality of the 'young man', Beaumarchais has moved away from the plane of philosophical enquiry and brought us back to Figaro's specific situation. This is a useful progression, but may not have been wholly a matter of conscious design. There are passages in Beaumarchais' writings, of which this may well be one, where he succumbs to the temptations of verbal virtuosity and neglects considerations of strict logical development. The style of this passage, which we shall discuss in a moment, is typical of these flights into eloquence.

But the rapid shift away from 'philosophy' should make us notice too that this contemplative and questioning passage occupies a very small proportion of the whole soliloquy. It would be unwise to take these reflections too seriously; Figaro is never set up as a profound thinker. The fact that he falls into an unwonted mood of serious speculation may be more important, dramatically speaking, than the philosophical issues he raises.

The sentence beginning, 'Forcé de parcourir . . .', and more especially its latter section, can be taken as a good example of Beaumarchais' manner when he launches into non-satiric eloquence. Eighteenth-century France is notably lacking in great poets, but in the writings of the outstanding *prosateurs* such as Voltaire, Diderot and Rousseau, one can see a keen sensitivity to the sensuous qualities of language – sound and rhythm – which are exploited in poetry. Beaumarchais shared this gift. One of his characteristic traits is the frequent use of triple rhythms, which begin here with the series: 'un assemblage informe de parties inconnues; puis un chétif être imbécile; un petit animal folâtre.' The phrase 'un jeune homme' begins a new sequence in which another three-fold group of phrases

qualifies the noun: 'ardent . . ., ayant . . ., faisant . . .'. The
mention of 'tous les métiers' introduces a pair of nouns, 'maître ici,
valet là . . .' which breaks the flow of triple comparisons and pre-
vents monotony. Then comes another set of three phrases, this time
dependent on adjectives: 'ambitieux . . ., laborieux . . .; paresseux . . .'. (The rhyme of the -eux ending helps of course to link
these phrases as a unit.) Finally three nouns, expressing activities
rather than qualities, round off the catalogue: 'orateur . . .; poète
. . .; musicien . . .'. The final qualification, 'amoureux par folles
bouffées', does not fall clearly into this pattern; one might indeed
expect it to fall into the group 'ambitieux, laborieux, paresseux'. It
does however introduce the subject of love and can thus lead Figaro's
thoughts on towards Suzanne.

The comprehensive list of qualities and activities is summed up
in another triple rhythm: 'J'ai tout vu, tout fait, tout usé.' Whether
this is a cry of weariness or, as Roger Pons contends, of triumph, it
leads into a statement of undoubted gloom: 'Puis l'illusion s'est
détruite . . .'. But what illusion has Figaro lost? Can it be the illusion of love, evoked by the word *amoureux*? In this case he is sum-
ming up the dramatic irony of the speech, since the love he now calls
an illusion was and is a reality; he himself is under an illusion which
is soon to be dispelled.

The final word of this sentence, '. . . désabusé', echoes the
previous 'tout usé', while 'illusion' and the repeated 'Suzon' again
pick up the -us- syllable. Such an effect seems deliberately calculated
from the beginning. But in the earlier versions of the speech Beaumarchais had followed 'Désabusé . . .!' with a development on the
final stages of human life, leading to 'une vile poussière, et puis . . .
rien!' After this, Figaro was to exclaim:

Brrr! En quel abîme de rêveries suis-je tombé, comme dans un
puits sans fond? Je suis glacé . . . J'ai froid. (*Il se lève.*) Au diable
l'animal! Suzon, Suzon, que tu me causes de tracas! J'ai sans
mentir, du noir un pied carré sur la poitrine. J'entends marcher. . . .

One can only applaud Beaumarchais' excision of this passage. The
reversion to the subject of the stages in human life would read oddly
after the intervening thoughts, while the progress of man's decline
and decay, and the physical chill it casts over Figaro, would merely
add a note of conventional sentimental gloom. Instead, the cry of

BEAUMARCHAIS

'Suzon!' immediately after 'Désabusé!' effectively stresses the internal rhyme, while the slightly trivial 'que tu me causes de tracas!' is strengthened to become, 'que tu me donnes de tourments!' In its exaggerated despair, together with, 'Voici l'instant de la crise!' this phrase is an ironic prelude to the gay revelations and reconciliations of the dénouement.

Critics who discuss *Le Mariage de Figaro* usually pass some verdict on the soliloquy, commenting on its placing or relevance or length. Outright condemnation is confined to the earlier critics.[11] In recent times, the tendency has been to find arguments in its favour.[12] In the last resort however a speech of this kind stands or falls by its effectiveness when the play is staged. Theoretical arguments about whether and how such a speech should be written may turn out to be pointless. In Molière's words: 'Je voudrais bien savoir si la grande règle de toutes les règles n'est pas de plaire, et si une pièce de théâtre qui a attrapé son but n'a pas suivi un bon chemin.'[13] The Figaro monologue is a *tour de force* which may require, like a Mozart aria, an exceptionally gifted performer to do it justice. But if the actor does possess sufficient skill, he will find that Beaumarchais has so organized the speech, in its shifts of mood and thought, in its variety of rhythms and cadences, that it can hold and move an audience, and carry them fittingly into the final happy resolution of Figaro's wedding-day.

NOTES
1 For details of the delays and difficulties before production, see F. Gaiffe, *Le Mariage de Figaro* coll. Les Grands Evénements littéraires, Amiens, 1928; Nouvelle édition, Paris, pp. 46–81.
2 On the social and political importance of Figaro's leadership of the vassals, see J. Scherer, *La dramaturgie de Beaumarchais*, Paris, 1954, p. 52.
3 J.B. Ratermanis and W.R. Irwin, *The Comic Style of Beaumarchais*, Seattle, 1961, pp. 90–3.
4 Roger Pons, 'Le monologue de Figaro', *Information Littéraire*, 1951, p. 118. (M. Pons provides an *explication* of the last section of the monologue, and raises a number of interesting points which limitations of space have prevented me from citing or discussing.)
5 For these variants see Beaumarchais, *Théâtre complet*, ed. Maurice Allem et Paul Courant, Paris, Pléiade, 1957, pp. 792–4.
6 Cf. Ratermanis and Irwin, op. cit., p. 100; and René Pomeau, *Beaumarchais*, coll. Connaissance des Lettres, Paris, 1962, pp. 147, 171.

« 166 »

7 *Théâtre complet*, p. 158.
8 Cf. Roger Pons, op. cit., p. 119.
9 On Beaumarchais' repeated references to his own career as 'bizarre', see P. Van Tieghem, *Beaumarchais par lui-même*, Paris, p. 52.
10 For a fuller exposition of Beaumarchais' philosophic views, see Van Tieghem, op. cit., pp. 41–52.
11 A useful summary of these views is to be found in F. Gaiffe, *Beaumarchais, Le Mariage de Figaro*, coll. Les Cours de Sorbonne, Paris, 1939, pp. 165–6.
12 Cf. Scherer, op. cit., pp. 70–1; and Pomeau, op. cit., pp. 171–3.
13 Molière, *Critique de l'Ecole des femmes*, vi.

*Source*

Caron de Beaumarchais (1732–99): *Le Mariage de Figaro*, Act v, sc. 3; in *Théâtre complet*, Bibliothèque de la Pléiade, ed. M. Allem and P. Courant, 1957, p. 347.

*Francis Scarfe*

## CHÉNIER

*Iambes:* 'Quand au mouton bêlant la sombre boucherie'

quand au mouton bêlant la sombre boucherie
    ouvre ses cavernes de mort,
patres chiens et moutons, toute la bergerie,
    ne s'informent plus de son sort.
5 les enfans qui suivaient ses ébats dans la plaine,
    les vierges aux belles couleurs
qui le baisaient en foule et sur sa blanche laine
    entrelaçaient rubans et fleurs,
sans plus penser à lui le mangent s'il est tendre.
10     dans cet abyme enseveli,
j'ai le même destin. je m'y devais attendre.
    accoutumons nous à l'oubli.
oubliés comme moi dans cet affreux repaire,
    mille autres moutons comme moi
15 pendus aux crocs sanglans du charnier populaire
    seront servis au peuple roi.
que pouvaient mes amis ? oui de leur main chérie
    un mot à travers ces barraux
eut versé quelque beaume en mon âme flétrie,
20     de l'or peut être à mes bourreaux . . .
mais tout est précipice. ils ont le droit de vivre.
    vivez, amis ; vivez contens.
en dépit de – – soyez lents à me suivre.
    peut être en de plus heureux tems
25 j'ai moi même à l'aspect des pleurs de l'infort.
    détourné mes regards distraits,
à mon tour aujourd'hui mon malheur importune.
    vivez amis ; vivez en paix.

IT IS A WEAKNESS in any poem, for its understanding and appreciation to depend to any great extent on background facts and circumstances which are neither explicit, nor implied in the text itself. The critic's first task, then, is to see how far the work is self-explanatory.

The text, as shown above, is reproduced from the manuscript, which in its original form occupies no more than about twenty square centimetres (or three square inches) on a narrow strip of thin brown paper. Although there are possible signs of haste in the sparse punctuation and the abbreviation of *infortune* to *infort.* in line 25, the hand is firm and even, and there are no words or spellings corrected, so that the text suggests a fair copy rather than a first draft.

From the spelling of such words as *enfans, contens, tems, barraux* (for *barreaux*), *beaume* (for *baume*), this is recognizable as being an eighteenth-century poem; the calligraphy, in any case, not being that of the previous century. The words 'De l'or peut-être à travers ces barreaux' show that the poem must have been written in captivity. 'J'ai le même destin' (as a sheep), 'crocs sanglans', 'bourreaux' (although the word was then used for both warders and executioners) reveal that the writer was in fear of imminent execution, like some sheep led to the slaughter. Such terms as 'charnier populaire' and 'peuple roi' make it clear, as other human victims are also mentioned, that the lines must have been written in a period of social upheaval when the masses had usurped the royal power. In the eighteenth century, this could only have been during the French Revolution. The reader will thus ascribe the poem to the period of the Terror, which lasted from August 1792 to July 1794. For those who recognize the *iambe* form, together with the above circumstances, the text cannot be ascribed to any poet but André Chénier, for other imprisoned and martyred poets such as Fabre d'Églantine are not known to have written *iambes*.

The poem, therefore, tells us so much about itself, that it is not to be dismissed as just a cryptic document or a meaningless fragment: it is recognizably written in verse, and the facts and sentiments which are expressed are reasonably complete and require little outside support.

However, the background may now be enriched with a few extraneous facts, such as, that André Chénier (1762–94), who took a constitutionalist but not royalist stand in 1789, after waging a newspaper campaign on behalf of the Feuillants against the Jacobins in 1791 and 1792 and 'conspiring' against them afterwards, was thrown into Saint-Lazare prison (now the Hôpital Lariboisière) in March 1794, without a warrant; that his family and friends did little to obtain his release, believing that he would be safer if they remained quiet; and that he was guillotined on the 7th Thermidor (25th July 1794), only two days before the fall of Robespierre. While he was in prison he wrote one or two Odes, which have survived, and a number of satirical poems of the above type, commonly called *Iambes*, the most personal of which appear to have been written in the very last days of his captivity. These irritable poems are mainly of a satirical intention, but they show occasional signs of an elegiac tone.

> Quand au mouton bêlant la sombre boucherie
> Ouvre ses cavernes de mort,
> Pâtres, chiens et moutons, toute la bergerie
> Ne s'informe plus de son sort.                              4
> Les enfants qui suivaient ses ébats dans la plaine,
> Les vierges aux belles couleurs
> Qui le baisaient en foule et sur sa blanche laine
> Entrelaçaient rubans et fleurs,                             8
> Sans plus penser à lui le mangent s'il est tendre.

These opening lines are a sardonic evocation and dismissal of the conventional pastoral imagery which, under Classical influences and that of Tasso and Ariosto, had dominated much of French poetry and painting from the sixteenth century onwards. Instead of presenting the 'poetic' *agneau* or lamb (the traditional plaything and sacrificial offering), the poet portrays a sheep entering the slaughter-house, it being the fate of pet lambs to become mere meat and food once we have done with them: there is no refinement of ritual, but the crude horror of the abattoir and the butcher's stall. The lines 5–8 in their serene smoothness are not just a parody, but at the same time are worthy of the great pastoral poets; yet they conclude on the savage pun, 'le mangent s'il est *tendre*'. The 'divine' La Fontaine, as Chénier called him, had long ago treated the pastoral convention ironically in such works as *Le Loup et l'Agneau* and *L'Homme et la Couleuvre*, but never with this coarse finality. After the treason of responsibility in the third and fourth lines (the shepherds, etc., being easily enough equated to rulers and ministers) the hypocrisy and fatuity of the effeminate courtly tradition of the Ancien Régime are rudely exposed. The poet's indignation leaves no room for surprise, as the key words 'sombre boucherie' and 'cavernes de mort' are given at the outset: but what began in violence ends in merciless wit, for which I know no parallel but W. B. Yeats's bitter rejection of the imagery of his early work in *The Circus Animals' Desertion*:

> . . . Now that my ladder's gone,
> I must lie down where all the ladders start,
> In the foul rag-and-bone shop of the heart.

Chénier now develops and applies his pastoral imagery, comparing himself and his imprisoned comrades with the slaughtered sheep:

> Dans cet abîme enseveli
> J'ai le même destin. Je m'y devais attendre.
> Accoutumons-nous à l'oubli.                    12
> Oubliés comme moi dans cet affreux repaire,
> Mille autres moutons, comme moi,
> Pendus aux crocs sanglants du charnier populaire,
> Seront servis au peuple roi.                    16

It can now be seen that the whole of the movement in lines 1–16 becomes a sustained simile. Dr Johnson wrote in his *Life of Pope*: 'A simile, to be perfect, must both illustrate and ennoble the subject; must show it to the understanding in a clearer view, and display it to the fancy with a greater dignity; but either of these qualities may be sufficient to recommend it. . . . A simile is said to be a short episode.' Johnson was speaking of heroic poetry, but most of his statements apply here. Chénier now raises his pastoral imagery to the human level, where it gains in seriousness, for the fate of a man is something more than that of a sheep: however, heroic values are reversed ironically, as is legitimate in satire. If he speaks first of himself, the risk of self-pity is avoided by the subsequent use of the plural, 'oubliés comme moi'. It will be noted that line 16, showing the human victims being served up as a dish for the mob (and, in fact, incidents of cannibalism were reported often enough during that period), is a perfect parallel to 'le mangent s'il est tendre'; so that the first part of the poem, and the circle of imagery, are correctly closed in obedience to the requirements of the Classical rhetoric.

> Que pouvaient mes amis? Oui, de leur main chérie
> Un mot à travers ces barreaux
> Eût versé quelque baume en mon âme flétrie;
> De l'or peut-être à mes bourreaux . . .           20

Mais tout est précipice. Ils ont le droit de vivre.
Vivez, amis; vivez contents.
En dépit de [Fouquier] soyez lents à me suivre.
    Peut-être en de plus heureux temps        24
J'ai moi-même, à l'aspect des pleurs de l'infortune
    Détourné mes regards distraits.
A mon tour aujourd'hui mon malheur importune.
    Vivez, amis; vivez en paix.        28

'Que pouvaient mes amis?' It is perhaps natural that, after reflecting on the fate of those in prison, the poet should turn to those outside and who were still at liberty. Letters, money to bribe his warders . . . a sudden fear for those friends, as well, the line 23 having to be completed by inserting the name of *Fouquier*, that is to say Fouquier-Tinville, the public prosecutor. With the same realism as that with which he had described the sheep, Chénier does not hesitate to express negative emotions which it is polite to conceal, to the extent of reproaching his friends and no doubt his family. These sentiments reach their lowest point in 'mon âme flétrie' which (even if 'flétrie' is used in its sense of 'branded') touches self-pity, and the sordid 'de l'or peut-être'. An elegiac note appears for the first time in lines 24–6. After exhorting his friends, not very convincingly, to live happily, he is forced to return upon himself and reproach himself for doubting them, and to evoke, in compensation, his own lapses of charity in the past. Unfortunately the poem is too short for the sad and bitter exclamation, 'A mon tour aujourd'hui mon malheur importune' to be softened by the generous last line although it comes as a refrain. However we take it, the second-last line imposes itself like a final reproach. The confession of moral guilt made by the poet largely destroys the initial comparison of his own fate with the sheep's, as the sheep was entirely innocent. The poet will go guilty to the grave: not guilty, perhaps, of the political crimes of which he is accused, but consciously guilty of past offences against one of the cardinal virtues.

The last line, 'Vivez, amis; vivez en paix' (which might also read, without a comma, 'Vivez amis' – i.e. 'Vivez en amis', live *as* friends, don't reproach each other as I have done), is thus intended to be very positive, and the last word; but it cannot adequately compensate for what went before. The general impression left on the reader is one of frustration. He goes away with 'infortune' and 'importune' ringing in his ears. Matthew Arnold once described his own poem *Empedocles on Etna* as being 'too painful to be tragic'. He meant by those words that his poem offered no catharsis or relief to the reader. For the moment, Chénier's *Iambe* suggests a like conclusion.

Perhaps something more may be learnt, from Chénier's manner of presenting his theme or themes. The first line, with its heavy alliteration, is of a frightening intensity, and the sound here is 'an echo to the sense'. The violent vocabulary and meaning of the first two lines, though suddenly suspended in the gentle, fluid movement in lines 5 to 8, find their climax in the revolting image and ugliness of sound of 'Pendus aux crocs sanglants du charnier populaire', a line whose concatenation is difficult to pronounce, while it has already been observed how 'servis au peuple roi' refers back to 'le mangent s'il est tendre'. But the 'poetic' effort, until now so thoroughly sustained, is abandoned in the second movement which begins after line 16. Now there is no further attempt to prolong the imagery or to invent new images, and all is related in plain prosaic terms, quietly and without overtones. The pastoral analogies are dropped and, apart from 'précipice', the only real link between the first and second movements is a slender one, the words 'oublié' and 'oubliés' which set the poet the question of How, If and Why he is forgotten by his friends. The noble resolution, 'Accoutumons-nous à l'oubli' is immediately broken. As for the rest, it was common enough for the eighteenth-century poets to escape from personal embarrassment into generalization, and Chénier himself had done so many a time, for instance in his change of the person of the verb in one of his London Elegies:

> Et puis mon cœur s'écoute et s'ouvre à la faiblesse;
> Mes parents, mes amis, l'avenir, ma jeunesse,
> Mes écrits imparfaits; car à *ses* propres yeux
> *L'homme* sait se cacher d'un voile spécieux.
> A quelque noir destin qu'elle soit asservie,
> D'une étreinte invincible *il* embrasse la vie . . .

The poet attempts something of that kind here, in lines 24–7, in order to find some excuse, either for his friends or for his shame at accusing them, but his continued use of the first person singular, 'j'ai moi-même', 'à mon tour', hinders the desired effect of rising above circumstances, which could only be gained by using some more impersonal form. As for the overall painfulness of the poem, analysis shows that we have here fifteen sentences in the space of twenty-eight lines; the longest two of them have five lines each, while nine are no longer than a line or a half-line. This is not commonly found in verse. The rhythm is thus harshly syncopated by the sense, for the most part, giving an unpleasant, jerky effect, suggesting either impatience or acute distress of mind, and thus reinforcing the sense of frustration that the reader finds in the logical meaning. The total meaning being that of the combined statements and modes of expression (apart from, of course, what we know about Chénier, and our general experience of poetry, which naturally enter into our interpretation and reaction), it is to be concluded that the rhythm and structure do nothing to reduce the general effect that has already been described.

As I have written elsewhere, in his last works André Chénier ventured at times into a kind of anti-poetry; and our present text is a fair but not extreme example of it. I also suggested that the *Iambes* reveal a spiritual struggle, in which Chénier painfully discovered how to transcend his personal egotism and dedicate himself and his gifts, for the time remaining, to all those who were suffering and oppressed; and some signs of that are already to be found in this text, although the transcendence was not fully accomplished until the last *Iambe*, 'Comme un dernier rayon . . .' Now it cannot be said with any certainty that the *Iambe* which we have just been reading is only a fragment; and yet, when examined as a poem in its own right, it somehow falls short of being a satisfactory poem, even if it be for other reasons than those which I have suggested.

The point now arises, whether the *Iambes* as a whole ought not to be considered, not exactly as a single poem, but as a single work? I mean by this, that the fragments and the finished parts all require each other, for a complete appreciation to be achieved. In that case the present *Iambe*, 'Comme au mouton bêlant . . .' gains much by being related to another piece, beginning 'On vit, on vit infâme . . .' which is on the same folio. In it, after describing the prisoners in Saint-Lazare amusing themselves in foolish ways in the prison yard, he concluded

Et sur les gonds de fer soudain les portes crient.

Des juges tigres nos seigneurs

Le pourvoyeur paraît. Quelle sera la proie
    Que la hache appelle aujourd'hui?
Chacun frissonne, écoute; et chacun avec joie
    Voit que ce n'est pas encor lui:
Ce sera toi demain, insensible imbécile.

That *Iambe* is certainly a fragment, although its sense is complete; for it is suspended on the word 'imbécile' which has no accompanying rhyme. But the last line might well have prompted Chénier to ask whether he, also, was nothing but an 'insensible imbécile', and thus to write the text which we have been considering. And, finally, the catharsis which both those pieces failed to achieve is found in his last-written *Iambe* (which I take to follow the piece under observation), 'Comme un dernier rayon . . .' which, after once again questioning the fidelity of friends to those who are condemned, rallies suddenly as the poet dedicates his pen to oppressed humanity.

Seen thus in the wider context of the *Iambes* as a whole, the piece 'Quand au mouton bêlant. . .' obviously gains in dignity and significance, for it shows the poet at the very moment of passing through his inferno, his crisis of conscience, before emerging purified. In it, he ceased for a moment to wear the mask or mantle of 'l'homme magnanime' to which he aspired but to which he was not yet fully entitled, and even bravely acknowledged mean thoughts and confessed to a lack of charity which lesser men are loath to admit, even to themselves. The poem thus amounts to a private spiritual confession, so that the catharsis could only be in himself, and not necessarily in the poem or in the reader. But this personal confrontation enabled Chénier to achieve that aesthetic and moral recovery for which his last *Iambe* is universally admired.

It is right and necessary for us to be on our guard against literary works which make a claim on us through their biographical or historical context – because a Chatterton died young, a Milton was blind, or the poem was written in exile, or when the poet was tubercular or aged ninety-six, or because he was one's uncle. However, every poem is an historical event, whether we like the fact or not, and this is the only justification for literary history. It happens that Chénier's poem is inseparable from an unusually dramatic personal situation, as well as a turning-point in the history of Europe. It presents a case in which the Writer's predicament and the historical moment are both of importance for the future of society and Letters; for it is the first intimation and perhaps the first literary expression of *l'univers concentrationnaire* in which twentieth-century man is learning to live. Apart from its intrinsic value, it is the forerunner of many works, few of which survive, clandestinely written and sometimes, like his, miraculously preserved, fragile things created against all the odds and in the most barbarous circumstances.

The subsequent course of history has only strengthened rather than weakened the claim of André Chénier's *Iambes* to hold a respected place in the literature of commitment and protest. At the same time, his confession of moral guilt foreshadowed that revision of conscience which was to be the main preoccupation of such writers as Dostoievsky, Rilke, Kafka, and with which the most sensitive writers of the present century have been anguishedly concerned. In its serious novelty, if the poem may be described academically as being 'too painful to be tragic', it has its place in a new type of genuinely tragic literature, perhaps imperfect but written directly from experience, in which the question of catharsis is either irrelevant or suspended; for catharsis might well suit an audience comfortably seated beside Aristotle in the stalls, but not those who are performing in the arena, where we all now find ourselves.

The pastoral poetry of which Chénier himself had given so many perfect examples, and which in this poem he was the first to cast away, took another hundred years to die its natural death, whether in the small beer of the Georgians or its last perfection in Valéry. It might be asked whether Chénier's *Iambes*, with their brutal writing out of brutal experience, were not one of the first symptoms of a crack in the literature of the West, a West in which innocence and the simplest human rights are flouted and insulted so constantly, that poetry is fast becoming impossible for those who would normally be sensitive enough to write it, or, indeed, to read it.

NOTE. A commentary of the above type is intended as a basis for discussion, for much more could be written about such a poem. In discussion I should expect to be asked such questions as what is an *Iambe*, and to reply with some 'technical' analysis. I would add that Chénier only mastered this form after long experiment with the alexandrine and the ode. It is a pity that he did not live longer to use the *Iambe* for other purposes, for (in the absence of such possibilities as Wordsworthian blank verse, or free verse) it could have offered a perfect alternative to the alexandrine couplet. Other questions might point to entirely different interpretations of the poem (such as, that Chénier merely described in realistic terms the normal condition of beasts and men, thus conveying, in any case, a pessimistic view of human nature which he subsequently revised in 'Comme un dernier rayon . . .'). However, I would reject any interpretation that takes insufficient account of an ironical intention. It might also be said that, in teaching, the confrontation with manuscripts does not often occur: here the answer is, why not? I have often circulated photo-copies of manuscripts, in a plastic cover, and they excited great interest among undergraduates. Finally, some might argue that the notion of catharsis has nothing to do with non-dramatic works. This is a matter of opinion, for the term has its uses outside the aristotelian context. It comes to mind as soon as questions are asked about intention or effect. If it reveals the 'painfulness' of this poem, it can also show up the essential triviality of works by . . . many writers whose reputation has been too cheaply earned.

*Source*
André-Marie Chénier (1762–94): *Iambes*, x, in *Poems*, ed. F. Scarfe, Blackwell, Oxford, 1961, p. 107.

*J.B. Barrère*

---

*HUGO*
**Extract from** *Booz endormi*

Pendant qu'il sommeillait, Ruth, une moabite,
S'était couchée aux pieds de Booz, le sein nu,
Espérant on ne sait quel rayon inconnu,
Quand viendrait du réveil la lumière subite.

65 Booz ne savait point qu'une femme était là,
Et Ruth ne savait point ce que Dieu voulait d'elle.
Un frais parfum sortait des touffes d'asphodèle;
Les souffles de la nuit flottaient sur Galgala.

L'ombre était nuptiale, auguste et solennelle;
70 Les anges y volaient sans doute obscurément,
Car on voyait passer dans la nuit, par moment,
Quelque chose de bleu qui paraissait une aile.

La respiration de Booz qui dormait
Se mêlait au bruit sourd des ruisseaux sur la mousse.
75 On était dans le mois où la nature est douce,
Les collines ayant des lys sur leur sommet.

Ruth songeait et Booz dormait; l'herbe était noire,
Les grelots des troupeaux palpitaient vaguement;
Une immense bonté tombait du firmament;
80 C'était l'heure tranquille où les lions vont boire.

Tout reposait dans Ur et dans Jérimadeth;
Les astres émaillaient le ciel profond et sombre;
Le croissant fin et clair parmi ces fleurs de l'ombre
Brillait à l'occident, et Ruth se demandait,

85 Immobile, ouvrant l'œil à moitié sous ses voiles,
Quel dieu, quel moissonneur de l'éternel été
Avait, en s'en allant, négligemment jeté
Cette faucille d'or dans le champ des étoiles.

THIS POEM forms part of the *Première Série* of *La Légende des siècles* (1859). Hugo has placed it in a first section headed: *D'Eve à Jésus*, the eight poems of which outline the spiritual ascent of mankind from the Creation to the Redemption. The sixth poem in the section, this idyll echoes the first poem, *Le Sacre de la femme*, and represents an essential stage in the divine plan, since, following the Bible, it tells of the encounter at Bethlehem – quite accidental, to outward appearance – between Boaz and Ruth, from whose union was to stem the line of David and of Jesus Christ:

Une race y montait comme une longue chaîne;
Un roi chantait en bas, en haut mourait un Dieu.

Written with the design of the whole volume in mind, this poem is dated in the manuscript 1st May 1859 – three months before the completion of the *Première Série*. It belongs, therefore, to the final phase of composition, when the poet, a little weary from the writing of other poems, lengthy and sombre, in which Evil sometimes triumphs over Good, was looking around for more light and hoping to compose some freer and less burdensome verse. (It was at this same period that he wrote *Le Satyre*, where, however, what looks like a fable at the start grows into a cosmic poem). The theme – for which there is a curious antecedent in an eighteenth-century poem, often republished, Florian's *Eglogue de Ruth et Booz* – might easily have been less seriously handled; and Hugo, for the fun of it, tried this elsewhere, applying the famous image and phrasing: 'Vêtu de probité candide et de lin blanc' (reminiscent of Milton's 'with native honour clad/In naked majesty . . .'), not to Boaz but to Ruth, and in rakish verse.[1]

But if some readers have responded to the sensuous atmosphere of the scene, to others it seems, and I think rightly, that what prevails here is an impression of purity and serenity. All that is best in mankind seems now to be making ready, and in what is to be his very birthplace, for the coming of God in human flesh. Just as in *Le Sacre de la femme* the first dawn of all seemed to the poet filled with a holy expectancy, so now this twilight is tinged with a holy quiet; or, as we read in another poem of *La Légende, Les Sept Merveilles* (ll. 15–16):

Les astres commençaient à se faire entrevoir
Dans l'assombrissement religieux du soir.

Furthermore, the expectation now is not explicitly of a child – as was made clear at the end of *Le Sacre de la femme* – but an expectation of light; yet of a child none the less, though this remains unknown. *Booz endormi*, the title, a curious title, daring at the time in its formulation (a proper noun followed by a participle) – Leconte de Lisle still writes 'le sommeil du Condor' – gives a first indication. Sleep, a state of inactivity, and the sleeper is Boaz, an old man. In this star-lit poem, made up of a series of panels, the poet takes care to provide for dramatic development. First, the portrait of the old man, a righteous man; his sleeping described in a couple of stanzas; a dream sent from God, Jacob's ladder here transferred to Boaz, the tree of Jesse, his grandson, growing out of him as it does in those medieval images admired by Hugo and described by him (in *Le Rhin* x at Cologne, and at the beginning of *Promontorium Somnii*). The eight stanzas we quote make up the last panel – the scene set for the carrying out of God's plan. Up to this point, Hugo has taken his lead from the Bible, transposing its verses (ll. 12, 25, 29, etc.) and in accordance with the spirit of its language expressing the old man's virtues in concrete imagery (ll. 7–8). Now, the poet dwells on the silence of the night, leading us to understand that behind this scene there is an author, namely God, who has brought it about, but has not admitted the actors into the secret of his purpose.

The atmosphere of simplicity and grandeur that has hitherto prevailed is now, in the stanzas under examination, going to take on a very moving beauty, and an impression is created of mystery, of a holy mystery. How does Hugo achieve this?

Several words suggest a waiting for something unknown. 'On ne sait quel rayon inconnu', as in Lamartine, denotes a manifestation, a communication from God's side of things, and doubly stresses its indefinable nature. This hoped-for beam, concomitant with the outburst of light at the moment of wakening, subtly introduces a symbolism of light. The sense of something unknown is strengthened by the intentional repetitions: 'Booz ne savait point . . .', 'Et Ruth ne savait point . . .' The unconscious state of Boaz is matched by the ignorance of Ruth; it is she who has taken the initiative in moving, as though she were being drawn towards him. The uncertainty of forms and movements contributes to the intended effect of vagueness: 'flottaient', 'sans doute obscurément', tone down the unexpected character, in this motionless night, of any movement, be it that of a breath of air, or of an angel. The noise of the streams is 'sourd', muffled – somewhat unexpectedly – by moss; the bells of the resting flocks do not jangle, they merely 'palpitaient vaguement'.

A whole range of expressions – so familiar to the poet of the *Méditations* – is thus brought to bear on the scene, so that it may retain an equivocal mobility even when fixed as it is in a *tableau vivant*. Hugo wants it that way. Nor is it by mistake that he has confused the dates and the places. Paul Berret has pointed out the topographical spread: Galgala, in the land of Benjamin, is by no means close to Bethlehem; Ur, towards the sources of the Euphrates in Chaldea is on the northern horizon and Jerameel or Jerimeel, altered by Hugo or in some unknown translation to Jérimadeth and reckoned by the Surrealists to be a sheer poetic invention thrown up by the rhyme, is down in the south. Such a selection, in Berret's view, helps to 'donner une idée de l'immensité de la nuit qui s'étend sur la Palestine'. This vastness extends, like the tree of the generations, to time also: still close to the Deluge – as in the fine expression from Bossuet modified here by Hugo ('Le monde était encore nouveau et pour ainsi dire tout trempé des eaux du déluge') – 'La terre . . . Etait encor mouillée et molle du déluge' – the time of the coming together of Boaz and Ruth is thus rooted in the changeless and unending time of God. This is, as the saying goes, 'the night of the ages'. And so, in these primeval times, the supernatural remains familiar and makes its presence felt; angels show the tips of their wings, and the blessing of God descends from the heavens: 'Une immense bonté tombait du firmament.'

The poet uses all his skill with words to suggest that nature is herself in an attitude of expectancy, her very being in suspense, waiting for an intervention from the side of the supernatural – and in this Hugo, a primitive in his own fashion, finds no difficulty in believing. In the stillness of this night great things are being made ready. The poet's intention becomes explicit in the famous line: 'L'ombre était nuptiale, auguste et solennelle.'

This is a well-balanced line, majestic and slow-moving like a procession, thanks to its nasal sounds or diphthongs. Hugo did not bring it off at the first attempt. The replacement of *heureuse* by *auguste*, though rhythmically satisfying, takes away from the expression of human feeling what it gives to the transcendent. Everything is meant to create in us the expectation that this simple pastoral scene will give rise to an important event not stated here, but which will take place later in history and determine the meaning of the scene. For the time being, it is a wedding that we are led to expect from this simple encounter, in the mildness of the evening, between a wealthy old peasant of Judah and a young, debt-burdened widow from Moab – and this is indicated, obliquely, by the epithet qualifying *l'ombre* in line 69.

The static character of the scene is strongly marked. Ruth's approach hardly disturbs the gentle drowsiness of the night. The poet loses no opportunity of reminding us that this is a sleep-scene: 'sommeillait', 'couchée', 'la respiration de Booz qui dormait' – itself mingling with nature, as though to suggest their common consent in the will of God – 'et Booz dormait', repeated in the next stanza, all these in turn stress the passiveness of Boaz, his docility under the divine purpose. 'C'était l'heure tranquille' – the poet springs this on us in a line that stretches out after the fashion of these reputedly fierce beasts – they have figured in a preceding poem on the subject of Daniel – when their chase is done. And Ruth seems overtaken by drowsiness herself, 'ouvrant l'œil à moitié sous ses voiles'. Everything suggests that Hugo is seeking to translate into poetry some picture, seen perhaps in the days when he visited the exhibitions – not Poussin's, where we see the woman at her gleaning, but rather Hersent's, which attracted much attention at the 1822 *salon*, and in which the figures are resting motionless.

The beauty and the simplicity of the scene are closely knit together and sustained by a very full and subtle pattern of sensations. One notes, for instance, sensations that are tactile: 'les souffles de la nuit'; olfactory: 'frais parfum'; auditory: 'bruit sourd des ruisseaux', 'Les grelots . . . palpitaient'; and above all visual: angels' wings, stars in the sky, the crescent moon. One is reminded by contrast of another fine but quite different picture of night, shot through with light like this one, but in a dynamic, not a static landscape – the scene of the wild chase in *Deux cavaliers dans la forêt* (*Contemplations*, iv, 12, ms. 1841, ed. 1853):

La nuit était fort noire et la forêt très sombre . . .
Les étoiles volaient dans les branches des arbres
Comme un essaim d'oiseaux de feu.

Here, on the other hand, we have a landscape at rest ('Tout reposait dans Ur . . .'), and lit by the heavens. All else, on earth, is blurred by a luminous penumbra. In relation to the stillness of things on earth, it is the heavens that seem to be alive, as proclaimed by the glimpses of blue angels. The verbs contribute to this effect: 'volaient', 'passer', 'tombait', 'jeté', though they are to be accounted for also on stylistic grounds, Hugo being concerned, as a matter of course, to substitute concrete verbs of action or of attitude for the repetitious *Il y a* of description.

One might be tempted to think that the two closing stanzas, towards which the whole poem moves, are given a treatment that is somewhat *précieux* – jeweller's work: witness the words 'émaillaient', 'croissant fin et clair', 'faucille d'or'. In fact, what the poet is speaking of are the lights that stand out against the dark sky. He stresses the dimensions of sky, 'immense' and 'profond', bringing out the sense of the grandeur of the heavens arched over the flatness of the landscape. The word 'firmament' has a Biblical significance – 'cloison qui soutient le ciel', says Littré; it designates accurately the vault of heaven against which the stars stand out – and in Hugo's mind, as in ours, it seems also to stand for a serenity that turns man's gaze upwards and his thoughts towards God, as we see from the opening lines of a poem in *Les Contemplations* (I, 4):

Le firmament est plein de la vaste clarté;
Tout est joie, innocence, espoir, bonheur, bonté.

This is the *bonté* that comes down like a blessing on the Moabite peasant girl, looking up into the sky and moved by the will of God. It is a peasant's way of looking at things that is condensed in the strength and beauty of expressions like 'fleurs de l'ombre', 'champ des étoiles'. The lovely and mysterious vision at the end expresses the object of her dreamy contemplation in her own idiom. Hypnotized by the still beauty of the night, she translates it into homely imagery – the reaper, the sickle – which the poet admirably complements with a qualification full of meaning: 'de l'éternel été', – thus referring us back to the days of the garden of Eden; and we do indeed find the same image applied in *Le Sacre de la femme* to Time the 'moissonneur pensif', gathering up the successive transformations of the species (l. 87). More appropriate however to the mentality of Ruth the gleaner, the image falls in with a group very common in Hugo – that of the 'ouvriers mystérieux', as he says, each with a characteristic gesture that 'fait penser'.[2] The relation between the two poems is quite clear: in a setting down-graded from that of Eden, but lovely still, we have the same glorification of the human couple. The first dawn of all, in which Adam and Eve take their delight, has for its counterpart the dawn awaited, after the day's toil, and from which the race will rise that is to save the world.

The mystery thus prepared for and half-divined is emphasized in the fabric of the verse during Ruth's dreamy questioning – left in suspense at the end of line 84: as P. Clarac has justly observed, 'une longue pause marque le départ de la dernière strophe dans laquelle la nuit semble s'illuminer: les sonorités deviennent plus claires progressivement; les coupes, nombreuses dans les trois premiers vers, permettent à la voix de se reposer pour lancer le dernier, tout d'une venue, dont la syllabe éclatante *d'or* fait un vers d'apothéose'. There is a holding back of the question, step by step, the circumstantial phrases, first in relation to Ruth, then in relation to the divine reaper, postponing time and again the complementary detail still required, and which is held in reserve until the closing line. The effect of this skilful building up of the sentence through the grid of the metre is combined with great variety in the placing of the pauses, very noticeable in this final stanza, which avoids monotony no doubt, but, more importantly, follows the hesitant musing of the subject with great flexibility.

This example enables us to pass on to some detailed remarks on the form and harmony of the verse. The expression is perfectly adapted to the ideas to be suggested or the feelings to be evoked. We noted earlier that certain verbs of motion suggesting animation in the heavens might well have resulted from the stylist's desire to replace the elementary verbs of description: *être* or *y avoir*, by verbs of action: instead of '*il y a* un arbre', we have instead: 'un arbre s'élève' or 'se dresse' or 'surgit'. Hugo excels in the use of such turns of speech, which are in keeping with the dynamic character of his poetry in general. But he does also have recourse to the bare verb *être*, and sometimes in the same passages. Thus in *Le Sacre de la femme*, one comes across such lines as

On sentait sourdre, et vivre, et végéter déjà

Tous les arbres . . . etc.

indicative of a 'vie excessive', alongside such simple statements as

La montagne était jeune et la vague était vierge . . .

So that here, besides expressive verbs like 'volaient' or 'émaillaient', we find the verb *être* six times (ll. 65, 69, 75, 77, 80), twice, that is, in a single line (75). This alternation testifies to the poet's careful elaboration of his verse. Line 75, moreover, results from the correction of a line so simple that it might be taken for a truism – 'En été, la nature est glorieuse et douce.'

The variant may not read very convincingly to someone who knows the Middle East, but the poet's intention is easy to discern from this apparently off-hand remark. Similarly, so successful a line as line 69 was brought off only at the cost of a sacrifice – the cutting out of the *bonheur* of this night, which he would no doubt have liked to retain. It all seems to be a matter of the fitness of the turns of speech and of the choice of words, allied to extreme care over rhythm and sound-values. If, in the final stanza, one is struck by the varied pattern of the pauses in the lines, in the preceding stanzas on the contrary their regularity gives an impression of peace. The abundance of liquid consonants (l, r) often in the same line, conveys the softness of the night (ll. 72, 75, 76, 78, 80). The alternation of spirants (f, s) with liquids evokes to perfection, without destroying the basic tonality, the gentle stirring of this peace by the night breezes, in line 83 and especially in lines 67 and 68:

Un frais parfum sortait des touffes d'asphodèle;
Les souffles de la nuit flottaient sur Galgala.

So successful an effect of evocative harmony would be almost unbearable, one might think, were it not for the abstract mattness of the two preceding lines. This is no matter of chance, any more than the phonetic make-up of line 83, in which, through an effect of transposition, the crescent moon at the beginning seems to stand out among the lesser lights at the end, where the sounds are progressively dulled. One must remember, of course, that an assessment of the inter-play of sound-values is meaningful only by virtue of the continual association that goes on in our mind between sound and sense.

These remarks, then, have brought out very clearly the poet's craftsmanship, as much a matter of control and self-restraint as of invention or felicitous expression. Berret has pointed out that 'la plus belle part du nocturne est une addition marginale' on the manuscript. Thus, as often happens with Hugo, it is by working over his text, by following up his chance inspirations, that he has brought his theme to fullness of expression: to use Valéry's language, there are fewer 'vers donnés' in Hugo than is generally supposed.

Another characteristic of this poem is its resolutely static character. Hugo excels in epic narratives centred on a combat, a pursuit on horseback, a clash, physical or mental, in the traditional manner. But he is also able, as in the present instance, to attune himself wonderfully well to a poetic mode quite estranged from his native forcefulness, just as, in his intimate lyrics, after the deliberate vehemence of *A Villequier*, he strikes the movingly simple notes of *Demain, dès l'aube*. If in the present text the scene achieves a kind of simplicity – though different from that of the poem just mentioned – it is by dint of subtle craftsmanship.

The imaginative theme of darkness out of which light springs is a familiar one in Hugo. This time, however, the night is not one of foreboding, but of trust, and throughout, until the coming of the dawn, the virgin light of the moon keeps watch. When dawn comes, it will not, like the first dawn of all in *Le Sacre*, be an 'abîme d'éblouissement', causing the poet to say: 'Autant que le chaos la lumière était gouffre.'

This is rather, so to say, a well-ordered and peaceable dawn, in which, in the words of *Le Sacre*, brightness

> Brillait au front du ciel inaccessible,
> Etant tout ce que Dieu peut avoir de visible.

Light is the primary element, then, in this scene. Visible in the old man's eyes, it is hoped for by Ruth, and shines forth unfailingly in the darkness of the sky. For the reader interested in poetic exchanges, a curious item is this line from Florian, in which light means nothing more than life: 'Au vieillard qui va perdre un reste de lumière.'

It may be that Hugo noticed it, and sensed all that he could make out of it in his own poetic idiom: 'Mais dans l'œil du vieillard on voit de la lumière' – by turning to account the symbolic value of this interplay between man and the heavens. Surely Claudel must have remembered Hugo's Boaz, when he took up the same motif in his own fashion for a poem on St John in his *Corona Benignitatis Anni Dei*:

> Maintenant Jean est très vieux et il est tout blanc de barbe et de crinière
> Et son visage aussi est si blanc qu'on dirait qu'il en sort de la lumière.

Among the poets, a good line never goes astray.

Notes

1 *Théâtre en liberté*, Reliquat, p. 465:
   Ruth, femme de Booz, apparaissait vêtue
   De clarté, d'innocence et d'ombre, au chérubin
   Qui, par un trou du ciel, la regardait au bain.

2 *Napoléon-le-Petit*, v. 6, Imprimerie Nationale ed., p. 126, the orator who sows ideas in Parliament: 'Une fois monté à cette tribune, l'homme n'est plus un homme; c'est un ouvrier mystérieux qu'on voit le soir, au crépuscule, marchant à grands pas dans les sillons, et lançant dans l'espace, avec un geste d'empire, les germes, les semences, la moisson future, la richesse de l'été prochain, le pain, la vie' (1851). In *La Fin de Satan* (ii, i, 3, p. 70), the image in lines written in 1859–60 refers to Christ:
   Les paysans, le soir, de sa lueur troublés,
   Le regardaient de loin marcher le long des blés,
   Et sa main qui s'ouvrait et devenait immense
   Semblait jeter aux vents de l'ombre une semence.
The image culminates in the magnificent evocation found in one of the *Chansons des rues et des bois* (ii, i, 3), where, as night falls (at Rochefort, in Belgium, 1865), the poet watches an old man casting 'la moisson future aux sillons':
   Et je médite, obscur témoin,
   Pendant que, déployant ses voiles,
   L'ombre, où se mêle une rumeur,
   Semble élargir jusqu'aux étoiles
   Le geste auguste du semeur.
The original impetus comes, in fact, from 'choses vues' while travelling. In *Le Rhin*, Reliquat, p. 490: 'Le semeur marche à grands pas et gesticule tragiquement dans la plaine solitaire, comme un poète qui fait son cinquième acte.' This might be compared with the earlier related image of the trappist-ploughman in 1837 (between Lier and Turnhout, in Belgium, *En voyage*, t. ii, p. 94): 'un trappiste qui défrichait, triste laboureur d'un triste sillon. C'était beau d'ailleurs par la pensée de voir cette robe blanche et ce scapulaire noir pousser deux bœufs (. . .). De temps en temps, il se retournait et le soleil couchant dessinait vivement par les ombres et par les clairs sa figure austère et sereine. Je ne sais si cet homme pensait, mais je sais qu'il faisait penser.' Similarly, in the *Chansons* poem, the poet was first struck by 'la haute silhouette noire'.

*Source*
Victor Hugo (1802–85): *Booz endormi*, ll. 61–88, in *La Légende des siècles*, ed. P. Berret, Paris, 1921, t. i, pp. 85–7.

*Peter H. Nurse*

# BAUDELAIRE
*Les Fleurs du mal: Les Aveugles*

*Les Aveugles*

Contemple-les, mon âme; ils sont vraiment affreux!
Pareils aux mannequins; vaguement ridicules;
Terribles, singuliers comme les somnambules;
Dardant on ne sait où leurs globes ténébreux.

5 Leurs yeux, d'où la divine étincelle est partie,
Comme s'ils regardaient au loin, restent levés
Au ciel; on ne les voit jamais vers les pavés
Pencher rêveusement leur tête appesantie.

Ils traversent ainsi le noir illimité,
10 Ce frère du silence éternel. O cité!
Pendant qu'autour de nous tu chantes, ris et beugles,

Éprise du plaisir jusqu'à l'atrocité,
Vois! je me traîne aussi! mais, plus qu'eux hébété,
Je dis: Que cherchent-ils au Ciel, tous ces aveugles?

INTRODUCTION. The sonnet: *Les Aveugles*, first appeared in a literary review, *L'Artiste*, in October 1860. When Baudelaire revised *Les Fleurs du mal* for a second edition in 1861, he included this sonnet, with only two small variants, in a newly-formed section which was called: *Tableaux Parisiens*.

At various times, the poet made it clear that the *Fleurs du mal* were not a haphazard collection of verse, but that the situation of each poem was carefully subordinated to an overall design. While, as critics have shown, there is room for argument about the precise nature of this design, it is evident that the book's different 'chapters' provide a record of Baudelaire's 'baromètre spirituel', and the title of the first chapter: 'Spleen et Idéal', already gives an indication of the dual rhythm which shapes the inner life of the poet, torn between moods of exaltation and despair. Born into an age profoundly marked by the restless sensibility of the Romantic movement, Baudelaire reflects more acutely than any of his contemporaries the disorientation of modern man in an industrial society increasingly dominated by materialistic values. At the heart of his inspiration is the experience of the soul, ever aspiring to transcend the bondage of the flesh and all the limitations of the finite world, yet always encountering defeat and disillusionment. In spite of the sublime moments of ecstasy, when art or love seems to offer an escape from behind the bars of Time and Space which make a prison of man's earthly existence, the ultimate result is an experience of inexorable *déchéance*: the Ideal retreats out of reach and Spleen reasserts its hold over the spirit.

The poems in the 'Tableaux Parisiens' represent a fresh stage of this eternal quest for escape from the confines of the self. Among the attributes of Spleen, according to Baudelaire, is the 'sensation d'isolement insupportable',[1] and one of the attractions of the Capital, with its seething life and infinite variety of spectacles, was that it offered 'le plaisir, sans cesse renaissant, de sortir de [soi]-même, pour [s'] oublier dans autrui'.[2] Two other passages in *Le Spleen de Paris* amplify this remark. Having proclaimed in *Enivrez-Vous* that:

Il faut toujours être ivre . . . Pour ne pas sentir l'horrible fardeau du Temps qui brise vos épaules et vous penche vers la terre, il faut vous enivrer sans trêve,[3]

he explains, in *Les Foules*, that the poet's gift for entering imaginatively into the life of those he sees around him in the crowded city is but another form of *ivresse*:

Le poète jouit de cet incomparable privilège, qu'il peut à sa guise être lui-même et autrui . . . Le promeneur solitaire et pensif tire une singulière ivresse de cette universelle communion.[4] It is significant, however, that eight of the poems which, in 1861, made up the 'Tableaux Parisiens', had already figured in the 'Spleen' section of the 1857 edition of the *Fleurs du mal*, a fact which is sufficient warning to us to be ready for the resurgence of the mood of defeat that once again appears in *Les Aveugles*. For Baudelaire, the life of the City will prove to be a mirror of his own soul: he will meet there the same anguished search after the Infinite, the same inescapable solitude.

It is in this sense that the 'tableaux' of Parisian life transcend the domain of purely descriptive poetry and reveal their essentially symbolic function. Mallarmé, with his maxim: 'Peindre non la chose, mais l'effet qu'elle produit', will complete the movement away from descriptive realism, but already in Baudelaire there is the characteristic emphasis of symbolist aesthetics on art as an instrument of self-analysis, and in *Les Aveugles*, no less than in the other 'tableaux parisiens', the poet illustrates the principle which was stated in his prose poem, *Les Fenêtres*:

Qu'importe ce que peut être la réalité placée hors de moi, si elle m'a aidé à vivre, à sentir que je suis et ce que je suis.[5]

SOURCES. The images of light and darkness, as metaphysical symbols of Good and Evil or Spirit and Matter, are as old as literature itself, and there was no novelty in Baudelaire's frequent use of them. Phrases such as 'les lourdes ténèbres de l'existence commune et journalière' abound in his work, and, in *Le Voyage*, for example, he compares human life to a 'mer de Ténèbres' on which we embark at birth. Almost equally common as a literary symbol is the theme of blindness, especially with the ironic twist, exploited by Sophocles in *Oedipus Rex*, according to which it is often the physically blind, like Teiresias, who are the seers, whereas there are those like Oedipus himself who 'have eyes but do not see their own damnation'.

While, therefore, the inspiration for *Les Aveugles* may well have come from Baudelaire's having met a group of blind men during his frequent wanderings through Paris, some of the symbolic implications of the spectacle lay ready to hand in the literary tradition and could well have been revived in the poet's imagination by contem-

PETER H. NURSE

porary sources. The three poems which precede *Les Aveugles* in the
1861 edition of *Les Fleurs du mal* are all dedicated to Victor Hugo,
whose *Contemplations*, published in 1856, contained the poem: *A Un
Poète Aveugle*, with its concluding lines:
 Le poète des sens perce la triste brume;
 Quand l'œil du corps s'éteint, l'œil de l'esprit s'allume.[6]
But the works most commonly quoted by critics as probable sources
of Baudelaire's sonnet are a book by Champfleury and a painting of
the elder Brueghel. Champfleury's *Hoffman, Contes fantastiques* (1856)
refers to 'cette seule manière de tourner la tête en haut, qui est propre
à tous les aveugles' and to the blind man's 'œil intérieur [qui] tâche
d'apercevoir l'éternelle lumière qui luit pour lui dans l'autre monde'.
At the same time, both Baudelaire and Champfleury could have found
mutual inspiration in Brueghel's famous painting: 'The Parable of
the Blind', where the grotesque elements of Baudelaire's vision are so
strongly foreshadowed. In his article of 1857 on 'Quelques Caricatur-
istes Étrangers', the poet wrote of the 'puissance de l'hallucination'
and of the 'monstrueusement paradoxales' qualities of Brueghel's
allegories,[7] and there seems little doubt that *Les Aveugles* reproduces,
especially in the first quatrain, something of the caricatural genius
of the Flemish canvas. In this, against a mockingly idyllic pastoral
landscape, with a church spire pointing to heaven, six men grope their
way forward, their sightless eyes looking upwards, unaware of the
stream into which they are about to fall. But while what Baudelaire
calls the 'capharnaüm diabolique et drolatique de Brueghel le Drôle'
certainly evokes the paradoxical fusion of the *terrible* and the *ridicule*
in the poem, the following detailed analysis will show that Baudelaire's version achieves a genuine originality of vision through the
admixture of a hint of Sophoclean irony.

ANALYSIS. The structure of the traditional French sonnet, as derived
from the Petrarchan model, with its division into two quatrains
followed by two tercets, lent itself particularly to the development of
a simple form of lyrical symbolism, where the poet first creates an
image of some natural spectacle and then, in the concluding tercets,
illustrates the symbolic significance of the image. A typical instance
of this process is Ronsard's celebrated sonnet: 'Comme on voit sur
la branche, au mois de mai, la rose', in *Les Amours de Marie*: here,
after evoking the glory of the May rose in its first bloom and then its

premature death, brought about by the beating rain or the excessive summer heat, Ronsard introduces in the ninth line the comparison with his own beloved ('*Ainsi*, en ta première et jeune nouveauté'), who also died, a victim of the Fates, at the very moment when her youthful beauty was in its finest flower.

In *Les Aveugles*, as we shall see in the ensuing analysis, Baudelaire also adopts something of the traditional structure, since he uses the tercets to develop more explicitly the symbolic meaning of his tableau and to suggest an analogy between his own predicament and that of the blind. At the same time, this structure is less schematic than in the Ronsard sonnet because of a dialectical movement in the poem whereby the original relationships and values are reversed: if the poet 'se traîne aussi', he is nevertheless ultimately conscious of being '*plus* hébété' than the blind.

(a) lines 1–4. The poem opens in a manner characteristic of the author of *Les Fenêtres*, for whom reality exists above all as a sounding-board for his own soul, enabling him to 'sentir que je suis et ce que je suis'. For here, where once more, as in *Les Sept vieillards*, we see the poet 'discutant avec [son] âme', this new spectacle of Parisian life provokes a highly personal reaction. In the manuscript version of the poem, Baudelaire had first written: '*Observe*-les . . .', but the substitution of the verb *contempler* not only gives the line a richer sound-pattern (increasing the assonance by adding two more nasal vowels to the three others in the same line), but also perhaps reflects the influence of *Les Contemplations* – which Hugo had called 'les Mémoires d'une âme' – with their philosophical meditation upon the mysteries of life. Confronted by these grotesque figures who move with the jerky stiffness of wooden models, the poet recoils in horror, and to convey the intensity of his reaction he uses a series of essentially affective adjectives: *affreux, ridicules, terribles, singuliers*, reinforced by the emphatic adverb: *vraiment*. The effect is heightened by the broken rhythms of the opening lines, which constitute a succession of exclamations, each of these being clearly divided off by marked pauses both at the cæsura and at the rhyme, while considerable use is made of alliteration to strengthen the exclamatory emphasis: the vibrant consonant *r* recurs six times in an accented position (*vraiment, affreux, pareils, ridicules, terribles, ténébreux*), and a similar alliteration of '*k*' is found in line 2, with *mannequins* at the sixth syllable balancing *ridicules* at the rhyme. There is likewise a repetition of the sibilant 's' in *singuliers* and *somnambules* in line 3, where Baudelaire adds another facet to his tableau: the comparison with sleep-walkers suggests the appropriate abstracted look of the blind and captures the uncanny atmosphere of a Brueghelian hallucination. Finally, in line 4, we have the first allusion to the blindness from which these creatures suffer; the manuscript shows that Baudelaire first wrote: '*Fixant* on ne sait où . . .', but the verb *darder* creates a highly effective oxymoron: with *darder* we associate such complements as *rayons*, whereas we are given the unexpected shock of *globes ténébreux*, the complete phrase evoking convulsive but frustrated effort.

(b) lines 5–8. The second quatrain shows Baudelaire departing from the normal rhyme-scheme of the traditional French sonnet form and following the Elizabethan precedent by introducing new rhymes; and this corresponds to a change in poetic tone. Whereas his first reaction was strong repugnance, he now ceases to judge and yields to the fascination of his subject, reminding us of the opening lines of the preceding poem, *Les Petites Vieilles*:

> Dans les plis sinueux des vieilles capitales
> Où tout, même l'horreur, tourne aux enchantements . . . [8]

What strikes the poet is that, in spite of their blindness, these figures keep their eyes raised to heaven – towards the source of all light. Here is the first indication of the symbolic content of the poem, for, although the word *ciel* is still written here without a capital letter, the adjective *divine* points to the religious element in the light-imagery. As though to stress the importance of this idea, Baudelaire introduces in line 5 a change of metre, using a trimeter instead of the tetrameters of the preceding lines: 'Leurs yeux, / d'où la divine étincel / le est partie'. [9]

The metric structure of lines 6–7 is more problematical, and another critic has referred with good reason to the presence here of 'une sorte de coïncidence du rythme binaire et du rythme ternaire'. [10] One is at first tempted to see a further use of the trimeter in line 7, but on closer examination it seems likely that, as in line 6, the accent is intended to fall on the sixth syllable, thus creating *rejets* at the cæsura, a technique which enables the poet to detach and throw into relief certain important words. Just as there is a running-on of line 6 into line 7 (leaving 'Au ciel' as a *rejet*), so too there is an *enjambement* at the cæsura of line 6, isolating and stressing 'au loin'. The same remark applies to 'jamais' in line 7, which runs on over the slight pause after the accented sixth syllable. The main result of this is to give the lines a highly dislocated rhythm, conveying appropriately the jerky, groping movements of the blind. Baudelaire perfectly fulfils Pope's dictum that 'the sound must seem an echo to the sense', for, just as it is in the nature of these blind men never to enjoy a moment's respite, so the successive *enjambements* prevent the alexandrines from giving that impression of harmonious completion that is only possible where rhythmic and logical groupings fully coincide. The effect is made more striking by the contrast with the final line of the quatrain which also echoes the sense: the physical and spiritual repose which is denied the blind is evoked in the unbroken flow of line 8, where the impression of heavy somnolence is increased by the presence of two four-syllabled words (including the proleptic adjective: *appesanties*) and the regular beat of $2+4$; $2+4$.

(c) lines 9–14. It was suggested above that, with the tercets, Baudelaire proceeds to develop more explicitly the symbolism of his subject, as is often the case in the traditional sonnet-form – an affirmation which depends largely upon the interpretation of the metaphor of the 'silence éternel' in line 10. Most previous commentators have seen here an allusion to death, but I think it more probable that the poet began by thinking of the related physical handicap of deafness, and was then carried by his literary imagination to a reminiscence of Pascal's famous *pensée*: 'Le silence éternel de ces espaces infinis m'effraie'.[11] In other words, Baudelaire associates the endless darkness that envelops the blind with the Pascalian view of the universe as a limitless *gouffre*, in which a *deus absconditus* vouchsafes no tangible sign of His presence. Indeed, in another poem of *Les Fleurs du mal*, with the title: *Le Gouffre*, Baudelaire specifically recalls Pascal's theme of 'l'aveuglement et la misère de l'homme . . . l'homme sans lumière, abandonné à lui -même,et comme égaré dans ce recoin de l'univers, sans savoir qui l'y a mis, ce qu'il y est venu faire, ce qu'il deviendra en mourant, incapable de toute connaissance', and the seventeenth-century text provides an invaluable commentary on the full implications of *spleen*.[12]

In line 10, with the apostrophe: 'O cité!', which is a *contre-rejet* interrupting the rhythm of the verse, the poet dramatically emerges from his 'contemplation'. What now provokes him is no longer the spectacle of the blind, but that of the turbulent city, whose clamorous pleasure-seeking shatters the silence and incites his indignation. The passage illustrates well a remark of Jean Prévost, who wrote of Baudelaire that: 'Comme Pascal encore, et comme tous ceux qui passionnent leur pensée, qui passionnent leurs regards, Baudelaire sent, voit et comprend par antithèses. Le tableau le plus important des thèmes baudelairiens sera un tableau de contrastes'.[13] It is these antitheses that give the poem its dialectical movement, for there is a clear contrast intended between those who, though physically blind, seek the light, and the complete spiritual *aveuglement* of the city (whose *divertissements* progress from the relatively innocuous verb: *chanter* to the crude animality of *beugler*).

In the 1860 version, line 12 read: 'Cherchant la jouissance avec férocité.' The superiority of the 1861 variant lies in the added symbolical significance of the noun: *atrocité*, by reason of its etymological origins: < *atrox* < *ater*, *atra* (black), recalling another aspect of *le noir illimité*.

Already in line 11, with the phrase: 'autour de *nous*', Baudelaire has indicated a new sense of kinship with the blind, but in line 13 it becomes clear that his original attitude of disdain has been completely reversed, for now he not merely shares with them their disability ('je me traîne aussi'); rather, he now sees (and, with the imperative: *Vois*! – effectively replacing the 1860 version: *Moi* – calls on the city to share his new insight) that his own predicament is worse, for he is 'plus qu'eux hébété'. In spite of their physical affliction, the blind would seem to have some sixth sense – denied to the poet – which might provide the key to the riddle of existence, a supernatural key, since it is to be found 'au Ciel' (this time significantly written with a capital letter).[14]

Line 14 poses the same metrical problem as was encountered in line 7. It could be read as a trimeter, the change of meter being designed to focus attention on the cry of anguish with which the poem ends:

Je dis:/Que cherchent-ils au Ciel,/tous ces aveugles?

On the other hand, by analogy with the *rejet* in line 7 (*Au ciel*), it is perhaps preferable to interpret the line as a binary structure, with an *enjambement* at the cæsura, in order to throw into relief the key-words: *au Ciel*.

Je dis:/Que cherchent-ils/au Ciel, tous ces aveugles?

CONCLUSION. There is an entry in Baudelaire's *Journaux intimes* which reads: 'Deux qualités littéraires fondamentales: surnaturalisme et ironie'.[15] In one sense, the two terms overlap, since 'surnatural-isme' signified for him the fact that the phenomena of the natural world have hidden meanings that go beyond their surface appearances – which is one of the conditions of irony. 'Surnaturalisme' is thus the essence of poetic symbolism, and *Les Aveugles* is a classic example of the process whereby 'dans certains états de l'âme presque surnaturels, la profondeur de la vie se révèle dans le spectacle, si ordinaire soit-il, qu'on a sous les yeux. Il en devient le symbole'.[16]

In some respects, it might be claimed that this sonnet lacks the poetic suggestiveness which synæsthesia gave to the best of Baudelaire's symbolism, and that the opening evocation of the *aveugles* relies too much on rather empty rhetorical adjectives (*affreux, terribles, singuliers*) and laboured similes (*pareils aux, comme, comme si*) – the kind of faults that led one critic to say that 'il y a dans Baudelaire un excès de matière sur le langage'.[17] On the other hand, this seems to me to be more than compensated for by the dramatic qualities of the poem, and that is where the deeper sense of Baudelaire's call for 'ironie' is illustrated. It is the kind of irony hinted at in the concluding stanza of the verses addressed to the reader of the *Fleurs du mal* – the 'hypocrite lecteur', whose complacency will be punctured as he comes to see how illusory is his own detachment and moral superiority.[18] For, in *Les Aveugles*, the poet dramatically re-enacts a similar ironic reversal of rôles, whereby the attitude that was at first provoked in him by the blind – a complacent attitude of disgust and horror – is finally turned against himself. Hence the justification for the use of the word 'dialectical' to describe the movement of this poem in which the initial oppositions are superseded and replaced by a higher truth. And it is only after this fresh truth has fully emerged that we become really aware of the element of ambiguity in the poet's first reaction to the blind. If they were '*vaguement* ridicules', was it not that he already sensed within them something potentially sublime? Indeed, if our analysis of the sonnet is correct, it is, like Baudelaire's *Le Cygne* (with which it is grouped), yet another 'poème des exilés', in which the blind move convulsively through an alien world, recalling the grotesqueness of the swan when marooned on land:

> . . . avec ses gestes fous,
> Comme les exilés, ridicule et sublime,
> Et rongé d'un désir sans trêve . . .[19]

NOTES

1 Cf. Baudelaire's letter to his mother, dated 30 December, 1857: 'Ce que je sens, c'est un immense découragement, une sensation d'isolement insupportable . . . C'est là le véritable état de spleen.'
2 *Œuvres complètes*, ed. Y. – G. Le Dantec and Cl. Pichois (Bibliothèque de la Pléiade), 1961; *Le Spleen de Paris*, p. 260.
3 Op. cit., p. 286.
4 Op. cit., p. 244.
5 Op. cit., p. 288.
6 *Les Contemplations*, ed. Garnier, 1957, p. 40.
7 *Œuvres complètes*, p. 1023.
8 Op. cit., p. 85.
9 Cf. M. Grammont: *Petit Traité de versification française*, Paris, 1947, p. 54: 'Tout changement de mètre, produisant un contraste, frappe et éveille l'attention, qui se porte aussitôt sur ce mètre nouveau, c'est-à-dire sur les idées qu'il exprime'.
10 Cf. P. Nardin: *Le Commentaire stylistique aux rendez-vous littéraires*, Dakar, 1958, p. 146.
11 *Pensées*, ed. Louis Lafuma (Editions du Seuil), 1962, p. 122 (fragment 201).
12 *Pensées*, p. 114 (fragment 198). The relevant passage of *Le Gouffre* is:
   Pascal avait son gouffre, avec lui se mouvant.
   – Hélas! tout est abîme – action, désir, rêve,
   Parole! [. . .]
   En haut, en bas, partout, la profondeur, la grève,
   Le silence, l'espace affreux et captivant . . .
13 J. Prévost: *Baudelaire*, Paris, 1964, pp. 85–6.
14 In the critical edition of *Les Fleurs du mal* by J. Crépet and G. Blin (Paris, 1942, p. 459) we are reminded how closely the sonnet reflects the poet's feelings, as expressed in a letter to his mother, dated 6 May, 1861: "Et Dieu!" diras-tu. Je désire de tout mon cœur (avec quelle sincérité, personne ne peut le savoir que moi!) croire qu'un être extérieur et invisible s'intéresse à ma destinée, mais comment faire pour le croire?
15 *Œuvres complètes*, p. 1256.
16 Op. cit., p. 1257.
17 B. Fondane: *Baudelaire et l'expérience du gouffre*, Paris, 1947, p. 352.
18 Traces of the influence of Hugo's *Contemplations* upon *Les Fleurs du mal* have already been indicated. Here is further possible evidence of such influence. In the Preface to the *Contemplations*, Hugo too had addressed his reader in the same way as Baudelaire: 'Hélas! quand je vous parle de moi, je vous parle de vous . . . Ah! insensé, qui crois que je ne suis pas toi!'
19 Op. cit., p. 82. This is a revised and expanded version of a commentary which first appeared in *L'Information littéraire*, January, 1967.

*Source*
Charles Baudelaire (1821–67): *Les Fleurs du mal*, in *Œuvres complètes*, Bibliothèque de la Pléiade, ed. Y. G. Le Dantec and C. Pichois, Paris, 1961, p. 88.

*A. W. Raitt*

# FLAUBERT
Extract from *Un Cœur simple*

« Fellacher garda longtemps le perroquet. Il le promettait toujours pour la semaine prochaine; au bout de six mois, il annonça le départ d'une caisse; et il n'en fut plus question. C'était à croire que jamais Loulou ne reviendrait. 'Ils me l'auront volé!' pensait-elle.

5 Enfin il arriva, – et splendide, droit sur une branche d'arbre, qui se vissait dans un socle d'acajou, une patte en l'air, la tête oblique, et mordant une noix, que l'empailleur par amour du grandiose avait dorée.

Elle l'enferma dans sa chambre.

10 Cet endroit, où elle admettait peu de monde, avait l'air tout à la fois d'une chapelle et d'un bazar, tant il contenait d'objets religieux et de choses hétéroclites.

Une grande armoire gênait pour ouvrir la porte. En face de la fenêtre surplombant le jardin, un œil-de-bœuf regardait la cour; une

15 table, près du lit de sangle, supportait un pot à l'eau, deux peignes, et un cube de savon bleu dans une assiette ébréchée. On voyait contre les murs: des chapelets, des médailles, plusieurs bonnes Vierges, un bénitier en noix de coco; sur la commode, couverte d'un drap comme un autel, la boîte en coquillages que lui avait donnée Victor; puis un

20 arrosoir et un ballon, des cahiers d'écriture, la géographie en estampes, une paire de bottines, et au clou du miroir, accroché par ses rubans, le petit chapeau de peluche! Félicité poussait même ce genre de respect si loin, qu'elle conservait une des redingotes de Monsieur. Toutes les vieilleries dont ne voulait plus Mme Aubain, elle les pre-

25 nait pour sa chambre. C'est ainsi qu'il y avait des fleurs artificielles au bord de la commode, et le portrait du comte d'Artois dans l'enfoncement de la lucarne.

Au moyen d'une planchette, Loulou fut établi sur un corps de cheminée qui avançait dans l'appartement. Chaque matin, elle

30 l'apercevait à la clarté de l'aube, et se rappelait alors les jours disparus, et d'insignifiantes actions jusqu'en leurs moindres details, sans douleur, pleine de tranquillité. »

Un Cœur simple, one of Gustave Flaubert's *Trois Contes*, first published in 1877, tells the story of Félicité, maidservant for almost fifty years to Mme Aubain, a widow living in straitened circumstances in the little Norman country town of Pont-l'Evêque with her two children Paul and Virginie. Félicité, humble, pious, selfless and devoted, attaches herself successively to a faithless suitor; to her employer's children until Virginie dies and Paul leaves home; to her nephew Victor, a cabin-boy who succumbs to yellow fever in the tropics; to Polish refugees, to cholera victims, to marching soldiers; to a repulsive old man mortally ill with cancer; and finally, when all human companionship has disappeared from her life, to a parrot called Loulou. When Loulou too dies, Félicité has him stuffed, and, setting him in a place of honour in her room, gradually comes to regard him with almost sacrilegious veneration, until, dying herself after years of privation and solitude, she has a vision of a celestial parrot receiving her into paradise. The passage quoted here occurs when the parrot, which Félicité has sent to Fellacher, a taxidermist in Le Havre, is returned to her and installed in her bedroom.

At first sight, it may look as though Flaubert is indulging in that taste for elaborate description of physical settings which is a marked feature of French fiction from Balzac's time onwards. The drabness of the scene, the meticulous listing of objects, the careful attention to visual clarity, the powerful sense of the presence of material reality – all this is paralleled innumerable times in the works of Champfleury, of the Goncourts, of Daudet or of Zola. Indeed, Flaubert too believed that a character could not be properly understood without reference to the milieu in which he lived. Mme Aubain's house, modelled on a real house in Pont-l'Evêque, has already been depicted in some detail, and if the description of the room itself is held back until a late stage in the story, that can be explained on the grounds that it only assumes its full significance for Félicité and the reader when the parrot comes to rest there.

Yet this passage has an unmistakably Flaubertian quality which sets it apart from similar passages in the novels of his contemporaries and makes one wonder whether he really is pursuing the same aim as they were. If one compares it with a paragraph of the Goncourt brothers' *Germinie Lacerteux*, the differences are striking. The situation is almost identical: the Goncourts are describing the room in which a maidservant, now approaching death, has lived for years in her mistress's house.

> Mademoiselle s'assit et resta quelques instants regardant cette misérable chambre de domestique, une de ces chambres où le médecin est obligé de poser son chapeau sur le lit, et où il y a à peine la place pour mourir! C'était une mansarde de quelques pieds carrés sans cheminée, où la tabatière à crémaillère laissait passer l'haleine des saisons, le chaud de l'été, le froid de l'hiver. Les débarras, de vieilles malles, des sacs de nuit, un panier de bain, le petit lit de fer où Germinie avait couché sa nièce, étaient entassés sous le pan coupé du mur. Le lit, une chaise et une petite toilette boiteuse avec une cuvette cassée, faisaient tout le mobilier. Au-dessus du lit était pendu, dans un cadre peint à la façon du palissandre, un daguerréotype d'homme.

In the first place, the Goncourts are much more obviously present in this description than Flaubert is in his. The first sentence is an authorial comparison of Germinie's room with other such rooms, and the sentimental exclamation with which it ends marks the pity which they themselves feel for their character and to which they wish to draw the reader's attention. Flaubert on the other hand has scrupulously avoided any perceptible editorial intervention; he has attained his effects by a seemingly impersonal cataloguing of observable facts. Secondly, Germinie's room is almost entirely anonymous. Except for the bed in which her niece had once slept, all the objects mentioned are devoid of any particular association with Germinie herself – even the subject of the daguerreotype is unidentified. That the Goncourts have simply imagined a room typical of those inhabited by servants is made manifest by the phrase 'une de ces chambres où . . .'. How different from Félicité's minutely individualized room, which only she could live in and which is filled with things which form part of the fabric of her life, and her life alone! Finally, although the Goncourts' celebrated *écriture artiste* is relatively restrained here, one is conscious of a contrived rhetorical effect in the phrase 'où il y a à peine la place pour mourir', and of an evident desire to strike a poetic note in the cadence 'l'haleine des saisons, le chaud de l'été, le froid de l'hiver'. In the Flaubert passage, the style is never allowed to draw attention to itself in this way; his is very much the art which conceals art.

The Goncourts then would seem to be using their description as a stage décor, into which are interpolated some sentimental comments on their character. Flaubert's motives and techniques are, despite superficial similarities, quite different. The description for him has a psychological rather than a decorative purpose. Félicité has reached a stage in her existence when, deprived of any normal outlet for her affections, she is forced to turn more and more to inanimate objects. After her human loves had come an animal love; now the animal too is dead, reduced to the status of an object among other objects, and it is these objects which henceforth will constitute the centre of her emotions. It is noteworthy that the only two people here said to be in contact with Félicité both treat her with cold indifference – Fellacher cannot be bothered to send the parrot back to her; Mme Aubain, far from giving presents to Félicité, simply discards things and takes no notice when her maid picks them up. Félicité's poor belongings are now invested with special significance; however mean or ridiculous they may appear, they form the focus for that need to love which is the outstanding feature of her character. Thus when Flaubert seems merely to be recording the contents of her room, he is in reality telling us about her inner life, but avoiding those abstract psychological terms which imply the intrusion of a commentator charged with categorizing and interpreting feelings for the reader's benefit.

Seen in that light, the description reveals an extraordinary richness of texture and cunning of exposition. The possessions which Flaubert lists in apparent confusion fall into three categories, each of which has its own function in making us share in Félicité's life. The first category comprises the standard furnishings of a maid's room in a somewhat dilapidated house – the oversized wardrobe, relegated from some larger bedroom, the table, the chest of drawers, the trestle bed, the mirror, the ewer, the chipped plate holding cheap soap, the combs. These few bare necessities evoke the poverty-stricken simplicity, the spartan plainness of Félicité's outward existence. The second category, that of the objects of piety which Félicité has accumulated, puts us in closer touch with her inner nature. Her collection of rosaries, religious medallions and images of the Virgin Mary, together with a holy-water stoup incongruously made out of a coconut, shows her to be extremely devout, with that naïveté bordering on superstition which has led her to multiply around her the material manifestations of religious belief. Last of all, but closely connected with the bric-à-brac of popular devotion, come the relics of her own past, treated by her with the same respect and veneration as the religious objects.

This third category is the largest and most complex. Many of the things Flaubert mentions we have not heard of before, but we presume that the watering-can, the ball, the exercise-books, the bootees have all belonged to one or other of the children whom Félicité has loved and lost. That an element of fetishism is involved in this hoarding of memory-laden objects is made apparent by the fact that she does not know how to read the exercise-books she so carefully preserves, and by the inclusion among her treasures of things which have no real meaning for her at all – a frock-coat which had belonged to M. Aubain, dead years before she entered his widow's service, a bunch of artificial flowers, the portrait of the Comte d'Artois which had evidently been handed on by Mme Aubain when his accession to the throne as Charles X and subsequent deposition in 1830 had made it hopelessly irrelevant. But among these heterogeneous souvenirs are some which we have met before and which recall the most intense emotional experiences of Félicité's life. The box made of seashells had been a present from her nephew Victor after one of his first sea-voyages; the geography picture-book had been Paul's, and his explanations of its illustrations had given Félicité her only literary education, forming the basis of what she imagined of Victor's travels in foreign parts; and the little felt hat once worn by Virginie had provoked the only moment of genuine communion with Mme Aubain which Félicité had ever had, when, sorting out the girl's clothes together after her tragically early death, they had both broken down in tears. The catalogue is thus a mixture of objects mildly comic because of their meaninglessness or their unexpected oddity, and of relics which, though tawdry in themselves, have the most moving emotional associations, and it is the mingling of the insignificant with the significant which wards off any danger that the reader might feel that his sympathies were being too systematically enlisted. Moreover, the fact that we, like Félicité, remember the part which some of these objects have played in her life, dispenses Flaubert from the necessity for any explicit commentary: a mere allusion is sufficient to re-awaken past emotion.

The order in which these three categories of objects are presented is very deliberately chosen for reasons which only later become clear. Flaubert begins, logically enough, with the wardrobe which obstructs the doorway and then catalogues the other main furnishings in a dispassionate tone. Next, with the brevity of what seems like casual indifference, he enumerates the objects of piety which one might find in the room of a devout but simple-minded old woman. Then there is a transitional comparison between the cloth on her chest of drawers and an altar-cloth, designed to make it clear that for her there is no real separation between orthodox aids to prayer and the relics of her own private cult of memory. The list of these relics concludes the paragraph. Into this atmosphere in which the sacred and the profane have been indissolubly mixed she introduces Loulou, the stuffed parrot which is all she has left to love, and this in its turn prepares for the consoling confusion of the final vision, in which the parrot, transfigured, appears to her as the Holy Ghost welcoming her into heaven. In that respect, the passage combines with a number of others to motivate the beatitude of her last moments: her literal understanding of the biblical imagery of the dove, the bright colours of the stained-glass windows in church, the childish picture on the *image d'Épinal* which reminds her of Loulou, the prominent position which he occupies among the religious paraphernalia of her room, the celestial ray of light which shines from his eye when the sun is reflected in it, the priest's permission for him to be placed among the decorations of one of the altars set up for the Corpus Christi procession. Here as so often in his works, Flaubert is unobtrusively advancing a psychological process which, because it is never defined in generalizing terms, exists only as a unique, irreplaceable and individual experience.

Something of the same intention is apparent in the effect of point of view which Flaubert attains in this passage. His primary aim in writing *Un Cœur simple* was, as he himself declared with a half-mocking exaggeration which should not blind us to his essential sincerity, to 'apitoyer, faire pleurer les âmes sensibles, en étant une moi-même'. But in choosing as the recipient of his pity an illiterate, unintelligent and inarticulate serving-woman, he was faced with the problem of making the reader live her life as she lived it, that is, without formulating any abstract opinions or even consciously meditating on her position. This he has done by discreetly adapting his own vision to that of Félicité. Not that he has used the stream-of-consciousness technique evolved by later writers, which would in any case have been excluded by the rudimentary nature of Félicité's vocabulary and intellectual equipment. What he does is to look at the world through Félicité's eyes but, with the utmost unobtrusiveness, interpret her vision with his own stylistic resources. Thus, if *Un Cœur simple* contains many descriptive passages like this one, consisting of apparently artless notations of an eminently concrete reality, it is because Félicité herself experiences the world above all through a series of physical contacts. Deprived of any faculty for abstraction, unable even to give her feelings coherent verbal expression, she has an inner life consisting essentially of pictures, and this is the quality Flaubert brings out in his descriptions. Descriptive writing has thus for him gone beyond its usual rôle of background to feelings or events, and has become the very fabric of life itself.

In the passage we are considering, the fact that we are being delicately placed in Félicité's position is indicated by one or two barely noticeable phrases of *style indirect libre*. This is Flaubert's favourite device for allowing us to follow a character's thoughts without interrupting the narrative flow, and at the same time establishing a deliberate ambiguity between what is said in the author's name and what is said in the character's name. When he writes: 'C'était à croire que jamais Loulou ne reviendrait', this is Félicité's anxious reaction to his prolonged absence. When the stuffed parrot on his branch is said to be 'splendide', this is Félicité's uncritical admiration. When the reference to 'le petit chapeau de peluche' is followed by an exclamation mark, this represents the pang of grief that shoots through Félicité whenever she catches sight of it. The plain, unadorned presentation of the contents of the room corresponds to the unquestioning, matter-of-fact way in which Félicité registers their presence – indeed, there is no outside observer comparable to 'Mademoiselle' in the Goncourt passage who might be supposed to be reporting the scene. By thus quietly manœuvring the reader into Félicité's position, Flaubert has made us feel with her from the inside, rather than pity her from the outside, and it comes as a natural climax to the story when we are induced to participate in a vision of which Félicité alone could have had knowledge.

The style too is appropriate to the evocation of Félicité's inner life. The simplicity of her nature gives rise to a corresponding simplicity of sentence structure, particularly noticeable where Flaubert inserts a colon after 'on voyait contre les murs', in order to make the bare, direct effect of an inventory. Almost all the sentences have as their basic content an uncomplicated statement of fact; just under half of them have no subordinate clauses at all, and only two have more than one. The only sentence of any length (the one beginning 'on voyait . . .') is especially elementary in its construction, with a single verb at the start governing a long list of noun objects. Otherwise the sentences here, as throughout the story, are short – their average length only just exceeds that of the sentences in *La Vénus d'Ille*, and Mérimée is noted for the clipped concision of his phrases. In imagery too Flaubert has eschewed any form of elaboration. In *Un Cœur simple* he has kept a very tight rein on the vigorous similes which had once threatened to run wild in *Madame Bovary*, and in this passage there is only one, the description of the chest of drawers 'couverte d'un drap comme un autel'. That is amply justified, both by its function in linking the overtly religious objects with Félicité's personal relics, and by its origin in the familiar surroundings of Félicité's daily life, which makes it the sort of comparison not unlikely to occur to her. The restraint of the style and the unembellished plainness of the physical impressions it records means that we tend to forget the presence in the tale of an omniscient and intellectually superior author, and think only of the simple figure of Félicité herself.

At the same time, the identification with Félicité is not complete, nor is it meant to be. Despite the absence of any explicit comment, we are in no doubt that the gilded nut so inappropriately stuck in the parrot's beak is in grotesquely pretentious bad taste, as is the stoup made from a coconut. We feel that there is something touchingly incongruous about the combination of junk-shop and chapel into which Félicité has turned her room. We smile at the absurd deference for any remnant of the past which leads her to keep the frock-coat of a man she had never met and a royalist propaganda picture years out of date. We are even conscious that her adulation of her defunct pet has its ridiculous side as well as its pathetic implications. The consoling tendency of the story depends on an unspoken irony: Félicité dies happily because she has a beatific vision – but the reader may well notice the sadness implicit in the non-committal phrase: 'elle *crut* voir, dans les cieux entr'ouverts, un perroquet gigantesque planant au-dessus de sa tête'. In the list of her treasures, Flaubert is careful not to end on the emotional high-point of Virginie's little hat, but to descend to the near-bathos of the frock-coat, the artificial flowers and the portrait. All these ironic touches act as correctives to over-involvement with Félicité and create the dual perspective which is one of the secrets of Flaubert's art.

The movement of the style reflects this double intention of making us simultaneously be at one with Félicité and see her as others might see her (though the naturalness of the transitions and the smooth integration of the two tones obviates any sense of dichotomy). The sentence relating the return of the parrot begins with a mock-pompous statement of magnificently fulfilled anticipation – 'Enfin il arriva', which is parodically reminiscent of Boileau's emphatic 'Enfin Malherbe vint'. Then, as the picture of the stuffed bird develops, it becomes ever more grotesque until it degenerates into the final absurdity of the gilded nut, the key word 'dorée' being suspensefully withheld until the end of the sentence. The abrupt juxtaposition of 'chapelle' and 'bazar', 'objets religieux' and 'choses hétéroclites', exemplifies the strangely assorted nature of Félicité's hoard, and the unusual word 'hétéroclites' (certainly not part of Félicité's vocabulary) is used because its sharp consonants and angular sound suggest the confused jumble of objects piled up in the room. The paratactic sentences, with their heavy preponderance of nouns over verbs, help to create the impression of a series of objects placed side by side and all considered in the same light by their owner. The magpie-like nature of Félicité's collecting instinct is brought out by the derogatory turn of phrase (emphasized by the inversion of the clauses): 'Toutes les vieilleries dont ne voulait plus Mme Aubain'. The material nature of the symbols of piety to which she is superstitiously attached is indicated by the brisk, detached air with which Flaubert lists her religious possessions, including, in a phrase so offhand as to seem almost shocking, 'plusieurs bonnes Vierges'. These devices subtly reinforce the impression of ridicule which emanates from Félicité's habits, if one looks at them without reference to the fact that her intelligence and upbringing prevent her from finding any more adequate exteriorization of her inner life.

There is then in most of the passage an ambivalence of tone consequent upon our being at once within Félicité and outside her. But the last sentence is notably different in its tone and rhythm. Up to this point, the movement of the sentences has produced either a neutral, impersonal impression (as in the laconic notations of facts, or the longer catalogue phrases) or an anti-climactic effect (the gilded nut as the crowning glory of the taxidermist's art, or the decline from meaningful relics to nonsensical survivals). The most characteristic sentence rhythm in *Un Cœur simple* is that illustrated here by the second sentence: two or more juxtaposed clauses arousing expectations of a final balancing element, and succeeded instead by a brutally curt phrase expressive of disappointment and frustration, which is the recurrent rhythm of Félicité's emotional life. The last sentence however moves quite differently. The rhythm spreads out into a slow and serene movement of fulfilment, with a long, calm sequence of words culminating in two harmonious and evocative phrases. The sound of the words enhances the sense of peaceful satisfaction; there are altogether twelve *l* sounds in the sentence, with no heavy consonantal groups to break the even flow of the soft vowels. This enables us to share almost physically in the feeling of nostalgic tranquillity which Félicité experiences when the contemplation of Loulou evokes for her, in the glowing golden light of memory, the moments of happiness she has known in the past. That the passage should eventually attain this sense of benediction is in accordance with Flaubert's consolatory intention in the story, and looks forward to the sustained and restful phrase with which it all ends.

The art of this passage, for all its apparently unassuming character, is thus brilliantly subtle and original. While seeming to restrict himself to bald description and factual narration, Flaubert has achieved a moving and profoundly human vision which is much closer to deep emotion than the surface reveals.

*Source*
Gustave Flaubert (1821–80): *Un Cœur simple,* in *Trois Contes,* ed. Raymond Decesse, Paris, Petits Classiques Bordas, 1965, pp. 80–2.

C. A. Hackett

RIMBAUD
*Illuminations: Aube*

*Aube*

J'ai embrassé l'aube d'été.

Rien ne bougeait encore au front des palais. L'eau était morte. Les camps d'ombres ne quittaient pas la route du bois. J'ai marché, réveillant les haleines vives et tièdes, et les pierreries regardèrent, et les
5 ailes se levèrent sans bruit.

La première entreprise fut, dans le sentier déjà empli de frais et blêmes éclats, une fleur qui me dit son nom.

Je ris au wasserfall blond qui s'échevela à travers les sapins: à la cime argentée je reconnus la déesse.
10 Alors je levai un à un les voiles. Dans l'allée, en agitant les bras. Par la plaine, où je l'ai dénoncée au coq. A la grand'ville elle fuyait parmi les clochers et les dômes, et courant comme un mendiant sur les quais de marbre, je la chassais.

En haut de la route, près d'un bois de lauriers, je l'ai entourée avec
15 ses voiles amassés, et j'ai senti un peu son immense corps. L'aube et l'enfant tombèrent au bas du bois.

Au réveil il était midi.

THE PROSE poem *Aube* is one of forty-two undated texts which editors of the poet's work have grouped under the general title *Illuminations*, a title for which we have only Verlaine's word that it was, in fact, Rimbaud's title. Verlaine also stated that it is an English word meaning 'gravures coloriées – *coloured plates*'. All of the *Illuminations* are, however, richer and more complex than Verlaine's statement suggests. *Aube* in some respects may indeed resemble a 'coloured plate', or a picture – and a remarkably luminous picture; but it is also an 'illumination' in a deeper sense: one of the rare moments when the 'Voyant' *sees*, and experiences an intense, if ephemeral, ecstasy.

A number of references to the dawn occur throughout Rimbaud's work. In *Le Bateau ivre*, dawn is 'un peuple de colombes'; in *Bonne pensée du matin* (which like *Aube* ends on the word 'midi') the summer dawn inspires the poet's 'bonne pensée' for the workers; the 'aurores' give to the conclusion of *Comédie de la soif* the same kind of purity and freshness that characterize *Aube; Promontoire*, one of the *Illuminations*, begins with 'l'aube d'or', and in another, *Ornières*, the summer dawn is the awakener of nature; while dawn is invoked in *Adieu*, the last section of *Une saison en enfer*, to mark both a conclusion and a fresh beginning. In *Aube*, one of Rimbaud's most characteristic prose poems, the dawn, 'cette heure indicible, première du matin' (as he says in a letter of June 1872 to his friend Ernest Delahaye) is personified and presented with another character, the child-poet. It is at once a picture, a story (at times reminiscent of a fairy-story), and a miniature drama. Above all, it is – to quote the title of one of Rimbaud's lost manuscripts – a 'chasse spirituelle'.

The poem begins with the last, but most important of a series of momentous events, and then reveals (as it were in flashback) how this event came about. The opening sentence announces an extraordinary fact in the most natural and simple language. It could stand by itself as a 'poème-phrase', for in eight syllables, rhythmically assonanted by the four 'e' sounds, Rimbaud has condensed the joy and the triumph which are the essence of the poem. The sentence recalls another opening line, by the English metaphysical poet Henry Vaughan: 'I saw Eternity the other night / Like a great *Ring* of pure and endless light'; but the comparison only emphasizes the un-metaphysical and un-mystical nature of Rimbaud's poem. A more relevant comparison is with the opening lines of his own lyric

*L'Eternité*: 'Elle est retrouvée / Quoi? – L'Eternité / C'est la mer allée / Avec le soleil.' For Rimbaud, Eternity is something as natural as this union between the sea and the sun and, in much the same way, the child and the dawn 'go together', and finally fall together. The first section is composed of two almost equal parts; the first made up of three sentences, the second of a single sentence, and together they form a contrasted sequence in which inactivity is followed by movement. In the first half, Rimbaud evokes the silence and the mystery of a sleeping landscape with its palaces, stagnant water, and encamped shadows. The word 'palais' is unexpected, but this is an enchanted world in which everything is transformed by the light of dawn and by the poet's vision. 'Les camps d'ombres', an original image, suggests the dormant vitality of the sleeping shadows (in contrast with the 'dead' water) which are ready to strike camp at the first light of dawn, or rather, at the first movement of the poet. It is he, the animator and life-giver, who awakens (or imagines that he awakens) the landscape. This awakening, as hushed and as strange as the previous immobility, is conveyed in the second part of the section by a quickening tempo; by a change from imperfect tenses of description to past tenses of action; and by the thrice repeated 'et', the last two being used, as in the Biblical manner, to give authority to the statement. In this long sentence each word is at once definite and rich with suggestions. 'Haleines' may refer to something as precise as the breathing of animals, or the early mists and breezes; 'pierreries' may be stones seen as precious stones (just as houses are seen as palaces), or stones covered with gleaming dew, or the dew sparkling in the light; 'ailes' may be the birds, or the darkness, silently taking flight. But the total impression, produced in part by the use of plural nouns and adjectives, is that of the actual presence, the warmth, and the vibrant potentiality of awakening life.

In the next sentence, the first words 'La première entreprise . . .' strike a grave yet naively heroic note as they announce a momentous event. Wonder and expectation are further heightened by variations in the rhythm; and by penetration into the wood, from the 'route' to a 'sentier', where we see – and feel – the first cool gleams of light (there is a difference of temperature between the 'haleines' that are 'vives et tièdes' and the 'éclats de lumière' that are 'frais et blêmes'). In this setting, a flower declares its name. Coming after so many words in the plural, 'une fleur', unaccompanied by any qualifying adjective, stands out with sharp clarity. This example of animism is reminiscent of other examples in the work of Nerval, Hugo, and Baudelaire; but Rimbaud's flower that speaks is unique in its utter naturalness. This climax is so simple as to be almost an anti-climax; but the apparent spontaneity is the revelation of a power (as godlike as the power to create by naming) that compels nature to reveal her secrets. The realization of this power produces the ecstasy which, in the following section, is expressed by laughter. The poet's laughter at the waterfall, a force that corresponds to his own exultant energy, is not an expression of harmony with nature in the Romantic manner, but rather pagan delight, pride, and even defiance. The rest of this section describes two contrary movements: the water falling, and the poet looking up. The sudden reversal of direction from 'à travers les sapins' to 'à la cime argentée' emphasizes the swiftness of the poet's perception of the 'déesse', and turns the moment of recognition into a *movement* of recognition. This is the real climax and it comes at the centre of the poem.

In a series of sensitively varied, and increasingly vital rhythms, the poem has progressed to this central point, from a shadowy expanse to flashes of bright colour, from 'dead' water to living water and a source of life – the dawn goddess. The personification may seem conventional, by contrast with that of the 'wasserfall',[1] where the adjective 'blond' and the verb 's'échevela' convey in a visual and dynamic image the impression of sunlight on water, tumbling between rocks and boulders. But the personification of the dawn as a goddess, precisely because it relates *Aube* to innumerable other dawns in literature, throws into high relief Rimbaud's skill in transforming a conventional 'figure' into a presence and a force.

From a momentarily static point, the poem opens out; and from 'Alors' to 'je la chassais' all is excited movement, first staccato, then continuous. Pursuit and flight are conveyed by nouns – 'l'allée', 'la plaine', 'la grand'ville' – which widen the perspective from the countryside to the town; and more explicitly by a series of verbs, the changes in tense and form suggesting the vicissitudes and the breathless continuity of the chase. But first there are three short sentences in which the poet seeks to unveil the mystery. The child waving his arms recalls the child in *Après le déluge* ('l'enfant tourna ses bras, compris des girouettes et des coqs des clochers de partout'); but whereas, in that first 'illumination', he was understood by the weather-vanes and the steeple-cocks because his action resembled theirs, in *Aube* he usurps the cock's function. It is he who announces to that usually vigilant herald of the dawn the presence of the goddess. But 'dénoncée', as well as having the sense of 'announced' may also mean 'denounced' because, in the child-poet's view, the dawn's flight implies treachery and guilt. The duration of the flight is effectively suggested in the next sentence by its length; by the present participle 'courant' (prolonged by the assonance of 'mendiant'); by the use of an imperfect tense ('fuyait') at the beginning, and another ('chassais') at the end, the last of these having the effect of immeasurably extending the movement and of carrying it over into the next section. The inversion of the previous order so that the goddess – 'elle' – is now placed at the beginning of the sentence, and the 'je' at the end, does more than introduce a change into the structure; it stresses the poet's inferior role as pursuer and suppliant. Far above him the dawn continues to light up the highest points, the 'clochers' and the 'dômes'; while he, now described as a beggar, runs along the 'quais de marbre'. His state as a 'mendiant' is underlined by contrast with the richness suggested by the 'marbre', itself an ironic echo of the 'palais' at the beginning of the poem.

A slower rhythm marks the penultimate section, which describes the end and the result of this 'chasse spirituelle'. We have moved from the 'quais de marbre' to 'en haut de la route'; where the laurels, which recall the classical legend of Apollo's unsuccessful pursuit of Daphne, stand as an ambiguous symbol of victory. The dawn, enveloped again in her veils, does not reveal her secret; and the child, although he embraces the goddess, only touches a fraction of her immense body. Together they fall at the edge of the wood. At the dénouement, the 'je' is generalized as 'l'enfant'; and the poem is given a universal application. Then time breaks into the timeless world of childhood: 'Au réveil il était midi'. The last line is as taut as the first, and its eight syllables re-echo the eight syllables of the opening line. But the tense 'i' sounds introduce a different note, and with the pause coming after the third instead of the fourth syllable, this line, unlike the first, is neither symmetrical nor perfectly balanced. These slight formal differences may indicate a certain disenchantment, but if there is disenchantment (and Rimbaud himself does not comment or explain) there is no self-pity in the final statement. Moreover, the first line, and not the last, may be intended to express the essence of *Aube*: rapture at having seen the beauty, and touched, if only 'un peu' and for a moment, the body of the dawn. Together, the brief opening and concluding lines express, in a 'visual lyricism', the enigma of the poem. They are like the arms of the child ('Oh! bras trop courts!' as Rimbaud exclaims at the end of *Mémoire*) which, while embracing, are unable to hold the dawn.

This poem of impressions, sensations, movement, and of awakening and developing vitality, has several possible meanings (and there seems no reason to follow modern practice and put the last word in inverted commas). *Aube* expresses the desire for a special kind of union with nature, and in it Rimbaud achieves one of his frequently stated aims, to live 'étincelle d'or de la lumière *nature*'. It also expresses his search for the 'future vigueur', the new kind of inspiration he mentions in *Le Bateau ivre*; and for the new visions, which were the aim of the 'Voyant'. In a more general sense, *Aube* is an aspiration towards purity and the ideal, unhindered and uncomplicated by remorse, Romantic ennui or Baudelairian spleen. On the human plane, *Aube* is the journey from childhood to 'maturity'; from the brief period when the child is a poet, creator and bearer of life; when things are always seen and felt 'for the first time'; and visions are a present reality, but abruptly disappear when we reach the midday of life. *Aube*, with its two main characters, the child and the dawn goddess, also represents and plays out Rimbaud's (and the child's) conflict with the mother, a struggle in which the 'coq' (symbol of the awakening of desire as well as of life) is an accomplice. The child and the dawn may also represent conflicting parts of Rimbaud's own nature, and in this respect *Aube* is related to other *Illuminations*, such as *Conte* and *Royauté*, where a momentary synthesis, or union, is likewise achieved.

With delicacy and power, concretely, sensuously, and with a pure immediacy, Rimbaud has not only expressed in *Aube* the beauty, the immaculate freshness, and the very feel of the dawn; he has also expressed, in symbolic form, his search for the completeness and fulfilment that he constantly sought, but was never able to achieve, except imaginatively, in creative moments of illumination, one of which is *Aube*.

NOTE

1 The presence of this German word in *Aube* has been used as 'evidence' for dating the composition of the poem after Rimbaud's visit, in 1875, to Stuttgart. Internal evidence suggests, however, that *Aube* was composed between 1872 and 1874. Rimbaud did not need to go to Germany in order to become acquainted with the word 'wasserfall' – its strangeness and its sound make it more suitable in this context than 'chute d'eau' or 'cascade'.

*Source*

Arthur Rimbaud (1854–91): *Illuminations*, in *Œuvres*, Classiques Garnier, ed. Suzanne Bernard, Paris, 1963, p. 284.

S. I. Lockerbie

APOLLINAIRE
*Alcools: Le Voyageur*

APOLLINAIRE

*Le Voyageur*

Ouvrez-moi cette porte où je frappe en pleurant

La vie est variable aussi bien que l'Euripe

Tu regardais un banc de nuages descendre
Avec le paquebot orphelin vers les fièvres futures
5  Et de tous ces regrets de tous ces repentirs
     Te souviens-tu

Vagues poissons arqués fleurs surmarines
Une nuit c'était la mer
Et les fleuves s'y répandaient

10  Je m'en souviens je m'en souviens encore

Un soir je descendis dans une auberge triste
Auprès de Luxembourg
Dans le fond de la salle il s'envolait un Christ
Quelqu'un avait un furet
15  Un autre un hérisson
L'on jouait aux cartes
Et toi tu m'avais oublié

Te souviens-tu du long orphelinat des gares
Nous traversâmes des villes qui tout le jour tournaient
20  Et vomissaient la nuit le soleil des journées
O matelots ô femmes sombres et vous mes compagnons
     Souvenez-vous-en

Deux matelots qui ne s'étaient jamais quittés
Deux matelots qui ne s'étaient jamais parlé
25  Le plus jeune en mourant tomba sur le côté

     O vous chers compagnons
Sonneries électriques des gares chant des moissonneuses
Traîneau d'un boucher régiment des rues sans nombre
Cavalerie des ponts nuits livides de l'alcool
30  Les villes que j'ai vues vivaient comme des folles

Te souviens-tu des banlieues et du troupeau plaintif des paysages

Les cyprès projetaient sous la lune leurs ombres
J'écoutais cette nuit au déclin de l'été
Un oiseau langoureux et toujours irrité
35 Et le bruit éternel d'un fleuve large et sombre

Mais tandis que mourants roulaient vers l'estuaire
Tous les regards tous les regards de tous les yeux
Les bords étaient déserts herbus silencieux
Et la montagne à l'autre rive était très claire

40 Alors sans bruit sans qu'on pût voir rien de vivant
Contre le mont passèrent des ombres vivaces
De profil ou soudain tournant leurs vagues faces
Et tenant l'ombre de leurs lances en avant

Les ombres contre le mont perpendiculaire
45 Grandissaient ou parfois s'abaissaient brusquement
Et ces ombres barbues pleuraient humainement
En glissant pas à pas sur la montagne claire

Qui donc reconnais-tu sur ces vieilles photographies
Te souviens-tu du jour où une abeille tomba dans le feu
50 C'était tu t'en souviens à la fin de l'été

Deux matelots qui ne s'étaient jamais quittés
L'aîné portait au cou une chaîne de fer
Le plus jeune mettait ses cheveux blonds en tresse

Ouvrez-moi cette porte où je frappe en pleurant

55 La vie est variable aussi bien que l'Euripe

*Le Voyageur* belongs to Apollinaire's first major book of verse, *Alcools* (1913). It was published in review form in September 1912, and was probably – although we do not know for certain – written only shortly before this date. The years around 1912, as we shall see, were a period in which Apollinaire's writing became subject to strongly competing pressures, and the main reason why *Le Voyageur* makes a claim on the attentions of the critic is that it seems to be a product of this underlying complexity of inspiration. While, at a first reading, it makes an immediate impact as an unusually forceful expression of melancholy and frustration, most readers would admit to being intrigued partly because of elements in the poem that they cannot at first understand. There are passages of what appears to be a cunningly contrived obscurity (ll. 32–47) and images of enigmatic simplicity (ll. 23–5), which in style sit rather oddly together. There is the highly fragmented form of the work, conveying a general impression of modernity but not revealing immediately any source of unity. These and other features suggest that the poem is the outcome of a variety of shaping forces, which the reader can only appreciate by going to some extent outside the poem to trace them to their source.

There are many directions in which one can turn in thus seeking a guide to one's reading. Biographical study of various sorts – the traditional resource of scholarly criticism – can be useful, and will be used briefly later in this essay. But it seems more immediately profitable to consider *Le Voyageur* first of all in relation to other works by Apollinaire. For our reading is conditioned above all by the interaction of themes, images and atmosphere on a purely literary plane, which does not necessarily connect directly with life. A work of literature is above all an imaginative experience, and what it connects with are other imaginative experiences in the work of the same writer. With them it makes up a distinctive literary world which has its own laws, patterns and texture. By surveying the relative part of this world we can determine much more exactly the kind of response we are expected to make, as readers, to any one particular work.

What such a comparison does in the case of *Le Voyageur* is to throw light on the poem's distinctive imaginative and emotional structure. It is a work which is built up, as the title suggests, round a theme of travel, but it is clear from the most casual reading that this travel, peculiarly restless and distraught, has more than ordinary connotations. One is thus led to relate it to a group of major poems in *Alcools* which similarly use a theme of travel, or more precisely a theme of wandering, in a very special way. This is a group of long poems, including *La Chanson du Mal-Aimé, Zone, Les Fiançailles* and *Le Brasier*, which are to some extent an inheritance from Apollinaire's Symbolist beginnings. In all of them there is a certain atmosphere in which wandering or *vagabondage* takes on some of the overtones of the Symbolist quest for an unattainable ideal. But while drawing on the overtones of the Symbolist allegory, these poems subtly renew and deflect it to other ends. First, the world through which the poet-hero wanders is no longer the languid, pseudo-medieval world of the fin-de-siècle writers. It is often, on the contrary, a modern scene of a big city at night, harshly lit by café and street lights, and presented as desolate and repelling. Secondly, the quest is not really directed towards an outside goal. It is rather an inner quest, a meditation by the poet on his own anxiety and unease. The function of the wandering motif is to magnify and give lyric poignancy to this meditation, so that the poet becomes an ideal figure expressing the anxiety of all men.[1]

It can be seen that the overall structure of *Le Voyageur* corresponds to this general pattern. The main thread of development in the poem is supplied by the succession of scenes through which the poet-traveller passes. But right from the start this wandering movement is linked to anguished memories. The third stanza establishes the dominating motif and metaphorical action. The disappearance over the horizon of the *paquebot orphelin* suggests the exclusion of the traveller from the hectic future – *les fièvres futures* – and all that this means in terms of engagement in the world. Instead he is turned back to the world of regret, remorse and memory. Although the poem moves rapidly from scene to scene, the obsessively repeated *je m'en souviens, souvenez-vous-en, te souviens-tu*, show that the journey is always through the past, in the inner landscapes of the poet's mind.

What is recalled is also not one, but many different forms of emotional pain. Line 17 might make one suppose, at first, that the poem has a simple source in an experience of disappointed love. But nowhere else does this note occur – nor does that particular use of the *tu* form. Although its use elsewhere is sometimes ambiguous, the general development of the poem, and similar cases in other Apollinaire poems, make it likely that in saying *tu* the poet is addressing himself. The *deux matelots* image with its elusive and enigmatic suggestion of death seems to imply a deeper and graver obsession than amorous pain: it arises almost like a spontaneous product of the subconscious. Similarly the line *Qui donc reconnais-tu sur ces vieilles photographies* would imply a return to different memories from the past. Such a wide-ranging sense of unease is only what one would expect from the narrative motif employed. As the wanderings of the traveller are on a vast and ill-defined scale – one night he is by the sea, on another he arrives at an inn near Luxembourg, on another he is in the wooded valley of a great river – so they will touch on all the various forms of buried anxiety within the self.

The wandering motif, therefore, plays an essential part in the poem. It acts as a heightened metaphor for a mind's restless exploration of its own fears and anxieties. Its function is to project physical perspectives which are blurred and fluid, and to suggest that the poet's inner experience is commensurate with the wide canvas of his wanderings. These suggestions of an infinite richness of experience are particularly sharpened in the two passages evoking feverish rail journeys. Here it is explicitly the landscapes of an urban, industrialized civilization that the traveller traverses, and he is shown as having been deeply marked by what he has seen. This ominous picture of modern civilization underlines, of course, the extent to which *Le Voyageur* connects with the Romantic and Symbolist tradition of retreat from the world into the confines of the self. But more particularly relevant is the part these passages play in reinforcing the picture of a traveller whose distress is all-embracing. Wandering eternally, focussing the anxieties of his companions – *ô matelots ô femmes sombres* – he becomes a symbol in his *vagabondage* of the surfeit of experience and the troubled depths of consciousness of the whole modern psyche.

*Le Voyageur* is, therefore, a poem turned towards the darker side of the self. A large part of its power to involve the reader lies in the glimpses it gives into forms of apprehension which, it suggests, are common to us all. It makes these felt not only in the restless movement of wandering, but also in the highly charged language, built round involved networks of images, which occurs in certain key passages.

The multiple suggestive power of these images, and the incantatory nature of the language in general, will be evident to any casual reader. But, here again, familiarity with Apollinaire's work as a whole will lead to enrichment of understanding. For one discovers on further reading that in all his writing – as in that of all great writers – there are recurring groups of images which attach themselves to his deepest feelings. These form fundamental patterns of his sensibility, which provide the reader with a clear guide to his creative intention, and a touchstone to the depth of the experience that produced the work.

One such group is composed of images relating to the sea. *L'Emigrant de Landor Road*, one of the poems springing from his unhappy love for Annie Playden, is concerned with a boat disappearing over the horizon and an ocean covered with flowers. Vessels pass over the horizon again in *Le Brasier* and *Les Fiançailles*, two poems related to *Le Voyageur* in theme and technique, and in *Onirocritique*, a prose poem which by its very title announces itself to be an exploration of the subconscious. It has to be noticed also to what extent such images are associated with musical cadence. Ships insinuate themselves into some of Apollinaire's most harmoniously introspective phrases, as if the image and the melodic line were joint products of the same instinctive impulse:

Mon beau navire ô ma mémoire
Avons-nous assez navigué
Dans une onde mauvaise à boire
Avons-nous assez navigué
De la belle aube au triste soir
    (*La Chanson du Mal-Aimé*)

Je tourne vire
Phare affolé
Mon beau navire
S'est en allé
    (*Souvenir du Douanier*)

If the atmosphere of foreboding is so firmly established in the opening section of *Le Voyageur*, it is largely through a similarly cunning association of incantatory phrase, disappearing ship and limitless sea. It matters little that the image of knocking on a door, in the first line, is formally rather distant from the image in the second line, evoking the straits of Euripos with their shifting tides. More important is the undulating musical quality of both lines, which fuses the element of distress and vulnerability present in both images, and carries a general flow of associations on to the images of ship and sea. An undercurrent of agitation is set up, conveying the impression of a personality open to, and endlessly swayed by, the tides and eddies of events. Once generated, it continues to spread through the poem. Not only is it revived in the closing lines, turning the poem tightly back on the associations with which it began; it runs also through the related image of the *deux matelots*, with its curiously naïve cadences, and its brief, dream-like snapshot of death. The fact that we again have a glimpse of sailors linked to ships in *Les Fiançailles*, at a point where the tone of the poem darkens, would tend to confirm a consistency of reaction by Apollinaire to these two motifs.[2]

This flow of associations reaches its most intense point in the passage of regular quatrains (ll. 32–47). It was a frequent practice of Apollinaire's to transplant whole passages from earlier works to later ones. Often such passages contain important images, to which their new context seems designed to give added force of meaning. Although the manuscript gives no help here, this set of quatrains looks like an example of such a technique. With its regular versification and mysterious atmosphere, the passage has a very self-contained appearance, and its main images are indeed among the most fundamental in Apollinaire's poetry. They are those concerned, firstly, with flowing water, and those concerned with shadows.

It is tempting to connect the imagery of flowing water with something Apollinaire himself said about his fear of passing time. In a letter in 1916 to Jeanne-Yves Blanc he wrote:

> Je n'ai jamais désiré de quitter pour ma part le lieu où je vivais et j'ai toujours désiré que le présent quel qu'il fût perdurât.
>
> Rien ne détermine plus de mélancolie chez moi que cette fuite du temps. Elle est en désaccord si formel avec mon sentiment, mon identité, qu'elle est la source même de ma poésie.[3]

This remark shows an unusual awareness of a dominating obsession at work as the very impulse of literary creation. While the area of obsession concerned is not exactly the same as that covered by images of flowing water, the two are close enough together to suggest that they are merely different forms of the same psychic pattern of insecurity. The truth of this might be borne out by one of

Apollinaire's most famous poems, *Le Pont Mirabeau*, where the fear of passing time is in fact expressed through the flow of water.

> Sous le pont Mirabeau coule la Seine
> Et nos amours
> Faut-il qu'il m'en souvienne
> La joie venait toujours après la peine
>
> Vienne la nuit sonne l'heure
> Les jours s'en vont je demeure
> . . . . . . . . .
> Passent les jours et passent les semaines
> Ni temps passé
> Ni les amours reviennent
> Sous le pont Mirabeau coule la Seine . . .

Images of flowing water are indeed much more numerous in his work than direct references to passing time. No doubt this is because flowing water, being a more archetypal image, can express many other forms of dread or insecurity as well, and because it is transmuted with such complete naturalness into music. One need hardly stress the intimate association of music and obsessive image in *Le Pont Mirabeau*, and one can find many similar examples, from the early Rhine poems to *Marie*, where the flow of the Seine and the flow of music jointly link intimate memories.

Shadows, too, haunt all Apollinaire's introspective poetry.[4] What is especially relevant is that in many contexts they signify a projection of his own deeper and more mysterious self. This is true first of his own shadow, which in *La Chanson du Mal-Aimé*, as in *Signe* and other poems, is a *ténébreuse épouse que j'aime*. But personal shadow is never distinguished firmly from shadows of other kinds. Just as his temperament was particularly fluid in its mysteriousness, always seeking a reflection of itself outside the self, so his own shadow always seems on the point of merging with others. This is exactly what happens in *Ombre*, a poem in which he annexes the many shadows of his dead war companions into his own, making of the whole a mobile and plastic image of his restless and questing personality.

We must expect, then, that a passage which begins with images of flowing water, and leads up to a particularly sustained play of shadows, will be a crucial one. Even before we have gone beyond the first two stanzas, the combination of powerful imagery and harmonious gravity of expression warns us that feelings of prime importance are involved. The impression of instability and wistfulness generated by the earlier images is now deepened and darkened by association with a more relentless sweep of water. The more undulating music of the earlier part gives way to heavily weighted vocabulary – *éternel, large, sombre, roulaient, mourants* – and the insistent movement of the alexandrine. Such a sense of endless flow goes beyond a mere evocation of passing time and comes near to a half-willing anticipation of death. The detail of dying glances borne on by the river occurs, also, significantly enough, in *Le Pont Mirabeau*, with the same sense of the whole of human life being swept away.

It is at this point of deepest introspection that the shadows appear – with such aptness that one cannot doubt that some process of assimilation of them by the poet, similar to the one in *Ombre*, has taken place. The shadows are so particularized, with their soldier-like appearance, their lances and stately movement, that it seems certain that they must indeed have belonged originally to a context where they had a more precise allegorical meaning. Yet it is totally impossible to find such a meaning in the present context. There is nothing in the poem with which soldiers carrying lances and weeping can connect – except the poet and his gathering apprehension. By removing this passage from its earlier context, therefore, Apollinaire has contrived to release the secondary and submerged associations of the image, at the expense of any more precise significance it might once have had. The wraith-like soldiers revert to the status of pure shadows, heavily tinged with sadness, and become available to express the projected anxieties of the poet himself.

In this way the strange shadow-play represents a point of culmination in the emotional and imaginative development of the poem. The obsessions which have been generated through the movement of wandering and the flow of images are brought together and exteriorized into an action of moving and weeping. A focal point is created in which a climax of dramatic representation expresses what cannot be put fully into ordinary statement. No doubt, in the reader's reaction to this, some cathartic element of release or liberation is involved. But the main satisfaction is the more precisely imaginative one of a sense of artistic order flowing from the arrangement of such deeply felt emotions into a cohesive network of music and imagery.

None the less, if this passage provides a focal point and source of unity, it is clear that the organization of the poem round it is loose rather than tight. Not every stanza looks in towards it with the same degree of concentration. In some parts we feel other pressures at work, for which we have not yet accounted. These pressures also must concern us on the literary plane, but it will help us to understand them if we glance briefly at the larger matters of Apollinaire's intellectual and artistic evolution from which they sprang.

If Apollinaire has an importance in the history of twentieth century art, over and above his excellence as a poet, it is because, despite his fundamentally introspective temperament, he became one of the most ardent champions of revolution and change in art. His enthusiasm for modernism came largely from two sources: his admiration for Cubist painting, and his fascination with the speed and vitality of the twentieth-century machine age. Increasingly – and especially from 1912 onwards – he came to feel that, in an age which was dynamic and capable of the most astonishing technological inventions, artists of all kinds had to find new forms – as the Cubists had – or sink into graceful decadence. His own contribution to artistic innovation came in experimental poems, written mainly in 1913–14 and later included in *Calligrammes*, his second major book of verse. They aimed principally at replacing the traditional form of poems as continuous statements with a type of fragmented, discontinuous structure, which, Apollinaire hoped, would suggest the concentration of multiple forms of energy in modern life.

These experiments did not produce a 'new' Apollinaire, but they did bring about some shifts in focus in his work and the modification of certain themes. In many post-1912 poems, Apollinaire moves confidently towards *les fièvres futures*, travel takes on optimistic associations, and the modern city is seen as a stimulating challenge. There can be no doubt, then, that in its essential themes *Le Voyageur* turns its back on modernism. Yet, written about 1912, it is near enough this modernism in point of time to have caught some of its atmosphere in its language and form. It is at these two levels, consequently, that new pressures can be felt in the poem.

What one finds, at various points, is a language quite different in tonality from the language we have so far considered. It is a language much more prosaic and sparse, stripped of harmonic overtones and halos of secondary meanings. It can be sensed, in some measure, in the passages evoking rail journeys, which have a new energy running through them. The language here, with its hectic accumulation of plurals and its pungent verbs, admirably catches the frantic note in our civilization. It can be seen, more especially, in the deliberate bareness of expression in several other places.

Both the passage evoking the *auberge triste* (ll. 11–17) and the *deux matelots* sequences flirt with prosaic understatement. In the one, the soaring figure of Christ is played off against three flat statements of drab normality, and an unemphatic cry of pain. In the other, a naïve and elusive type of harmony, on the first appearance of the image, is contrasted with a subtly flatter, unrhymed, pattern of phrasing on its second appearance. The sadness and anxiety communicated in each case gain more power by the deliberate restraint imposed on the language. The *deux matelots* image, especially, must be considered exceptionally successful in making a maximum appeal to the imagination in a minimum of unelaborate words.

In this sense, such passages imply an alert confidence in the expressive power of language, very different from the excessive obscurity accumulated round words at the latter end of the Symbolist movement. The whole emphasis in the language is still thrown on the evocation of a state of feeling lying beyond words, but it is evocation achieved without leaning on borrowed responses. Possibly the best example of all is to be found in the three lines which follow the central passage of quatrains (ll. 48–50). In complete contrast to it, they adopt the most laconic conversational tone. While the main image of a bee falling into the fire is concerned with death of a sort, it is death evoked without any traditional emotive support. The line is even unrhymed, and without any particular cadence. One could hardly come nearer to a sequence of words which, outside the context of the poem, would be quite neutral. Yet, within this context, it is alive with associations of incandescence suddenly eclipsed at the end of summer – and so, of happiness irretrievably lost. It is an example of language reduced to its simplest components, and then recharged with poetic force in a way unique to one poet's sensibility.

This alertness of language is matched, of course, by an alertness of form. It is true of many Apollinaire poems that they are built up on a principle of abrupt juxtaposition. In part this reflects the contradictory and fluctuating nature of his temperament, and his desire to give full play to it. In part it stems from an aesthetic fascination with variety of texture, and the formal contrast of one part of the poem with another. This was one of the effects achieved by the technique of transferring passages from one context to another.

In *Le Voyageur*, however, what was once an occasional and instinctive practice has become a conscious and sustained interest in fragmentation of structure. It is no longer a matter of one obviously imported passage – like the passage of quatrains – providing one clear point of contrast. There is a general break-up of the poem into multiple fragments, all varying in tone, texture and shape. The reader has to pass from incantatory or urgent single lines to the prosaic rhythm of *Un soir je descendis*, the feverish tempo of the railway passages, the remote brevity of the *deux matelots*, the elaborate and troubling obscurity of the passage of quatrains, and the laconic tone of *Qui donc reconnais-tu. . . .* With such constant switches in tone and tempo, variety of texture begins to assume an autonomous status in the reader's reaction to the poem. This does not detract from the emotional and psychological impact of such switches. Read in one way, they continue to suggest the unruly stream of consciousness. But, increasingly, their value as sharp splinters of form begins to count as well. The reader can hardly escape the feeling of tension imparted to the structure by the repeated changes in the point of attack, and the resultant diversity of formal patterns.

This is still a long way from a random assembly of fragments. The poem remains sufficiently organized through its schemes of imagery as it is loosely contained in the basic framework of the wandering motif. The repetition of certain fragments has also an unobtrusive tightening effect. But, in general, the illusion, very pleasingly achieved, is of a certain unpredictability of design. Fernand Fleuret once claimed, indeed, that he and Apollinaire composed the poem together in a light-hearted game of improvization.[5] Although the story cannot literally be true, one can see how, within limits, Apollinaire might have drawn inspiration from such an exercise, perhaps as a starting point. It was of a kind to encourage him to keep the poem as open as possible to happy accidents, and thus approximate to that daring polyvalence of form which he was already admiring in Cubist paintings. It was especially in his experimental poems that he took up this challenge of the work of literature as an open, multi-directional construction. But already in the jig-saw of shapes in *Le*

*Voyageur*, jostling each other for the reader's attention, one has a foretaste of things to come.

Such immediacy of form and language makes a considerable difference to the final impact of the poem on the reader. He can feel, combined with the anxious meditation which provides its main theme, an openness and alertness of mind which is seeking, none the less, to extend the expressive power of literature. The work reveals an introspective sensibility, certainly, but not one wrapped up in its own cocoon. It remains fully alive to the changing atmosphere and pace of the twentieth century, and capable of inventing new forms to respond to them.

And this reminds us, finally, that while a poem is first and foremost a pattern of forms on the purely literary plane, it must lead us out eventually to human and cultural concerns much larger than itself. In broad literary terms, Apollinaire looks back instinctively to the great tradition of French poetry stemming from Baudelaire. He explores deep sources of unease within the self in a rich harmony of language undoubtedly inherited from Symbolism. But at the same time he is caught up in new enthusiasms, and looks eagerly for new forms of self-expression. It is in this sense that his writing is subjected to strongly competing pressures. The full range of such pressures is not evident in this one poem, of course. But, if it is read sympathetically, there are enough of them to broaden our understanding of the complex relationship between a man and his cultural situation. This means that *Le Voyageur* cannot be a particularly ordered and reposing work of literature: the diverse sets of forces in it are too strong for that. But it does remain, undoubtedly, a record of human experience of the greatest interest, and an effort of literary expression of considerable vitality.

NOTES

1 I have enlarged on this point in *Alcools et le Symbolisme* in *Guillaume Apollinaire 2*, éd. Décaudin, Minard, Paris, 1963, and developed it in *Le rôle de l'imagination dans Calligrammes (Deuxième Partie)* in *Guillaume Apollinaire 6*, Minard, 1967.

2 Michel Décaudin has connected the *deux matelots* with a childhood photograph of Apollinaire and his brother dressed in sailor suits. See M. Décaudin: *Le Dossier d'Alcools*. Droz et Minard, Geneva and Paris, 1965, p. 133.

3 G. Apollinaire: *Lettres à sa Marraine*, Gallimard, 1951, p. 72.

4 One of the most striking manuscript changes in his work occurs in *Les Fiançailles*, where the two lines:
   Et sombre éveil si faible je me rappelle
   Les passantes ce soir n'étaient jamais jolies
were changed to:
   Et sombre sombre fleuve je me rappelle
   Les ombres qui passaient n'étaient jamais jolies
With the introduction, in successive lines, of flowing water and shadows, this is an outstanding example of a poet seeking out a familiar, deeply felt pattern of imagery.

5 F. Fleuret: *De Gilles de Rais à Guillaume Apollinaire*, Mercure de France, Paris, 1933.

*Source*
Guillaume Apollinaire (1880–1918): *Alcools*, in *Œuvres poétiques*, ed. M. Adéma and M. Décaudin, Bibliothèque de la Pléiade, Paris, 1962, pp. 78–80.

Germaine Brée

# PROUST
*Du Côté de Chez Swann*: 'Combray'

« Cette année-là, quand, un peu plus tôt que d'habitude, mes parents eurent fixé le jour de rentrer à Paris, le matin du départ, comme on m'avait fait friser pour être photographié, coiffer avec précaution un chapeau que je n'avais encore jamais mis et revêtir une douillette de
5 velours, après m'avoir cherché partout, ma mère me trouva en larmes dans le petit raidillon contigu à Tansonville, en train de dire adieu aux aubépines, entourant de mes bras les branches piquantes, et – comme une princesse de tragédie à qui pèseraient ces vains ornements, ingrat envers l'importune main qui en formant tous ces nœuds avait
10 pris soin sur mon front d'assembler mes cheveux,* – foulant aux pieds mes papillotes arrachées et mon chapeau neuf. Ma mère ne fut pas touchée par mes larmes, mais elle ne put retenir un cri à la vue de la coiffe défoncée et de la douillette perdue. Je ne l'entendis pas : 'O mes pauvres petites aubépines, disais-je en pleurant, ce n'est pas vous
15 qui voudriez me faire du chagrin, me forcer à partir. Vous, vous ne m'avez jamais fait de peine! Aussi je vous aimerai toujours.' Et, essuyant mes larmes, je leur promettais, quand je serais grand, de ne pas imiter la vie insensée des autres hommes et, même à Paris, les jours de printemps, au lieu d'aller faire des visites et écouter des
20 niaiseries, de partir dans la campagne voir les premières aubépines. »

---

* Indirect quotation from Racine's *Phèdre*, Act 1, scene 3.
Que ces vains ornements, que ces voiles me pèsent!
Quelle importune main en formant tous ces nœuds,
A pris soin sur mon front d'assembler mes cheveux?

SITUATION OF THE PASSAGE. 'Combray' is the title of the opening section of *Du côté de chez Swann*, the first part of Marcel Proust's seven-part novel, *A la recherche du temps perdu*. It is also the name of the small provincial town where the narrator and protagonist of the novel, an only child, would come at Easter from Paris with his parents. Proust introduces us to Combray by a somewhat circuitous path. A speaker, who, we do not know – nor where he is, nor what he does – recalls certain past impressions which over many years occurred at night, as he lay in bed between consciousness and deep sleep. Combray is one of the names that would frequently emerge as he awoke with the quasi-physically remembered presence of a childhood bedroom; and Combray is the first place on which the narrator then focuses his and our attention as he begins to unfold the story of his life.

The Combray room recalls his Tante Léonie's house at the centre of the small town and the two walks that the family habitually took: either 'du côté de chez Swann', in the direction of Méséglise-la-Vineuse, past Tansonville, the château of Charles Swann, an acquaintance who occasionally dropped in on the family; or 'du côté de Guermantes', toward Guermantes, the estate of the aristocratic landowners of feudal descent, the Duc and Duchesse of Guermantes. Around the Swanns and the Guermantes, quasi-fabulous people yet real, the child's aspirations and rêveries were vaguely polarized. Life in Combray is presented in two contrasting panels. The first centres on a childhood drama that took place one evening when, because Swann had come to dinner, the little boy had had to go to bed without his mother's goodnight kiss. Much longer, the second evocation introduces us to a sunlit, multi-faceted Combray, wrapped in the golden atmosphere of summer, and to a childhood world, slowly becoming an adolescent world of delight, excitement and rêverie.

The two walks belong to this facet of the narrator's memories, leading out of Combray, toward the inaccessible regions and people that inhabit them and the child's daydreams simultaneously. In leisurely fashion the narrator ends this re-creation of Combray with a composite description of those two walks in which he fuses impressions of many summers, studded with a few sharply etched, specific incidents. The selected passage occurs very early in the evocation of the walks 'du côté de chez Swann', soon after one such momentous incident: the boy's first glimpse of 'une petite fille rousse, à la peau semée de taches rousses' – Gilberte Swann – whom he sees through a hawthorn hedge in bloom as she stands in the park of Tansonville. Around the inaccessible Gilberte, instantly, his vague dreams of romance crystallize.

STRUCTURE. Introduced brusquely into the narrator's account of the walks along Swann's way, by a time-association – 'Cette année-là', i.e. the year he caught his first glimpse of Gilberte Swann – the passage is a small self-contained unit that seems somewhat arbitrarily inserted into the tightly woven descriptive pages with which it does not merge. The facts are few and simple: on the morning of the family's departure from Combray to return to Paris, the boy disappears. His mother finds him in tears in the 'raidillon' of Tansonville where he has gone to say good-bye to the hawthorns. The central motif, the 'adieu aux aubépines' (l. 6), is not directly linked to what comes immediately before the passage, the child's infatuation with Gilberte Swann; it only faintly recalls the vivid, lengthily developed scene of the encounter with Gilberte and the hawthorns in bloom. The narrative line is given in three rapid stages, marked by the use of the past-definite tense: 'ma mère me trouva en larmes. . .'; 'elle ne fut pas touchée . . . mais elle ne put retenir un cri . . .'; 'je ne l'entendis pas . . .'

The episode itself falls into two parts, both highly theatrical, leading to and from a central image: a 'dressed-up' little boy, hugging the branches of a hawthorn bush meanwhile trampling his hat and curlers underfoot, unaware that his mother is watching him. The theatricality is underscored by an indirect quotation from Racine's *Phèdre* associated with one of the more intensely dramatic moments in the play, the appearance on stage of the dying queen.

A first single long sentence – eleven lines – sets the stage of the action, with all the specific circumstances of the time and occasion pertaining to the incident. It finally comes to rest on the central image of the child, the main character already on stage, acting out his part in an outburst of self-pity and self-dramatization. The second part, 'Je ne l'entendis pas', focuses solely on the child, whose violent reactions give way to an emotional verbalization of his despair culminating in a solemn pact with the hawthorns. Between the two parts the spotlight shifts an instant to the mother: 'Ma mère ne fut pas . . . perdue.' The sentence orients the scene away from the anticipated outcome suggested by 'ma mère me trouva . . .' toward the subsequent 'je ne l'entendis pas', relegating the child's mother to the rôle of external witness. The stage is thus set for what is in effect an inner drama, theatrically projected in acts and words by the child before an uncomprehending witness. The recall of the outer circumstances of the episode raises a central question: the underlying nature of the child's grief and of his relation to the hawthorns. Proust offers no comment, explanation or further outcome.

ANALYSIS

(1) *Point of view and tone: the two spectators*
At first reading, it is apparent that there are two spectators to the scene: the mother and the narrator; and one actor, the child. The scene in the 'raidillon', following 'ma mère me trouva . . .' is observed through the mother's eyes. But the narrator holds her under his own observation: he objectively notes her feelings, 'elle ne fut pas touchée . . .' and the otherwise unnoticed 'cri'. Omniscient, he sets the narrative tone, intervening in appearance only once through the reference to *Phèdre*. The comparison of the child with a 'princesse de tragédie', Phèdre, on that tragic morning when she meets her fate, underscores the semi-rueful, gently ironic tone that suffuses the narrative, placing the reactions of both mother and child within the same perspective. The mother's concern for the trampled hat and 'douillette perdue' and the child's melodramatic action and words are thus seen from outside but lighted from within with a kind of tender yet ironic humour.

(2) *The third point of view*
(a) *The emotional build-up.* Fusing in a single whole the events that culminate in the child's emotional outburst, Proust suggests without formulating them the latent psychological tensions that led to the child's actions that particular morning. They involve the 'festive' ceremonial family preparations for departure, in which he is forced to participate and an inner distress that repudiates them and finds its outlet in the violent scene enacted and the pact with the hawthorns. The theme of resentment is obliquely introduced through the narrator's seemingly objective specifications, then bursts through in the child's actions and words. That year, the arbiters of his fate, his parents, arbitrarily change the ritual departure, fixing the date 'un

peu plus tôt que d'habitude.' The inner reluctance of the child, that morning, is manifest in the relation suggested by the use of the 'on', which puts the preparations in a specific perspective, the child's, subconscious though it be: 'on m'avait fait friser . . . coiffer . . . un chapeau . . . revêtir une douillette de velours . . .' The accumulating irrational grievance is directed more specifically against the hat – 'que je n'avais encore jamais mis', new, a negation of the past. The unrecognized resentment against his parents' indifference to his distress leads up to an indirect indictment – by contrast with the hawthorns 'qui (ne voudraient pas lui) faire du chagrin, (le) forcer à partir', which never made him suffer. The Phèdre quotation then underscores the emotional underground revolt, with its allusion to the 'importune main'. For the child, the trampling of the hat and curlers, the sacrifice of the *douillette* torn by the hawthorn branches is at one level a repudiation of the importunate 'on' that forced him to put them on – clearly his mother. And her reaction corroborates his sense of outrage: she does not even guess at the depth of his distress, finds him only 'après l'avoir cherché partout' and has a thought only for the ruined hat and velvet jacket.

(b) *The pact with the hawthorns.* The separation from the hawthorns is a small drama in three acts.

(1) an act left unexplained: the child's resolution to take leave of the hawthorns.

(2) the violent, two-faceted enactment of grief and revolt: the hawthorn clasped, personified, seized as unique refuge; and the rejection of the parental order: the destruction wrought on hat, curlers and jacket.

(3) the verbalization of the inner drama, first directly recorded as spoken, then indirectly reported by the narrator.

Against the outer world of social reality, the world represented in his eyes by the routine obligations of departure and his parents' callous indifference to his inner feelings, the child sets up a subjective magic relationship with the hawthorns, resting on their permanent accessibility – 'les jours de printemps' – and his own future freedom and will, 'je leur promettais, quand je serais grand . . .' Nature, symbolized by the hawthorns, is, romantically, projected as responding to his emotional needs: 'la campagne', 'les jours de printemps', 'les aubépines' contrasting with 'la vie insensée des autres hommes' and their 'niaiseries'. The hawthorns thus provide an alleviation of the child's grief. His immediate situation is generalized, his solitude is translated into terms of moral superiority and his unreasoned sorrow into self-justification at the expense of the 'vie insensée' of those – including his parents – who sacrifice feeling to society. The 'parting' is transformed into the assertion of a secret and lasting union and the child's grief is thus assuaged.

DETAILED EXAMINATION. There are some curious features about the passage, in spite of its careful patterning.

(1) Its brusque insertion into a tightly textured description of the walks along Swann's way: an occasional, but rather rare occurrence in *Du côté de chez Swann*, the most carefully wrought part of Proust's novel in which Proust tries to weave each episode inextricably by thematic associations into a continuous flow of narrative and description.

(2) Throughout 'Combray', Proust presents his protagonist through what a critic has called 'different age-layers arbitrarily compressed'; this, to some extent, the narrative use of the inter-play of memory and association authorizes. But, in this case, the discrepancies are rather violent. Even in the 1890s – approximately within the fictional date of this episode – the child with ringlets could hardly be of an age to make the solemn vow at the end; the boy who 'that year' had stood transfixed staring at the little girl in the park is at least eight or nine – too old for curlers.

(3) The central scene – the child hugging the hawthorn branches while stamping on hat and curlers – can hardly be visualized realistically given the nature of hawthorn bushes.

(4) Useful though it be in setting the scene in perspective, the quotation from Phèdre seems quite awkwardly forced into the long initial phrase.

A rapid glance at a discarded early draft of a quite different incident, published in a posthumous volume of fragments, entitled *Contre Sainte-Beuve*,* throws a good deal of light both on these puzzling features and on our understanding of the over-all significance of the episode in the thematic development of Proust's novel.

GENESIS OF THE INCIDENT. Proust, around 1908, seems to have been experimenting with a narrative set in a semi-autobiographical,

* See the Appendix, pp. 251–3.

semi-fictionalized framework – a conversation with his mother, who, at the time he was writing, had recently died. Within this framework he evoked, at one time, an incident, clearly a childhood memory, involving the entire Proust family, father, mother and the two boys, Marcel and Robert, which he developed in considerable detail with obvious relish.

Robert, the younger brother, is the central figure in the incident which Proust develops at length. Robert, who we are told is five-and-a-half, has been dressed up and had his hair curled with a double end in view: he is going to be photographed, then will go away with his mother on a visit to friends. He has been told that he must leave his pet goat behind. He disappears with the goat, and is found talking to it and hugging it in great despair. At the sight of his mother his despair turns into defiance; he tears the ribbons from his hair and stamps on them, yielding finally only before the stern intervention of M. Proust.

The incident is described from the semi-mocking, semi-affectionate point of view of the older brother, and amusingly transposed through Proust's deliberate adoption of the mock-epic style. Proust builds up the puerile incident by elaborate parallels between Robert and the royal children painted by Velasquez and English painters (he seems to have had Reynolds more specifically in mind); and by contrasting Robert's devastating royal rage and 'queen of tragedy' attitudes with his attire. The 'nœuds' of ribbon that Robert tears out of his hair lead quite naturally within this context to Phèdre's '. . . que ces nœuds me pèsent'. Significantly the whole episode seems to have been manipulated by Proust with a latent purpose in mind. Robert's violent despair is brief; in contrast, throughout, Marcel suffers a mute and deep distress at the imminence of his mother's departure. Thus stylistically manipulated and interpreted, the incident is at one remove from reminiscence. But it refers us back to Proust's life, it is a form of semi-fictionalized autobiography in the Romantic tradition, an oblique demonstration of the depth of the young Proust's affection for his mother and heroic efforts at self-mastery. Most of the elements of the 'Combray' situation are there, quite recognizably. At first glance the two episodes seem to have a common theme, the distress of children arbitrarily parted from something – a goat, hawthorns – or, in the case of Marcel, the elder brother, someone they love.

But from reminiscence to fiction, crucial changes have taken place.

(1) Proust has done away with the 'indiscriminate confusion of circumstance', lovingly elaborated in the early draft. Only two people are involved, the child and his mother. But even this is deceptive. The mother has no part in the child's grief, she is merely a witness.

(2) What transforms the incident radically – in spite of the slight consequent implausibility – is that, in the 'Combray' incident, the child's grief is caused by his separation not from a possession (the goat) nor from a person (his mother), but from flowers, the hawthorns.

Because of the hawthorns, the incident changes context and moves out of the world of reminiscence into the fictional universe of the novel, thence the vow which has no counterpart in the original anecdote.

BASIC THEME AND SIGNIFICANCE. The hawthorns play an essential rôle in the world of Combray. In a double garland they decorate the altar of the Church in the month of May, sculptured flowers and real. 'It is in the month of May, I remember, that I began to love hawthorns', remarks the narrator. They seemed then to the child 'inseparable from the mysteries in the celebration of which they participated', all the more enigmatic because they were both sacred and yet 'they were alive and belonged to the realm of nature'. Emblematic flowers, too, linked with the profane mysteries of love, their sensuous scent and presence were associated with the presence of an ambiguous young girl, Mlle Vinteuil.

When in the Tansonville 'raidillon' the child saw the hawthorn in bloom, the white then the pink, he had contemplated them with a rare degree of concentration. Screening his eyes with his hands, he tried to capture 'le sentiment qu'elles éveillaient en moi', in vain. Proust spares no pains in his setting of atmosphere and mood. The silence is complete except for 'un invisible oiseau' whose 'note prolongée' accentuates the stillness under a sky 'devenu fixe'. The hawthorns 'charm' the child, enthrall him quite literally. He feels called upon to elucidate the 'obscure and vague' emotion that relates him to the flowers. The theme introduced is the theme of a vocation, a 'call'; and all the associations in the lavish description are with the sacred flowers in the church.

It is from this association that the short episode of the 'adieu' derives its meaning. The child is in fact being cut off from something essential to him, symbolized in the flowers. For the sudden appearance of Gilberte, polarizing his emotions, has already created a sharp division and confusion in himself. Hence the irony of his vow. For he will indeed spend years in paying calls and listening to silly chatter: ambiguous, the hawthorns will first lead him only to Gilberte and to the salon of the beautiful Odette Swann. After this scene the hawthorns virtually disappear from the novel, the 'raidillon' of Tansonville evoking only Gilberte. Once only, in his later adolescence, far from Combray, the boy sees a hedge of hawthorns, but without flowers and he rather ashamedly recalls his unkept promise. Only at the end of a long odyssey will he return by an inner path to that initial encounter – and recognize its meaning, the long unheeded call to recreate in words the intense perception of their living beauty, which otherwise would be lost.

CONCLUSION. It seems clear that, after the vivid evocation of the child's encounter with Gilberte, Proust felt the need to stress the deeper significance of the episode, introducing one of the many unobtrusive signposts that point to the nature of the narrator's real adventure, his slow discovery of his vocation as artist, his final unquestioning assent to the apprehension of life implicit in the child's intense aesthetic reaction to the hawthorns, and in his deep grief at being parted from them, a grief not fully understood by him. We can thus follow to a certain extent the process by which Proust reached back to a scene that must have been vividly present in his memory since he had so carefully elaborated it once already, and integrated it into his novel. The original protagonist of the scene was, we note, not Marcel Proust, but his brother; this points to the ambiguous character of the 'I' in *A la recherche du temps perdu*, a fictional self not to be confused with the author's. It is clear too that the integrating factor here is not *memory* but a conscious æsthetic pattern, a design, whose purpose is not, as in the initial version, auto-biographical in kind. Because it was not completely fused into the whole, because it could in some measure be traced to its source, the episode gives us an insight into the almost overwhelming complexity of Proust's novel and of the mind that conceived it.

*Source*
Marcel Proust (1871–1922): *A la recherche du temps perdu*, ed. P. Clarac and André Ferré, Bibliothèque de la Pléiade, Paris, 1954, t. I, pp. 144–5.

Elle devait partir, je l'ai dit, avec mon petit frère, et comme il quittait la maison mon oncle l'avait emmené pour le faire photographier à Evreux. On lui avait frisé ses cheveux comme aux enfants de concierge quand on les photographie, sa grosse figure était entourée d'un casque de cheveux noirs bouffants avec des grands nœuds plantés comme les papillons d'une infante de Velasquez; je l'avais regardé avec le sourire d'un enfant plus âgé pour un frère qu'il aime, sourire où l'on ne sait pas trop s'il y a plus d'admiration, de supériorité ironique ou de tendresse. Maman et moi nous partîmes le chercher pour que je lui dise adieu, mais impossible de le trouver. Il avait appris qu'il ne pourrait pas emmener le chevreau qu'on lui avait donné, et qui était, avec le tombereau magnifique qu'il traînait toujours avec lui, toute sa tendresse, et qu'il 'prêtait' quelquefois à mon père, par bonté. Comme après le séjour chez Mme de Z . . . il rentrait à Paris, on allait donner le chevreau à des fermiers du voisinage. Mon frère, en proie à l'accablement de la douleur, avait voulu passer la dernière journée avec son chevreau, peut-être aussi je crois se cacher, pour faire par vengeance manquer le train à Maman. Toujours est-il qu'après l'avoir cherché partout nous longions le petit bosquet au milieu duquel se trouvait le cirque où on attelait les chevaux pour faire monter l'eau et où jamais n'allait plus personne, sans certes nous douter que mon frère pût être là, quand une conversation entrecoupée de gémissements frappa notre oreille. C'était bien la voix de mon frère, et bientôt nous l'aperçûmes, qui ne pouvait pas nous voir; assis par terre contre son chevreau et lui caressant tendrement la tête avec la main, l'embrassant sur son nez pur et un peu rouge de bellâtre couperosé, insignifiant et cornu, ce groupe ne rappelait que bien peu celui que les peintres anglais ont souvent reproduit d'un enfant caressant un animal. Si mon frère, dans sa petite robe des grands jours et sa jupe de dentelle, tenant d'une main, à côté de l'inséparable tombereau, de petits sacs de satin où on avait mis son goûter, son nécessaire de voyage et de petites glaces de verre, avait bien la magnificence des enfants anglais près de l'animal, en revanche sa figure n'exprimait, sous ce luxe qui n'en rendait le contraste que plus sensible, que le désespoir le plus farouche, il avait les yeux rouges, la gorge oppressée de ses falbalas, comme une princesse de tragédie pompeuse et désespérée. Par moments, de sa main surchargée du tombereau, des sacs de satin qu'il ne voulait pas lâcher, car l'autre ne cessait d'étreindre et de caresser le chevreau, il relevait ses cheveux sur sa tête avec l'impatience de Phèdre.

Quelle importune main en formant tous ces nœuds,
A pris soin sur mon front d'assembler mes cheveux ?

'Mon petit chevreau, s'écriait-il, en attribuant au chevreau la tristesse que seul il éprouvait, tu vas être malheureux sans ton petit maître, tu ne me verras plus jamais, jamais,' et ses larmes brouillaient ses paroles, 'personne ne sera bon pour toi, ne te caressera comme moi! tu te laissais pourtant bien faire; mon petit enfant, mon petit chéri,' et sentant ses pleurs l'étouffer, il eut tout d'un coup pour mettre le comble à son désespoir l'idée de chanter un air qu'il avait entendu chanter à Maman et dont l'appropriation à la situation redoubla ses sanglots. 'Adieu, des voix étranges m'appellent loin de toi, paisible sœur des anges.'

Mais mon frère, quoiqu'il n'eût que cinq ans et demi, était plutôt d'une nature violente, et passant de l'attendrissement sur ses malheurs et ceux du chevreau à la colère contre les persécuteurs, après une seconde d'hésitation il se mit à briser vivement par terre ses glaces, à trépigner les sacs de satin, à s'arracher, non pas les cheveux mais les petits nœuds qu'on lui avait mis dans les cheveux, à déchirer sa belle robe asiatique, poussant des cris perçants: 'Pourquoi serais-je beau, puisque je ne te verrai plus?' s'écriait-il en pleurant. Ma mère, voyant les dentelles de la robe s'arracher, ne pouvait rester insensible à un spectacle qui jusqu'ici l'avait plutôt attendri. Elle s'avança, mon frère entendit du bruit, se tut immédiatement, l'aperçut, ne sachant pas s'il avait été vu, d'un air profondément attentif et en reculant se cacha derrière le chevreau. Mais ma mère alla à lui. Il fallut venir, mais il mit comme condition que le chevreau l'accompagnerait jusqu'à la gare. Le temps pressait, mon père en bas s'étonnait de ne pas nous voir revenir, ma mère m'avait envoyé lui dire de nous rejoindre à la voie ferrée qu'on traversait en passant par un raccourci derrière le jardin, car sans cela nous aurions risqué de manquer le train, et mon frère s'avançait, conduisant d'une main le chevreau comme au sacrifice, et de l'autre tirant les sacs qu'on avait ramassés, les débris des miroirs, le nécessaire et le tombereau qui traînait à terre. Par moments, sans oser regarder Maman, il lançait à son adresse tout en caressant le chevreau des paroles sur l'intention desquelles elle ne pouvait se méprendre: 'Mon pauvre petit chevreau, ce n'est pas toi qui chercherais à me faire de la peine, à me séparer de ceux que j'aime. Toi tu n'es pas une personne, mais aussi tu n'es pas méchant, tu n'es pas comme ces méchants,' disait-il en jetant un regard de côté à Maman comme pour juger de l'effet de ses paroles et voir s'il n'avait pas dépassé le but, 'toi tu ne m'as jamais fait de peine,' et il se mettait à sangloter. Mais arrivé à la voie ferrée, et m'ayant demandé de tenir un moment le chevreau, dans sa rage contre Maman il s'élança, s'assit sur la voie ferrée et nous regardant d'un air de défi ne bougea plus. Il n'y avait pas à cet endroit de barrière. A toute minute un train pouvait passer. Maman, folle de peur, s'élança sur lui, mais elle avait beau tirer, avec une force inouïe de son derrière sur lequel il avait l'habitude de se laisser glisser et de parcourir le jardin en chantant dans des jours meilleurs, il adhérait aux rails sans parvenir à l'arracher. Elle était blanche de peur. Heureusement à ce moment mon père débouchait avec deux domestiques qui venaient voir si on n'avait besoin de rien. Il se précipita, arracha mon frère, lui donna deux claques, et donna l'ordre qu'on ramenât le chevreau. Mon frère terrorisé dut marcher, mais regardant longuement mon père avec une fureur concentrée, il s'écria: 'Je ne te prêterai plus jamais mon tombereau.' Puis comprenant qu'aucune parole ne pourrait dépasser la fureur de celle-là, il ne dit plus rien. Maman me prit à part et me dit: 'Toi qui es plus grand, sois raisonnable, je t'en prie, n'aie pas l'air triste au moment du départ, ton père est déjà ennuyé que je parte, tâche qu'il ne nous trouve pas tous les deux insuportables.' Je ne proférai pas une plainte pour me montrer digne de la confiance qu'elle me témoignait, de la mission qu'elle me confiait. Par moments une irrésistible fureur contre elle, contre mon père, un désir de leur faire manquer le train, de ruiner le plan ourdi contre moi de me séparer d'elle, me prenait. Il se brisait devant la peur de lui faire de la peine et je restais souriant et brisé, glacé de tristesse.

*Contre Sainte-Beuve*, 292–6. Gallimard, 1954.

*Roger Cardinal*

# BRETON
'Au beau demi-jour de 1934'

Au beau demi-jour de 1934
L'air était une splendide rose couleur de rouget
Et la forêt quand je me préparais à y entrer
Commençait par un arbre à feuilles de papier à cigarettes
5 Parce que je t'attendais
Et que si tu te promènes avec moi
N'importe où
Ta bouche est volontiers la nielle
D'où repart sans cesse la roue bleue diffuse et brisée qui monte
10 Blêmir dans l'ornière
Tous les prestiges se hâtaient à ma rencontre
Un écureuil était venu appliquer son ventre blanc sur mon cœur
Je ne sais comment il se tenait
Mais la terre était pleine de reflets plus profonds que ceux de l'eau
15 Comme si le métal eût enfin secoué sa coque
Et toi couchée sur l'effroyable mer de pierreries
Tu tournais
Nue
Dans un grand soleil de feu d'artifice
20 Je te voyais descendre lentement des radiolaires
Les coquilles même de l'oursin j'y étais
Pardon je n'y étais déjà plus
J'avais levé la tête car le vivant écrin de velours blanc m'avait
    quitté
Et j'étais triste
25 Le ciel entre les feuilles luisait hagard et dur comme une libellule
J'allais fermer les yeux
Quand les deux pans du bois qui s'étaient brusquement écartés
    s'abattirent
Sans bruit
Comme les deux feuilles centrales d'un muguet immense
30 D'une fleur capable de contenir toute la nuit
J'étais où tu me vois
Dans le parfum sonné à toute volée
Avant qu'elles ne revinssent comme chaque jour à la vie changeante
J'eus le temps de poser mes lèvres
35 Sur tes cuisses de verre

radiolaire

roue brisée

soleil d'artifice

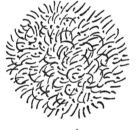

oursin

grand soleil (tournesol)

THE SURREALIST practice of automatism, the uncritical recording of what is dictated by the *voix surréaliste* of the unconscious mind, tends to produce poetry which flows unimpeded, without the normal restraints imposed by principles of expression or form. It is true that most of André Breton's published poems are not authentic 'automatic' texts, for, like most Surrealist poets, he recognized the need for a certain degree of *arrangement en poème*, as Eluard called it – the need to give some shape to the *materia prima* of poetry offered by automatism. However, such arrangement is usually restricted to ensuring that the poem observes syntax, presents a sequence of events, and ends on an impressive note. This means that there is no deliberated 'message', nor formal shaping in any conventional sense.

Faced with such a text as Breton's 'Au beau demi-jour de 1934',[1] the reader would not expect to derive much profit from conventional methods of elucidation. If modern poetry has accustomed him to the notion that a poem may have more than one level of meaning, Surrealism seems to encourage him to accept the validity of *any* meaning which he thinks he discerns. Also, since the principal agent in the creation of the poem is the unconscious, any 'meaning' must be of a primarily irrational nature. It might then seem that an *explication de texte* is an impossibility as far as Surrealist poetry is concerned; for surely there can be no real 'explanation'? One can indeed make no definitive rational statement about a kind of poetry which does not set out to be meaningful. Nonetheless, some basis for agreement is afforded by the fact that readers of European background are able to react to given irrational images or symbols in more or less similar ways; they are at least able to follow, if not to sympathize with the personal interpretation proposed by another reader. It is on the optimistic assumption that even irrational texts tend to mean something to the average conscious mind that I put forward the present interpretation, in the hope that, although it is inevitably a statement informed by subjective reactions, it may have some objective validity.

SYNTAX AND STRUCTURE. The poem presents a straightforward sequence of events that take place in relation to a protagonist, the poet or lover (*je*). He is trying to satisfy his desire for the woman he loves (referred to as *tu*). But whereas the subject of most of the sentences is in the first person, it is significant that the poet does nothing very decisive. No verb of which *je* is the subject has any real force:

> je me préparais
> je t'attendais
> je ne sais comment
> je te voyais
> j'y étais/je n'y étais plus
>> (the second statement cancels out the first)
> j'avais levé la tête (a minimal action)
> j'étais triste
> j'étais où tu me vois (no specific place is indicated)
> j'eus le temps de poser mes lèvres
>> (though this is the most important action carried out,
>> it is attenuated, for the action-word *poser* is not the main
>> verb in the sentence).

It is evident that the protagonist is a passive figure, and that things happen to him without his being able to control them. This passivity is complemented by an atmosphere of languid expectancy, conveyed by the repetitious imperfect tense. This is sustained throughout, until the decisive intervention of the past historic towards the end of the poem. This has dramatic effect: all at once, after so much indecision and delay, there is a specific, single action, and a quickening of rhythm that suggests a sudden, urgent awareness of time. Indeed, there is *just enough time* for the poet to kiss his beloved before she disappears from reach.

The poem possesses a coherent referential structure, for most things mentioned can be found in the countryside. Many references are to natural life (plants and animals: *rose, rouget, forêt, arbre, nielle, écureuil, grand soleil, libellule, bois, muguet*), though some indicate the presence of man (*cigarette, roue, ornière*). One can start reading the poem on the assumption that it is about a man walking in a forest. But this is not all, for this dominant sphere of references is counterbalanced by references to entirely different spheres: jewelry, fireworks, and, above all, aquatic life (*eau, coque, mer, radiolaires, oursin*). Some of these references convey an impression of wilful extravagance on Breton's part. One does not ordinarily expect a Surrealist to send us to the dictionary to look up a word such as *radiolaires* (a kind of minute protozoa). But even such preciosity has its effect on the reader, and cannot fail to contribute to the *dépaysement* that most Surrealist poems achieve.

ATMOSPHERE AND MOOD. Despite the precise indication of time in the first line,[2] the atmosphere of the poem is one of dreamlike uncertainty, as though what goes on in the poem were unaffected by ordinary time, forming part of a realm that is divorced from everyday life. The poet evokes a world of pure metamorphosis, which he expresses above all through *metaphor*. The sequence of images, always changing and incoherent (at least on a preliminary reading), reveals a world which is essentially unstable, a world in which perspectives shift constantly and all things are subject to incredible transformations. The sense of instability is typically Surrealist, and the reader must expect to be unsettled. At the same time, to savour this sensation of uncertainty, to feel that one is thrown completely on one's own resources in a world of fragile and unreliable things, can be a source of a pleasure highly poetic in its ambiguity, deriving as it does from the fascinating postulation of a domain which is so manifestly unreal. That the poet wishes this strange world *were* real, is evident from the wistful tone of the poem. The reader feels that he is witness to the conjuring-up of an illusion which the poet presumably hopes will be meaningful to him, though it is an illusion that can only last, like one of Rimbaud's *Illuminations*, for a fleeting moment.

IMAGERY. Since imagery is the *raison d'être* of all Surrealist poetry, it is important to consider the kind of images that Breton uses.

A Surrealist mind thrives upon abrupt comparisons and analogies. 'Le mot le plus exaltant dont nous disposions, est le mot COMME, que ce mot soit prononcé ou tu', writes Breton in an article on the 'analogical principle'.[3] Whether it is the result of deliberate choice, or whether it is an inherent feature of automatism, Surrealist poetry usually takes the form of an unrelieved 'firework display' of images, which confuse the reader by their irrational brilliance. In order to sustain this favourite effect, the Surrealists have by and large discarded words like *comme* or *tel que*, since these expressions have come to be considered as painstaking and even pedantic, inasmuch as they alert the reader to the fact that a comparison is being made. Explicit analogy in the form of simile has given way to 'modern' imagery as understood since Apollinaire and Reverdy, whereby the poet provokes the abrupt encounter of words, thrusting disparate entities together in the most unpredictable, most violent way. In the present poem, Breton makes use of 'compact' or incisive images; the predicative metaphor ('L'air était une splendide rose') or the genitival metaphor ('mer de pierreries'). These formulations lose no time in pairing tenor and vehicle, relying on one insignificant word to provide the syntactical link. This being common Surrealist practice, it is striking that, towards the end of the poem, Breton should twice use the almost 'obsolete' word *comme* to introduce an image. In a context of bold and unhesitant metaphor, the cautious simile slows down the flux of images. This effect of *ralentando* is important in that it allows a lull before the final thrust of the genitival metaphor 'cuisses de verre'. This appears at the very end as the triumphant culmination of the poem.

VISUAL PATTERNS. One of the weaknesses of the Surrealist poetic method is that it does not allow for the careful elaboration of a theme that will arouse the reader's more slothful responses and convey a recognized emotion. It is characteristically Surrealist that the images in Breton's poem should be predominantly *visual*. The Surrealist rarely troubles to develop a single image in a given context, so that the reader can usually only react at the visual level, as it were glimpsing images briefly as they shine and fade in swift succession. He is in the position of spectator rather than participant. At first, he is bound to feel *dépaysé* as he looks at what is essentially an *untouchable*, indeed a dematerialized world, existing only in so far as an image may be said to exist – as a mental object without substance.[4] However, if the images in the poem are classified, a pattern does begin to emerge, suggesting a certain visual coherence. The things 'seen' by the reader can be grouped under the headings of colours or effects of light; of circular shapes; and of separating pairs.

1. *Colours or effects of light*[5]
    red = une splendide rose couleur de rouget
    blue = roue bleue
    white = papier à cigarettes
          ventre blanc
          velours blanc
    dazzle = reflets
          mer de pierreries
          tu tournais nue
          soleil de feu d'artifice

wan light = demi-jour
       blêmir
       luisait hagard
  transparency = cuisses de verre

2. *Circular shapes* (see illustrations p. 257)
  roue brisée
  grand soleil de feu d'artifice
  radiolaires
  oursin

3. *Separating pairs*
  métal – sa coque
  coquilles de l'oursin
  deux pans du bois écartés
  deux feuilles centrales d'un muguet
  tes cuisses de verre

A preliminary orientation may now be proposed. The point of the poem must be found in large part in the patterns formed by the images and points of reference, and these seem to me to relate above all to a fundamentally Surrealist vision.

There is a fairly recognizable progression in the mention of colours and hues: one has the impression of a dematerialized world in which more or less vivid colours stand out against paler ones. These are in turn outshone by the more dazzling effects of light, which lead ultimately to an effect of complete transparency – pure, colourless light. This aspect of the poem may be thought of as an illustration of the emotional force of desire: in the supreme moment of the lover's vision, the physical world becomes transparent, and all is revealed to him.

It is interesting to note the pattern of references suggesting circular shapes. Though these seem more gratuitous than the effects of light, they appear to illustrate a similar idea: grouped around the image of the Catherine-wheel, and suggesting the blinding dazzle of a sudden miraculous apparition, these circular shapes are metaphors of the poet's state of mind: in the giddy instants of poetic vision, the world appears to spin.

A further aspect of the same Surrealist vision seems to be indicated by the sets of pairs which separate. Here, things moving apart suggest freedom ('Comme si le métal eût enfin secoué sa coque') and revelation. This revelation is certainly of an erotic nature, but not exclusively so. The marvel revealed by the parting of leaves or of thighs may equally well be a poetic vision.

ANALYSIS. The scene is set in a paradoxical way. On the one hand, the reader finds the precise, reassuring detail (it is 1934), and, on the other, he is faced with an initially disconcerting metaphor. The day, though dim, is beautiful, and the air is a splendid rose (ll. 1–2). This indication of the colour red is made explicit by the reference to red mullet.[6] If the *demi-jour* is that of daybreak, then the image is really quite conventional, and is indeed very close to Homer's 'rosy-fingered dawn'.[7] Thus the poem does have a straightforward beginning, though it soon plunges into incoherence.

There is a mood of expectancy as the protagonist prepares to enter a forest.[8] At the forest's edge he comes across a remarkable tree: it has cigarette-paper leaves (ll. 3–4). This suggests flimsiness, a feature that occurs throughout the poem. There is nothing hard or resistant in a world in which all things partake of the fragility and fluidity that typify Surrealist poetry.

The fifth line presents a problem which can frequently arise in poetry lacking punctuation. Michel Butor has shown that Apollinaire, the first French poet to abandon punctuation completely, may have deliberately intended that syntactical ambiguity should play a rôle in his poetry.[9] Breton's poem offers an example of such ambiguity, for there are at least two ways of punctuating lines 3 to 11. One can either place a full-stop after 'dans l'ornière' (l. 10) or after 'papier à cigarettes' (l. 4). In the first case, the two principal subordinate clauses in lines 5 to 11, introduced by the conjunctions *parce que* and *que*, would belong to the first sentence, and therefore constitute explanations of the statement about the tree in line 4. In the second case, these clauses would be attached to the statement in line 11.

The first instance, though syntactically plausible, presents something of a *non sequitur*. The fact of there being odd foliage on a tree is explained by the fact that the poet is waiting for his beloved. One could think of this as an apparent flimsiness caused by the lover's expectancy, an emotional state which a Surrealist mind readily appreciates as being capable of reducing the customary rigidity of objects. That is, the ordinary characteristics of the tree are transformed when witnessed by the passionate lover. However, this explanation does not progress well when one considers the subsequent clauses (ll.

6–10): the second explanation of the tree's appearance is that, wherever the lovers go, the beloved's mouth is the nigella whence rises a blue wheel. This offers no straightforward meaning.

I feel that the second possible punctuation offers a more accessible meaning, and I propose to read the lines in this way (i.e. with a full-stop after *cigarettes* in line 4, and a comma after *ornière* in line 10). The marvellous things that begin to occur as the poet enters the forest ('Tous les prestiges se hâtaient à ma rencontre') are the result of the lover's expectancy ('Parce que je t'attendais'). This is a clear statement of the Surrealist idea that love can determine certain manifestations of the surreal. But this is not all. Looking at the intervening lines (ll. 6–10), one wonders what to make of the startling juxtaposition of mouth, flower, wheel and rut. Various interpretations are possible. A simple solution would be to read this as a purely irrational image, whose function would be to denote the irrationality that Surrealism always associates with love. In prosaic terms: when the lovers walk together, marvellous things can happen, the beloved herself being the source of extraordinary revelations. To go further, one might take *bouche* as indicating a kiss, in which case the wheel that constantly rises up could well denote a sensual experience, one which attains a peak before fading away (*blêmir*, l. 10).

But this is not a conclusive explanation, and only as far on in the poem as line 19 does a hint come as to what the 'roue bleue diffuse et brisée' might mean. It is the reference to 'un grand soleil de feu d'artifice' that finally provides a solution. This can be read as a composite expression bringing together the terms 'un grand feu d'artifice' (a grand display of fireworks) and 'un soleil', a Catherine-wheel. It is now possible to see a reference to this type of firework in lines 9 to 10. There is a wheel which scatters blue sparks ('roue bleue diffuse'), and which rises up and then fades away after falling to the ground ('qui monte/Blêmir dans l'ornière'). The adjective *brisée* would seem to be arbitrary, unless one recalls that St Catherine of Alexandria, who gave her name to the firework, was tortured upon a wheel which, in miraculous circumstances, she broke.[10] In most pictorial representations, she is shown with her emblem, a broken wheel which, moreover, bears spikes around its rim. This particular shape recurs later in the poem.

These lines now become clearer if one sees the Catherine-wheel, spinning and giving off sparks, as an effective metaphor of the kiss, suggesting an overwhelming or vertiginous sensual experience, that dazzles the lover and makes his head spin. What remains obscure is the reference to the flower nigella.[11]

The poet has now entered the forest, an enchanted domain where marvellous things can happen.[12] The first apparition of *le merveilleux* is the squirrel, which clings to the poet in a strange way, its white underbelly against his heart (ll. 12–13). This appears to be a metaphor for the poet's feelings. Associations of softness, purity and tremulousness indicate an innocent acceptance on the part of the poet as he faces a magical world of images over which he has no control. There follows a list of marvels, that evince themselves in a very 'fluid' way.

The word 'fluid' aptly describes the process of careless metamorphosis that goes on in Surrealist poetry. Dissimilar things merge together, the ordinary characteristics of objects are disrupted without warning or apology, and all logic is swept aside in a flood of adjectives and nouns. The infinite malleability of words promotes the infinite malleability of things.

In Breton's poem, the earth, normally a matt surface, becomes smooth enough to give off reflections more impressive than those of water (l. 14). It is as though earth has become an element more fluid than water itself.[13] This is explained in the poem in terms of a similar denial of the ordinary characteristics of a substance (l. 15): to speak of metal shaking off its (hard) shell is to suggest a reversal of the normal character of metal. It is no longer hard, but discloses its inside, soft as the inside of an egg . . . The image is one of freedom, the shaking-off of all restrictions. Now anything seems possible. The hardest substances must yield to the poetic imagination, and allow the poet's eye to penetrate to the heart of things.

The next apparition is that of the beloved, lying naked upon a sea of jewels, and turning towards him (ll. 16–19). There may be a connexion between this sea and the reflections on the earth (l. 14), an explanation being that the earth is covered with jewels that glint in the light like the fireworks referred to a few lines later. The poet seems to be looking down at this vision (he raises his head when it fades, l. 23). On the other hand, these may be incoherent images best appreciated as indications of the poet-lover's capacity for perceiving marvellous changes in the world about him.

For a moment, the poet sees the beloved present before him, lying outstretched upon the surface of the sea. This can suggest a water-sprite, or *ondine*, and this was a favourite association of Breton's for his wife Jacqueline.[14] As she turns, her nakedness – the whiteness of her body – becomes dazzling light. It is interesting to observe that the single word *nue*, constituting a line in itself (l. 18), occurs precisely halfway through the poem, thereby indicating that the beloved's nakedness is the focal point of the poet's attention. The reference to the Catherine-wheel in the next line suggests that her beauty utterly overcomes him: that is, he is as dazzled as if he had looked straight at such a firework, or indeed at the sun itself.

The phrase 'un grand soleil de feu d'artifice' is, however, extraordinarily complex. If 'un soleil de feu d'artifice' signifies a Catherine-wheel, the expression 'un grand soleil' taken by itself means, as Breton has noted elsewhere, a kind of sunflower (*tournesol*). This flower is closely associated with his first meeting with Jacqueline, related in 'La nuit du tournesol'.[15] Though it is doubtful that Breton intended such an allusion, it is also worth noting that *le soleil* can signify an ostensory in the form of a radiating sun.

The cumulative effect of what I feel to be complementary readings must surely be that the apparition of the beloved impresses the poet in an almost mystical way. She is almost motionless, yet the effect she has upon him is so exciting as to call up the firework image. It is a moment of wonder in which both amorous and poetic desire are concentrated upon the same radiant image.

The next lines (ll. 20–21) are obscure. Like some supernatural being, the beloved seems to descend towards him[16] from above, as though emerging from a cluster of radiolaria. The abrupt, ecstatic cry 'Les coquilles même de l'oursin j'y étais' suggests that at this particular moment the poet is lucky enough to join her.

It is important to note the similarity in appearance of the two types of aquatic creature mentioned. Radiolaria and sea-urchins are spherical in form, with emerging spines.[17] Such a configuration is highly reminiscent of the spiked wheel, the Catherine-wheel and the sunflower already mentioned. Thus it is easy to associate the references to these creatures with the miraculous apparition of the beloved. They would seem likewise to have metaphorical connotations of vertigo and dazzlement: the naked beloved appears as a central form whence lines of light radiate like spines. One might alternatively think of the prickly spines (*radioles*) of the sea-urchin as suggesting touch sensations indicative of the lover's febrile desire. The phrase 'les coquilles de l'oursin' implies an opening-up of the soft interior of the creature, a change from hardness to unresistant softness like that of line 15. This is very likely a sexual allusion.[18]

There now comes an interruption of the even flow of the poem as the poet corrects himself: 'Pardon je n'y étais plus'. All at once, he is either in a different place, or no longer grasps what is going on. He has obviously lost his marvellous vision: his beloved is no longer present, and he no longer feels himself to be close to the centre of this poetic universe. The emotion of tremulous desire, symbolized by the squirrel at his heart, is thwarted.

The disappearance of the squirrel at this moment is only stated indirectly. The 'écureuil (au) ventre blanc' (l. 12) is now referred to as 'le vivant écrin de velours blanc' (l. 23). The association of sounds, almost amounting to an echo, makes it clear that Breton is putting forward a metaphor which coincides with that of the squirrel. The jewel-case and the squirrel being identified, the idea of the poet's emotion is associated with jewelry. Indeed, the feelings of half-fearful expectancy symbolized by the tiny animal clinging to his heart are very much akin to the emotion he felt on seeing the sea of jewels on which his beloved was lying. One might also see an equivalence between the *vivant écrin*, with its soft, velvet-lined interior, and the opened sea-urchin.

The disappearance of the squirrel/jewel-case means that the poet is deprived of his vision, and is sad. This sadness is expressed unambiguously (l. 24), before being mirrored in the scene around him (l. 25). The sky seen between the leaves shines with a harsh light, like that on a dragonfly. Though one might expect a dragonfly to represent something poetically appealing, the context indicates that this is an allusion to something the poet finds unattractive. His reaction is to turn from this disappointing prospect by closing his eyes (l. 26). However, the gesture of renunciation is forestalled, and before he can close his eyes, he is suddenly granted a splendid final vision. The wood slides back like two panels opening, and then falls down completely without a sound – a perfectly magical occurrence (ll. 27–8). Images of this kind – walls splitting open, veils being torn – often appear in Surrealist writings, and denote the sudden irruption of surreality. Here, the poet is able to *see through* the wood, and so perceive a new level of reality. In a simile that is drawn out at length in preparation for the *frisson* of the last image, the two panels are compared to two leaves of a huge lily-of-the-valley that are drawn apart (l. 29). The reader, imagining the parting of these leaves, at once sees in his mind's eye the delicate white bell-like flowers on the stem within.

The huge flower of the analogy is large enough to completely enfold the night (l. 30). The line suggests a mood of physical excitement, of heady scents and nocturnal passion, where delicate and seductive sensations are fused. As the wood falls back, the poet sees through to the supreme manifestation of surreality, the woman he loves. The vision is granted in conjunction with a striking synæsthetic image: 'Dans le parfum sonné à toute volée', which equates scent and sound. The tiny bell-like flowers of the lily-of-the-valley are no doubt at the origin of this image.

The moment is one of mystical absorption: the lover is possessed by an overwhelming feeling of the sacred, for he is in the presence of the marvellous object of his desire. His beloved shows herself to him as though she were the supreme miracle he had hoped for. But the poet has only a short moment in which to enjoy this emotion, and so the poem ends on a note of urgency. In a kind of trance and with the utmost reverence, he pays homage to her beauty. Before her thighs return to an unstable daily life, as they must do each day (l. 33), he is able to kiss them.

Thus a sequence of predominantly visual images ends with a reference to touch. All that has been merely seen, passively witnessed, is suddenly brought closer by a surprising fusion of perceptions, and then by actual contact. A dramatic *dénouement* occurs at the very end of the poem as expectancy is fulfilled and the lover, mentally and physically bemused by the awesome presence of his beloved, carries out an act which is not unlike a sacramental ritual. He kneels and communes perfectly with her in an intimate kiss (ll. 34–5).

But this is not a delirious, passionate kiss: it is a strangely *chaste* gesture. The poet's lips touch her thighs – which suggests erotic contact – and yet these thighs instantaneously become glass – a detail which at once attenuates the eroticism and makes of the kiss an expression of sublimated desire. Warm thighs become cold glass, flesh becomes transparent: a substance is transmuted. Thanks to the force of desire (or of poetic vision), the woman's body is transformed into something perfect through which the world can be seen as new, in a pure light that transcends colour. It is as though the dominant fluidity of the poem achieves crystallization at the last: a feeling of meaningful form, of crystalline perfection emerges spontaneously from the Surrealist flux. It is true that glass may suggest fragility and thus ephemerality. Yet it can also denote transparency and purity, glass being, along with crystals and diamonds, a favourite image of perfection for Breton.[19] Therefore, although the moment of revelation may not last for Breton the lover, the perfection of this image achieves a kind of permanency for Breton the poet.

CONCLUSION. Despite some *longueurs*, Breton's poem is a dramatic success. A mood is evoked, and then developed into tension, which is resolved by a final incident. The emotional effect of the poem is to satisfy the reader's taste for something more or less unsettling, whilst avoiding too thorough an assault upon normality. One can still relate to this 'unsettled world', and the poem is surely successful at evoking emotions far enough removed from ordinary emotions to be called 'poetic', but close enough to them to be still thought of as genuine. If the poem offers the reader an insubstantial fantasy, the experience of that fantasy is nonetheless vivid enough to be meaningful to him.

The fascination of Breton's poem derives from its allusions to at least three experiences. It is firstly an account, in Surrealist terms, of a lovers' rendez-vous in a forest, in which expectancy leads up to fulfilment. Secondly, the poem treats of a Surrealist quest, the poetic search for surprising visions, following similar lines of progression (expectancy, disappointment, and eventual satisfaction). Finally, it is a poem that by virtue of this thematic progression bears witness to a fundamental concern in Surrealist poetry, the search for the perfect image. For if the random exploration of possibilities within language, as carried out in Surrealism, has as its aim the discovery of a truth not ordinarily accessible to reason, then Surrealist poems, full of images – some surprising, some disappointing – are products of a vital poetic experiment. They represent the more or less impressive results of an attempt to hit upon the perfect image that, like the philosophers' stone, will turn dull reality into perfect gold.

Breton's poem may be read in these terms, for, progressing to a climax which confounds the normal processes of perception and reason, it sets the stage for a final image to gleam magnificently before the reader. To my mind, the dazzling last image constitutes the main achievement of the poem, which closes, after a succession of half-successful fireworks, with this highly impressive poetic illumination, one that continues to glow within the reader's mind.

NOTES

1 The poem appeared in *L'Air de l'eau*, Editions 'Cahiers d'Art', Paris, 1934 (no pagination), and was reprinted in *Poèmes*, Gallimard, Paris, 1948, pp. 137–8.

2 Cf. an equally misleading poem in *L'Air de l'eau* which begins 'Il allait être cinq heures du matin' (*Poèmes*, p. 141).

3 André Breton: 'Signe Ascendant' in *La Clé des champs*, Sagittaire, Paris, 1953.

4 Cf. Nicolas Calas: 'L'image donc n'est pas autre chose que la sensation d'un objet non perçu – ce serait une forme à laquelle la matière fait défaut.' (*Foyers d'incendie*, Denoël, Paris, 1938, p. 51.)

5 This classification omits those items, such as *bouche* and *oursin*, which do not convey a forcible impression of colour.

6 I take *rouget* to mean 'red mullet', a kind of gurnard. According to the *Grand Larousse Encyclopédique*, this fish is yellow in colour; but since the form of the word suggests redness, it may be assumed that Breton has a *red* fish in mind. It may be noted that the word has several other meanings. It can refer to cow-wheat; the harvest-bug; a disease of pigs; a variety of apple; etc. In the sixteenth century it signified menstruation. My interpretation is perhaps as arbitrary as Breton's choice of the word in the first place.

7 Elsewhere, Breton uses a similar image: 'l'air taillé en rose' (*Poèmes*, p. 199).

8 Though his actual entry is not stated explicitly, the phrase ' à ma rencontre' (l. 11) suggests that he does move forward into the forest.

9 Cf. his article on Apollinaire in *Répertoire III*, Ed. de Minuit, Paris, 1968.

10 Such an explanation would be more convincing if one were dealing with a poem by Nerval. It is quite likely that Breton intended no such reference at all!

11 An association of ideas may be seen between the nigella (love-in-a-mist), which grows in cornfields, and the reference to a wheel in a rut (ll. 9–10). On the other hand, there exists an entirely distinct word *la nielle* which signifies a type of blight affecting wheat (smut or purples). This is black in colour, which may account for its association with the flower, which has poisonous black seeds. (Both words should be distinguished from *le nielle*, meaning niello, or inlaid enamel-work.) In the circumstances, Breton seems to have left his reader with a wide range of possible meanings, though I can find no satisfying interpretation.

12 The forest is Romanticism's legacy to Surrealism. It frequently appears in Surrealist writings as a *lieu privilégié*, a mysterious domain associated with night, enchantment and eroticism. The present context calls to mind Breton's admission ' J'ai toujours incroyablement souhaité de rencontrer la nuit, dans un bois, une femme belle et nue . . .' (*Nadja*, Gallimard, Paris 1928, p. 46). A similar fantasy in his *Poisson Soluble* (ch. 24) shows that Breton was fond of this idea.

13 I find it more poetic to read this passage as a *rêverie* in the Bachelard sense, whereby the imagination penetrates the ordinarily unyielding substance of the earth; although it could be argued more prosaically that these reflections are simply caused by puddles in the ruts previously mentioned, and that these have turned the forest floor into a kind of mirror reflecting the trees ('profonds reflets').

14 Cf. 'La nuit du tournesol' in *L'Amour fou*, in which Breton reveals that, previous to their meeting, Jacqueline had in fact worked in a music-hall in a kind of aquatic ballet. It may be legitimate to associate the title of Breton's collection *L'Air de l'eau* with the *ondine*, who, like the dragonfly mentioned later on (l. 25), is a creature that moves at the limit of air and water.

15 Cf. *L'Amour fou*, Gallimard reprint, Paris 1966, pp. 55–6. Breton mentions the expression in connexion with his poem 'Vigilance', which also deals with the theme of a moment of magical vision. This poem contains the line ' Je vois les arêtes du soleil', which also corresponds to the present context, and points to a quite remarkable unity of visual imagery in Breton's poetry.

16 Taking *descendre* to be intransitive, one can read this as indicating that the beloved is an intangible emanation deriving from a cluster of microscopic organisms. It is less helpful to take the verb as transitive.

17 This applies to at least one type of radiolaria, though there is a wide variety of shapes. Most seem to have perforated skeletons, according to a sketch in the *Grand Larousse Encyclopédique* (1903). A sketch in the 1951 *Petit Larousse Illustré* shows a spherical form with pseudopodes (spines) radiating from it. A similar sketch in the *Encyclopaedia Britannica* (1964, article on 'Protozoa') is very reminiscent of a Catherine-wheel. (See illustrations p. 257.)

18 Gratuitous references to such creatures as the sea-urchin, the oyster, the turtle and the axolotl are a feature of the poems in *L'Air de l'eau*. It is possible, of course, that sea-urchins did have particular significance for Breton. A reference to a sea-urchin in his poem 'Fata morgana' (cf. *Poèmes* p. 188) is mentioned by Micheline Bounoure in an article on the symbolism of this creature, following a text by Jean Palou on the same theme, 'De l'œuf de serpent à l'oursin' (*La Brèche* No. 2, May, 1962, pp. 45–8). Philippe Audouin contributes a further article, 'De près et de loin' (*La Brèche* No. 4, Feb. 1963, pp. 37–41). These texts reveal a whole 'constellation' of esoteric symbols: *oursin, hérisson, châtaigne, étoile, œuf de serpent*, etc., which represent the principle of life, the primordial fire, and immortality. The *oursin* has alchemical significance, and Breton's sensitivity to the poetic qualities of esoteric symbolism is well-known. However, any undertones of alchemical allegory in the poem seem to me to be accidental. I prefer to take the present reference as a sexual one, bearing in mind that Surrealism does conceive of desire as a force capable of effecting a 'transmutation' of reality.

19 In *L'Amour fou* (p. 14), Breton writes of the 'artistic lesson' given by crystals, which take on the qualities of hardness, regularity and lustrousness with an altogether admirable spontaneity.

*Source*
André Breton (1896–1966): *Poèmes*, Gallimard, Paris, 1948, pp. 137–8.

Margaret M. Callander

---

*JOUVE*
Pays d'Hélène

JOUVE

*Pays d'Hélène*

C'est ici que vécut incomparable Hélène

Ici l'ancien lieu de verdure et d'argent
Les larmes de rochers
Un soupir bleu mais des déchirures pensives
5 Un noir éclatement de rocs argentés

Inhumaine inimaginable en robe à traîne
Qu'elle était belle vêtue de rochers
Et costumée des fleurs de l'herbe! Dans les grand soirs
Des maisons hautes blanches et nues, grillagées

10 Qu'elle était nue, et triste! et quel amour aux mains
Et quelle force aux reins de sa splendeur rosée
Qu'elle avait pour aimer et pour vivre! et quel sein
Pour nourrir! et les douces pensées
De son ombre! et comme elle sut bien mourir

15 Dans un baiser rempli de palmes et de vallées.

On voit ici ses larmes
Conservées dans ce couloir vert du cimetière
Un immense noyer endormi par le jour
Tient à ses pieds les tombes perles de couleur

20 Quand le noyer touche aux glaces penchées
Étincelantes du glacier de l'autre bord
Où cinq dents d'argent difformes du malheur
Luisent
Sur le gouffre harmonie d'éternelle chaleur.

25 Prairie du jour! avec les flots et les forêts
De maigre vert et les roches du ciel
Ta pureté céleste cri cruel
Fait mal, comme une morte ici marchait.

Hélène aimait-elle glaciers et noyers
30 Passait-elle son bras nu sur ces montagnes
Baisait-elle de sa robe les prairies,
Dans les yeux de son amant jeune espérait-elle
Et la lumière d'or ?

Loin, les rochers d'Hélène
35 Découpés par le soleil des funérailles
Luisaient au milieu des dents noires et dures
Et le soleil se déchirait religion pure.

Pays d'Hélène takes its place in the unified sequence of poems called *Hélène* and first published separately in 1936. This group forms the first part of *Matière céleste* (1937). The poem is an elegiac meditation on the pervasive presence of a dead and beloved woman. It therefore can be fairly easily related to a familiar poetic tradition, especially as it is cast in a recognizable lyrical form. The mourning of a surviving lover, a connection set up between love and death, the evocation of an earthly tomb coupled with a eulogistic lament, these are the associations that this theme suggests in its metamorphoses through classical or Renaissance or nineteenth-century literature, through Dante and Shakespeare, Ronsard and Mallarmé. Since such associations will inevitably come into play in some measure, this view of the poem is tantamount to seeing it 'for itself', that is, as an artistic unity important for what its specific language and imagery can achieve, independent of its creator and its genesis. Alternatively the poem may be seen as so intimately bound up with its author's life, psychological identity, and creative singularity as to be inseparable from such data. Again, it is possible to approach it as an integral part of a particular creative development, one element in the unity of one man's work.

A compromise would seem desirable. Certainly this poem is wholly accessible to linguistic analysis and to a fairly detailed appreciation by any reader. Too close an identification of its elements with biographical detail might well prove a dangerously limiting approach. But it is difficult not to believe that a poem that has been conceived as part of a sequence will not gain from being seen in this context. Its autonomy must be the dominant concern, but it would be foolish to neglect available knowledge if a wide interpretation rather than an 'explication de texte' is being attempted, so long as this is seen as at all times ancillary.

However this pattern must remain very flexible. Clearly, if one is dealing with a well-known and well-documented poet, with Hugo or with Baudelaire for example, his general conceptions and attitudes need only be alluded to. With Jouve we are concerned with a poet who is not well known to the common reader, and whose metaphysical and psychological attitudes are peculiarly individual. Glosses, therefore, seem necessary on the major terms used throughout his poetry as well as in the poem under consideration.

'Peut-être est-ce avec Hélène que l'œuvre de Jouve donne forme à son vrai *mythe*':[1] this is Jean Starobinski's assessment of the importance of the Hélène figure for Jouve. Her image dominates *Matière céleste*, appears in *Kyrie* (1938) and *La Vierge de Paris* (1946), and forms a link with Jouve's prose fiction of this period through the character of Hélène de Sannis in *Dans les années profondes*.[2] Jouve offers precise documentation for all the incarnations of this figure in *En Miroir* (1954),[3] and this is augmented in conversations recorded by René Micha.[4] The figure is a composite one, and the three women who go to form it were known to Jouve at widely separated periods in his life. The most unexpected evidence, however, is that the last of these women, the one who meant most to Jouve, was not dead when the *Hélène* sequence was written, nor did he know that she was in fact to die some two years later. Likewise, the mountain landscape which might seem to be her essential context was not connected with her in reality, although well known to Jouve himself. The question of genesis is seen, therefore, to be prophetic-seeming and oblique.

Jouve's attitude to love and death cannot be separated from his religious preoccupations. One of his lines of development leads to the idea of sacrifice, with, of course, the sacrifice of Christ as an extreme exemplar. A specific example of human sacrifice is seen in *Dans les années profondes*, where the death of Hélène de Sannis at the moment of sexual union releases in her young lover a new spiritual being. The clear parallels in atmosphere and imagery between this story and *Matière céleste* allow us to presuppose this event behind the poetic manifestation of Hélène. It may well be argued that a metaphysic so contorted that within it an act of substitution appears essential to salvation denies the human reality of the Hélène figure and lessens the dignity and pathos of the lament. However, in artistic terms she offers a principle of enrichment; through her it becomes possible for Jouve to re-orientate positively his whole poetic world. From this point of view *Pays d'Hélène* is important because in it words do not have their previous significances, and because it consolidates hitherto tenuous evidences of grace and possibilities of reconciliation.

In *Le Paradis perdu* (1929) Jouve had exemplified his need to redefine the theological basis of his poignant and daily sense of the reality of original sin. Since this sin is here identified primarily with the sexual union of Adam and Eve, Jouve can conclude – 'O Péché! . . . Tu te nommeras Vie ou Eve à jamais',[5] and this emphasis seems inescapable to him. The certainty is developed in *Sueur de sang* (1935) where an intense, turbulent and disturbing amalgam of explicitly Freudian material and Christian imagery displays the interrelation of 'inconscient, spiritualité et catastrophe',[6] seen by Jouve as terrifying and incalculable, and appearing even more obscure than in Blake or Baudelaire. However, Jouve's hope of salvation and his knowledge of sublimation combined to call into question the irreversibility of this condition. He offers the formula 'Le péché devient mouvement',[7] suggesting that it is man's responsibility to provoke a dangerous but crucial dynamism, escaping from a doomed and repetitive act not by abstention but by transformation.

This ambivalence of 'la belle puissance érotique humaine'[8] is paralleled for Jouve by that of death. Here he was seeking formulation for the differing views: death as the termination of life, the wages of sin, and an element in all unsanctified experience, the 'natural' trend of man's spirit seeming so resolutely to be towards a mortal violence, destruction and apathy – and at the same time death not only as a prelude to a new life but, more urgently, as a quickened force of grace for this earth. 'O double Mort! Tu es l'absolu du péché de la terre, et tu es sans doute le réceptacle de l'esprit saint, selon que Dieu se tourne'.[9] Finally, some divine intervention must set its seal on any such experience.

In the first line of *Pays d'Hélène* the powerful clear-cut statement of the essential fact of the poem appears in a perfect isolated alexandrine. The finality of the past tense, the constructional freedom that allows for 'pauses' around 'incomparable', the terminal force given to the name 'Hélène', all these things go to increase the sense of a momentous event and a majestic presence. The whole of the rest of the poem, with its consistent use of a different past tense, evokes retrospectively the living presence of Hélène as it is identified with a particular landscape of grass and snow.

There is no trace in the poem of the anecdotal, no circumstantial recall of past happiness, no conventional word of mourning for present loss. The exclamation or question form for certain lines, the use of 'on voit', suggests a human response to the death of Hélène. The poem is warmed by the oblique evocation of physical and emotional union. But there is no specifically individual lover figure, no 'je' whose emotions may be charted, partly because for Jouve this evocation crystallizes at a point just beyond the individual, and partly because it is conceived as the celebration of a mystery.

Characteristics of the first line recur throughout the poem, the name Hélène appears twice more, towards the end, and is each time placed with emphasis at the beginning or the end of a line. (It is debatable whether Jouve means there to be an allusion in this name to the Greek Helen, as an exemplar of memorable beauty and erotic power, or whether the sound of the name made an appeal to him.) In this, a relatively early work of Jouve's poetic maturity, he shows a mastery in the use of spacing, for lines, phrases, and words. Punctuation is minimal; the two or three commas are used to create special pauses, perhaps as in music; the more frequent exclamation marks and the question mark emphasize a sense of awe and wonder, and help to determine the suggestion of a celebratory almost liturgical stylization of form; much less noticeable full stops terminate certain groupings. But most of the rhythmic movement of the poem is brought about by the relation of pauses to the placing of words and phrases, and the conjunction of certain words and groupings, due in part to lack of punctuation. To this must be added the effect of Jouve's habitual syntactical and grammatical freedom, and the particular form chosen here in which lines of unequal length appear in semi-regular groups of four or five. All this conveys the feeling of an undefiant but integral independence in artistry.

When the 'ici' of the first line is repeated and identified as 'l'ancien lieu de verdure et d'argent' Jouve has set in motion the endlessly flexible and allusive process by which Hélène is totally identified with all the features of a defined landscape, so totally that they eventually seem to exist only in her. The subtle and rapid interplay of these images may recall perhaps something of the more dazzling conceits in the Shakespearian sonnets that Jouve had at this period begun translating. It may be noted that this landscape can be identified as the Alpine Soglio, in the Engadine, a place singled out by Jouve for the mysterious sense of significance in its beauty: 'A Soglio, pourrait-on dire sans nulle littérature, les imaginations de la mort et de l'amour se fondent en un fracas splendide . . . Les caractères du mythe existent dans les formes mêmes de la nature'.[10] Mountains and snow, grass and trees form a simple but contrasting whole, and it is the play of these elements that is reflected in Hélène's body, her hair and eyes, her bones and limbs.

It is the contrasts within the landscape that Jouve accentuates in lines 3–5, either in the conjunction of unexpected elements – 'Les larmes de rochers', 'noir/argentés', or by the overt use of 'mais'. Its 'humanization' is established in 'larmes', 'soupir', and 'pensive', while the terms 'déchirures' and 'éclatement', recalling the original geographical formation of the landscape, suggest an energy or violence of the natural elements that have here, as elsewhere in the poem, sexual connotations. It is interesting that in this, one of the longest poems of the cycle, the expression is still very concentrated, so that the phrase 'Les larmes de rochers' seems an elliptical version of, for example, 'Les monts brillants sont des réceptacles de larmes';[11] however, Jouve does here have wide scope for his allusive method in which certain features or images recur in changing manifestations and relationships. The 'larmes' which are here identified with the scattered areas of ice become later the 'tombes perles de couleur' of the funeral landscape (l. 19).

The juxtaposition of the goddess-like figure of Hélène suggests a calm domination, as though the contrasting elements of the first 'verse' are to be seen as held at a point of tension, with still a dangerous potential, but subject to an overriding influence. Evoking an Hélène who is the 'genius loci', 'vêtue de rochers Et costumée des fleurs de l'herbe', an Hélène who is the paradigm of generous love, Jouve uses a meditatively exclamatory style for the phrases whose repeating and answering rhythms emphasize the key words, that sequence of adjectives, nouns and verbs that is swept towards the climax of 'mourir'. A pervasive but restrained sensuality is suggested by the rich use of many plurals, by the placing of an abstract noun (splendeur) with a material term (rosée), by the initial tempering aloofness of 'inhumaine' and 'inimaginable'. All possible aspects of Hélène and the area of experience connected with her are touched upon: beauty, majesty, power, a strain of melancholy, and a relationship set up between the realities of physical passion (as in the assonanced 'mains', 'reins' and 'sein') and the positive emotional and spiritual force of 'aimer' and 'vivre' and 'nourrir', all very simple words but given a richness of significance by their positioning, parallel or antithetical. There is in fact a movement from the descriptive static evocation of Hélène to a point where the gathering momentum suggests that she is not only an active and generous participant in the act of love but is in some sense in control of the orientation of her experience. She seems to mobilize the dynamism of her acts in such a way that death does not differ from them in kind

and is treated as the necessary condition that allows for the gift of
regenerated life. The concept 'mourir' appears unexpectedly at the
end of a series of affirmatory phrases, but its significance is not terminal; it gives place to the rush of warmth and richness in the
isolated line 'Dans un baiser rempli de palmes et de vallées'. Jouve is
attempting the difficult task of integrating the idea of death into life
and at the same time suggesting a spiritual triumph over it. He does
not give a statement of this intention, but tries for a solution in
purely poetic terms, in accordance with his view of poetry as 'la vie
même du grand Eros morte et par là survivante'.[12]

The idea of the 'baiser rempli de palmes et de vallées' reminds us
how consistent Jouve's imagery is with the context of an Alpine
scene, because 'palmes' affords an apparent deviation. Its Biblical
echoes, its suggestion of richness and of spiritual victory serve to
emphasize a supreme experience at this the climax of the poem. This
leads to a further reflection: perhaps imagery is a misleading word to
use of this poem where we seem to be experiencing the insurgence of
a total imagined world whose features are being enumerated. Some
elements in Jouve's style recall Baudelaire, but he is certainly not
using the Baudelairean method of moving perceptibly from a limited
physical experience in the real world towards the freedom of a vast
imaginary world. The type of creative vision is closer to Rimbaud's,
but a better parallel would be perhaps with the *Spiritual Canticle* of
St John of the Cross, where a whole landscape is identified with, and
as it were created by, the object of love.

In the next section of the poem Jouve returns to the landscape,
evoking features already named and introducing new ones, but here
a closer relationship is set up with Hélène's death. The landscape is
seen as her tomb, the allusions become funereal. The words 'cimetière', 'tombes', 'funérailles' are used, but the constructions seem to
emphasize that this is not a new function for the landscape; it seems
always to have reflected the death as well as the life of Hélène. In 'ce
couloir vert du cimetière', in the idea of the 'tombs' at the foot of
the walnut tree, there is a powerful attempt to suggest a simple
indivisible reality. In this group of thirteen lines there is no direct
reference to Hélène, but the whole development is unified by a
mysterious intensity of feeling. The walnut tree recalls the tradition
of planting trees upon tombs, rocks and ice are seen as gravestones,[13]
but there is no bitterness of grief. The walnut tree performs a strange

unifying function as it stretches out and seemingly touches the high glaciers while its roots are in the soil below the green of the valley.

But Jouve does not mean to present a wholly softened world. The sharp contrast between bare peaks and lush valley is at all times maintained, and this contrast is used to increase the sense of a remarkable unifying principle that can transcend contradiction while embodying it. 'L'autre bord' becomes more than a geographical fact, it reveals a difference of significance. The 'cinq dents d'argent difformes du malheur' represent the pain and suffering of death, and the harsh and menacing elements in human life, but they also suggest the austere, almost inhuman climate of spiritual 'dénuement'. They are the 'dents noires et dures' (l. 36), but it is their relation with the 'gouffre harmonie d'éternelle chaleur' that produces the 'pureté céleste cri cruel'.

The last two quoted phrases illustrate Jouve's frequent use of juxtaposition where a simile might possibly be expected. Indeed his use of constructions here suggests identification rather than comparison, and the relation of subordinate to main is minimized. The absence of a half-expected 'si' in 'comme une morte ici marchait' changes a suggestion into a conviction.

At line 25 there is a new crystallization around the idea of the 'Prairie du jour'. In the latter sections of the poem light, day, the sun are recurring allusions, and seem related to the idea of life itself. An uneven sweeping rhythm runs from 'Prairie du jour!', so strong that the enumerative technique used by Jouve can in no way appear static. There is the ripple of the Alpine meadow, expressed in a sea image ('flots' also suggests the revivifying waters of grace, as well as carrying a sexual allusion), and a movement up through the more austere green of the conifers to the mountains above and the sky, and for Jouve this cannot be separated from the overwhelming and haunting quality of its spiritual identity. Alliteration underlines these effects, and reminds us of the frequent use of assonance in this poem and of Jouve's consistent attention to sound groupings (at their most apparent in contrasts between quick harsh sounds and rich long ones, e.g. 'cinq dents d'argent difformes du malheur' / 'le gouffre harmonie d'éternelle chaleur').

A parallel to lines 6 to 15 appears in more concentrated form in lines 29–33 where there is the most intimate and direct evocation of Hélène's relationship to the landscape and to her lover. Its simplicity is qualified by the sense of wonder and mystery conveyed by the question form. Here, as elsewhere in the poem, Jouve does not address Hélène directly; all memory, speculation and statement is indirect, and this is one of the ways in which Jouve stresses her strange power. Even here she seems a divinity: 'Passait-elle son bras nu sur ces montagnes'; at the same time the warmth of her presence is suggested in the repetitive verb constructions. A more personal sense is here given to her love by the introduction of 'son amant jeune', and the word 'jeune' recalls that the Léonide of *Dans les années profondes* is indeed very much younger than Hélène de Sannis, and that one of her rôles is a maternal-seeming one, alluded to also in the 'quel sein Pour nourrir!' of lines 12–13. The life-giving strength of this love is related to the 'lumière d'or' of the sun,[14] shortly afterwards to be identified as 'le soleil des funérailles',[15] and ultimately to be used as the image of sacrifice, suggesting tenderness and violence and a spiritual perfection: 'Et le soleil se déchirait religion pure.'

In this last 'verse' there is, then, a withdrawal from direct human contact; the final line offers an oblique rendering of the poem's subject and an indication of the scope of its final significance. The data are similar to those in lines 1 to 5 but there is a sense both of a greater humanization and of a greater aloofness. 'Loin' has the same distancing effect as 'ancien' but a more final effect. The rocks now belong specifically to Hélène and the sunset landscape appears arrested for ever in a spiritually determined stasis, in spite of the effect of the verbs. It is the rocks and the light that at the end are emphasized. The 'cinq dents noires et dures' retain their menace even when integrated into the spiritual pattern; it is the light that holds all the elements together in their triumphant tension.

The natural world is as tainted by original sin as the human person, in Jouve's eyes, and he called Satan a 'vraie puissance obsidionale de la terre'.[16] The sense of release and transformation in this poem cannot therefore be overestimated. Elsewhere he may express it with a greater sense of plenitude –

Elle s'en va gonfler jusqu'au haut des arbres
Elle couvre le plus froid du fronton de la nature[17]

or with a more precise suggestion of spiritual distillation:

Le péché remontant jusque dans son sourire
Défait la terre et la transforme en air;[18]

Here, however, the expression is more oblique, and the effect less clear-cut. Remoteness, poignancy, and a dark and painful intensity are complemented in the final lines by the effects of light and the feeling, conveyed by the tense, of an unmeasurable spiritual trans-formation in its moment of unseen action.

Jouve calls the poet 'le créateur des valeurs de la vie';[19] here it is solely with regenerate life that we have to do. Through the Beatri-cean figure of Hélène unregenerate matter, lover and landscape alike, is touched by a grace and granted a new harmonious life with its own melancholy beauty and privileged intensity. In the sequence of Jouve's work the dark and violent precipitate of passion that dominates *Sueur de sang* gives place to a diffused and spiritualized sensuality. The poem *Pays d'Hélène* impresses most, perhaps, by the quality of its unity. There is an obvious kind of unification, as in the major use of the two stated colours, green and silver-white, with the accompaniment of blackness and the glow of flesh and sunlight. Then there is the more subtle repetition and varying of motifs in a way closely allied to music. This is a poem to which words like simple and sophisticated do not seem to apply. It is elaborate and emphatic, and its subtleties are not the result of controlled simplicity; there are apparently deliberate checks to any easy lyrical flow. But it has an extraordinary purity and poetic integrity, a rich poignancy and a strange quality of beauty. There is a sureness about it, both aesthe-tic and spiritual, that seems to come from a rare unity of imaginative intensity.

NOTES

1 *Pierre-Jean Jouve, poète et romancier*, La Baconnière, Neuchâtel, 1946, p. 45.
2 In *La Scène capitale*, Gallimard, 1935.
3 pp. 67–78.
4 In *Poètes d'aujourd'hui*, no. 48, Seghers, Paris, 1956, pp. 55–62.
5 *Le Paradis perdu*, p. 106.
6 *Poésie*, Mercure de France, Paris, 1964, p. 125.
7 *Commentaires*, La Baconnière, Neuchâtel, 1950, p. 69.
8 *Poésie*, p. 130.
9 *Commentaires*, p. 47.
10 *En Miroir*, p. 76.
11 *Poésie*, p. 222.
12 *Poésie*, p. 129.
13 Cf. 'ses larmes marbres', *Poésie*, p. 227.
14 In *Dans les années profondes*, Hélène is described as 'une femme hélianthe'.

15 Cf. another evocation of the sun as a death-image: 'vers l'autre plus cend-reux soleil', *Poésie*, p. 224.
16 *Commentaires*, p. 69.
17 *Poésie*, p. 231.
18 Ibid., p. 226.
19 Ibid., p. 129.

*Source*
Pierre-Jean Jouve (b. 1887): *Poésie* I–IV, 1925–38, Mercure de France, Paris, 1964, pp. 218–20.

C.H. Wake

---

ÉLUARD
L'Extase

*L'Extase*

Je suis devant ce paysage féminin
Comme un enfant devant le feu
Souriant vaguement et les larmes aux yeux
Devant ce paysage où tout remue en moi
5 Où des miroirs s'embuent où des miroirs s'éclairent
Reflétant deux corps nus saison contre saison

J'ai tant de raisons de me perdre
Sur cette terre sans chemins et sous ce ciel sans horizon
Belles raisons que j'ignorais hier
10 Et que je n'oublierai jamais
Belles clés des regards clés filles d'elles-mêmes
Devant ce paysage où la nature est mienne

Devant le feu le premier feu
Bonne raison maîtresse
15 Etoile identifiée
Et sur la terre et sous le ciel hors de mon cœur et dans mon cœur
Second bourgeon première feuille verte
Que la mer couvre de ses ailes
Et le soleil au bout de tout venant de nous

20 Je suis devant ce paysage féminin
Comme une branche dans le feu.

24 novembre 1946

THIS POEM celebrating the ecstasy of the lover in communion with his beloved acquires a certain pathos from the fact that it was written only four days before the death of Éluard's wife Nusch. They had been happily married for seventeen years, and Nusch had been a constant inspiration in the life of a poet whose main theme was love and who needed to live his love in order to write about it. *L'Extase* is to be found near the beginning of *Le Temps déborde* (1947). This volume is almost entirely devoted to the expression not only of Éluard's grief but also of the intense, hopeless despair he felt after the loss of his wife. Two poems after *L'Extase*, Éluard records Nusch's death:

Vingt-huit novembre mil neuf cent quarante-six

Nous ne vieillirons pas ensemble.

   Voici le jour

     En trop: le temps déborde.

Mon amour si léger prend le poids d'un supplice.

Seen side by side, these two poems reveal one of the essential features of Éluard's personality. His desire for absolute joy was so great that when he lost it, it was replaced by an almost equally absolute despair. The tension between these two states is one of the most striking aspects of Éluard's poetry.

The essential nature of the poet's ecstasy, as expressed in *L'Extase*, is contained in the first line of the poem: 'Je suis devant ce paysage féminin'. It is a state of contemplation. It is an all-absorbing contemplation, with the implication of a distance between the poet and his beloved. Like the child lost, as only a child can be, in his contemplation of the fire, the poet is mesmerized by his *paysage féminin*. 'Souriant vaguement et les larmes aux yeux' is grammatically ambiguous, with striking effect. Does it refer to the child or to the poet? The ambiguity brings the two together in a kind of poetic shorthand. *Paysage* is the strongest word in the first line. The poet probably intends us to think of a country scene, so that the effect of this image is to suggest something aesthetically beautiful, with only a hint of sensuality. It also suggests that love is a whole 'world', not just the limited external appearance of a person. Reference to the beloved's femininity, and therefore, in a love poem, to her sensual appeal, is relegated to second place by the use of an adjective, *féminin*. This word simply establishes the sex of the poet's *paysage*, but almost obliquely, and personifies the metaphor. The opening words of the poem are in a form of words frequently found in lyrical poetry. At the side of *paysage*, they are almost unobtrusive, but they are brought to life by the simile in line 2. The first line sets the scene, while the second helps to establish the mood. This is because the latter is a more precise, simple everyday image which the reader visualizes immediately. The word *feu* refers metaphorically to the same reality as the word *paysage*, and of course in lyric poetry it has old associations with the love theme. But the two words are contrasted by the essential passivity of a *paysage*, and the essential vitality of a fire. The alliteration on *feu/féminin* emphasizes the link between the two lines and perhaps already points to the way the theme will develop.

The second half of the first stanza introduces the notion of communion between the lovers, but a communion which still has a basic element of separation. 'Devant ce paysage où tout remue en moi' is deliberately paradoxical to make the image more striking. Its meaning is clarified in the next two lines by the image of the mirrors and the word *reflétant*. *Remue* therefore describes the reflection of the woman/*paysage* in the poet's eyes. The repetition of *devant*, the picture of separate mirrors, the *deux corps nus* all emphasize separation. But they are united on a spiritual level. *Où tout remue en moi* conveys effectively the intimacy and yet separation of the lovers. The image of the mirrors is frequently found in Éluard's poetry. In this poem, alongside predominantly natural imagery, it has something of the air of a conceit, a little reminiscent of John Donne.*

The eyes have always fascinated people, not only poets. Because of their mysterious quality, like the depths of a bottomless pool, they seem to be a direct external link with the soul. They certainly have this association for Éluard. In this poem he suggests it, for instance, in the line: 'Belles clés des regards clés filles d'elles-mêmes'. Éluard adds a dimension to this image with the notion of mutual reflection and the consequent 'metaphysical' idea of communion. Perhaps the strongest emotional desire of the lover is to be completely united physically with the beloved. This is impossible because of the distinctness of the lovers' bodies (*deux corps nus*). But we are a long way, here, from the sensuality of physical love. Everything suggests, instead, the notion of purity: the underlying theme of contemplation, the 'metaphysical' nature of the mirror image, and, influenced by

* The theme and imagery of this poem closely resemble Donne's *The Extasie*.

these, even the phrase *deux corps nus*. The overall effect of this first stanza is to suggest a static state of contemplation, with the hint of an undercurrent of vitality in the words *feu* and *remue*. The mirrors reflecting one another suggest that all else is excluded, a theme also taken up, by implication, in lines 8 and 16. Ecstasy would not be ecstatic if it did not seem eternal, for the abolition of time is of the essence of this state. Thus eternity is suggested, not only in the endlessly reflecting mirrors, but also in the phrase *saison contre saison*. Metaphorically it is associated with the *paysage* image, and it is given a certain emphasis because it is not idiomatic. It is probably a concentrated version of two usually distinct phrases: *en saison* and *à contre-saison*.

The second stanza is encased in the predominant image of the first: the *paysage*. It also adds a new dimension to it. The poet can lose himself in this *paysage féminin*: 'me perdre / Sur cette terre sans chemins et sous ce ciel sans horizon' (l. 7). In the same way as time is abolished, so too is the need for a sense of purpose (*sans chemins*). Love, or rather ecstasy, is an end in itself. In addition, the joy of ecstasy is boundless (*sans horizon*). The overall impact of this line, as I have already indicated, is the exclusion of everything foreign to the poet's joy. It is absolute.

The second stanza is centred, however, around the dominant word *raisons* and the two lines:

Belles raisons que j'ignorais hier
Et que je n'oublierai jamais.

They are striking because they are abstractions in a poem otherwise based entirely on imagery. Éluard's purpose is to show that, unlike the real or everyday world, where the rational and experience are distinct, in complete love they are identical (*clés filles d'elles-mêmes*). His reasons for loving cannot be divorced from his experience. This is linked, I think, with the idea common to poets of Éluard's generation, that the rational is artificial and to be avoided; all that counts is concrete reality or experience. Éluard makes his point in this poem by transforming the rational into the concrete. When it is first used in line 7, the word *raisons* is associated, intentionally, with its usual meaning. This is emphasized by adding *tant de*: 'J'ai tant de raisons'. The sort of thing anyone might say. He next refers, not to the idiomatic and more usual *bonnes raisons*, but to *belles raisons*, a word much more appropriate to a *paysage*, to a woman, than to the rational. In other words, the word *raisons* is now associated with the concrete, the aesthetic. His next step is to repeat, not *raisons* but *belles*; *raisons* is replaced by *clés*, metaphorically and visually more closely associated with the poet's theme of the experience of complete happiness in love (so much so that it brings tears to his eyes: *les larmes aux yeux*, line 3, and *s'embuent*, line 5). The transformation is completed in the last line of the stanza by the return to the basic image of the poem: 'Devant ce paysage où la nature est mienne'. The word *nature* is the culmination of the return to the concrete; it contrasts completely with the original meaning of *raisons*. The possessiveness of *mienne* further intensifies this state of affairs. In line 14, the next stanza, Éluard returns to his *raisons* and this time actually refers to *bonne raison*. But he can do this quite safely because the word has already been redefined for the imagination. *Bonne* now has a gently ironical flavour which once and for all completely undermines the usual meaning of the phrase.

Lines 9 and 10, already referred to, reflect a practice not uncommon in Éluard's poetry: a statement in intellectual terms coming in the middle of a poem characterized by its imagery. It has the effect of emphasizing the presence of the imagery, but I think its main purpose usually is to make with complete clarity a point the poet holds to be of great importance. These two lines express two such ideas: firstly, that the poet's ecstasy is an entirely new experience, without antecedents and without roots in the past (*que j'ignorais hier*), and secondly, that it has irrevocably altered his life (*Et que je n'oublierai jamais*). In this poem, the suggestion is that he has never loved like this before, but elsewhere Éluard tells us that each time one loves it is an absolute experience, a complete renewal. An example of this is these lines from *Vivre*:

J'ai vécu plusieurs fois mon visage a changé
A chaque seuil à chaque main que j'ai franchis
Le printemps familial renaissait . . .
. . . . . . . . . . . . . . . . . . . . . . . . . . . . . . . . . . . .
Mon âge m'accordait toujours
De nouvelles raisons de vivre par autrui
    (*Le Livre Ouvert* 1)

The third stanza returns to the imagery of the first two lines, but this time the fire is given the place of first importance. It opens the stanza and it is no longer merely a simile dependent on a more important image. The association between the images of the first lines of the poem is recalled here by echoing the last line of the second stanza and the first line of the third stanza: 'Devant ce paysage. . ./ Devant le feu.' The establishment of the fire image as one of primary importance, on the same level as the *paysage* image, prepares us for the dramatic confrontation of the two images in the last two lines. The specific theme of this stanza is that love is the fundamental human experience. It is the focal point for all other experience: *premier feu, bonne raison maîtresse, étoile identifiée*. As he wrote the first line of this stanza, Éluard may well have been thinking of an earlier, celebrated poem of his, *Pour Vivre Ici*, in which the fire stood for the essential reality of life when all else is unobtainable. Throughout his poetry, the image of the fire always remained the chief symbol of life and of love.

Je fis un feu, l'azur m'ayant abandonné,
Un feu pour être son ami,
Un feu pour m'introduire dans la nuit d'hiver,
Un feu pour vivre mieux.

All the imagery in this stanza suggests convergence towards a focal point. We are left with a single, *bonne raison maîtresse*, which is the *premier feu*, the *étoile identifiée*. Similarly, *second bourgeon, première feuille verte* concentrates the imagination on a focal detail. These images all lead up to the last line of the stanza: 'Et le soleil au bout de tout venant de nous'. The centre of the poet's world (*au bout de tout*) is the sun, the symbol of life and joy, warmth and happiness throughout Éluard's poetry. It is another form of the fire image. But it is not only the centre, the heart of the love universe; it is brought into being by the communion of the lovers (*venant de nous*). This image could, of course, simply express location, but I think it has this notion of creation by the lovers because the poet tells us there is only one sun and that it can only exist when they are in communion. The primary function of the image in line 18 – 'Que la mer couvre de ses ailes' – is to suggest protectiveness. It echoes line 2, where the poet-lover is likened to a child, and it looks forward to the last line of the poem: 'Comme une branche dans le feu'. And, of course, the preceding line, which it qualifies, talks about new birth, that delicate stage of life – and love – which needs protection of a maternal kind. The sea, like the mother bird, folds the lovers in its wings. The sea may symbolize their ecstasy. There may, too, be a deliberate intention on the part of the poet to make a pun on *mer/mère*. The idea of the mother is definitely contained in the line, and one cannot help thinking back to the child in line 2. The image of the sea as something protective and maternal is, of course, deeply rooted in the Romantic subconscious.

The images of the *paysage* and the *feu* having been placed now on the same level, the poem reaches a dramatic climax in the last two lines. This is produced by the paradoxical linking of *devant* and *dans* by *comme*, and is made all the more striking by the visual quality of the image: *comme une branche dans le feu*. The themes of contemplation and identification are brought together in a single experience. The mirrors have, as it were, merged. The *enfant devant le feu* has become *une branche dans le feu*, while at the same time the poet remains *devant ce paysage*. So far in the poem, separation through contemplation has been emphasized, and so has a kind of metaphysical identification. The suggestion contained in the last new image is distinctly physical; it probably refers, in poetic terms, to the physical act of love. Yet it is not really sensual, for it seems to suggest, perhaps because of the rest of the poem, that the poet is consumed in a kind of spiritual holocaust of love. This has already been prepared to some extent by lines 18 and 19, which hint at a kind of vertigo which draws the poet into the depths of his love, and in retrospect we realize that the image in line 2 suggests this as well: the hypnotic effect of the fire could lead to the child falling into it. But to return to the grammatical paradox: linked by *comme, devant* and *dans* are equated, indicating that contemplation and physical identification are one, occurring simultaneously. This bears out something we have already noted. The poet is passive in his ecstasy; it is something that happens to him. First he is a child, then he is a branch. Everything associated with the beloved is protective, maternal. From passive contemplation he passes to passive identification, absorbed by the *feu féminin*. The absence of a verb in the last line – for example, *jetée* or even some form of the verb *être* – not only reinforces the notion of simultaneity mentioned above, it also emphasizes the poet's essential passivity. The poem has, literally, come full circle. The repetition of the same form of words at the beginning and at the end indicates that contemplation and identification are simultaneous, that the poem is about a state of being and that it does not describe a state that develops or changes. This is what one would expect ecstasy to be.

Having examined the theme in some detail, it is important now to look a little more closely at the imagery and the structure.

In the first line, the real (*féminin*) is subordinated to the metaphorical (*paysage*) by reversing the normal order of comparison. In addition, by making the reference to reality an adjective, the real is further pushed into the background. There are only two other references in the poem – *deux corps nus* (l. 6) and *nous* (l. 19) – which remind us that *paysage* is metaphorical. The same kind of effect is achieved with the image of mirrors, but is heightened here because the object likened to mirrors is only implied. I have already indicated the significance of lines 9 and 10, which do not belong to the realm of metaphor. Because the imagery is so predominant, because it is, for the most part, visual, and, chiefly, because it is nearly always presented as if it were literal fact, the reader cannot avoid reading the poem as if the imagery was the primary subject matter. This technique is typical of Éluard's poetry and is inherited from his experience as a Surrealist. The visual effect of combining such apparently unrelated objects as a countryside, two naked bodies, fire, mirrors, the sun, the sea, a star, wings, etc., has the literal effect of a Dali painting.

As unrelated as they may seem on a visual level, the three main images (*paysage, miroir, feu*) are brought together in different ways. They are all, for example, related to the sun image. The sun (like the star at night, l. 15) is the centre of the geographical universe, the *paysage*. The mirrors in the first stanza refer to the eyes of the lovers, and the sun expresses their final communion, that single eye into which they have merged. One immediately associates the fire with the sun, and there is an obvious link between *premier feu* and *le soleil au bout de tout*. In other words, the three main images all lead to the sun, immediately before the poem's climax. At this point, it seems as if the sun ceases to be something contemplated at a distance, and the lover falls into its flames. *Au bout de tout* prepares us for *dans*, which is its culmination. It recalls Éluard's earlier poem, which has already been mentioned, *Pour Vivre Ici*: 'J'étais comme un bateau coulant dans l'eau fermée'. This incorporation into a greater whole is a second unifying feature of the imagery: the poet before the countryside; the child before the fire; the image of the child itself suggests the small in a great world; the vastness of the poet's universe, described in lines 8 and 16, a factor which is emphasized by the way these lines expand into sixteen syllables as the universe itself fills everything and by the verb *perdre*; finally, there is the reflection in the mirrors and the branch in the fire. Most striking of all these images is line 18: 'Que la mer couvre de ses ailes'. This has nothing to do with the Pascalian sense of man's insignificance in the world. It expresses the poet's need to protect his love, which is something infinitely marvellous, infinitely delicate (*second bourgeon première feuille verte*) and which nevertheless fills his universe to the total exclusion of all else – 'Et sur la terre et sous le ciel hors de mon cœur et dans mon cœur'. Indeed, Éluard sought in perfect love, whether based on love between a man and a woman or on compassion for humanity as a whole, a release from the tensions of life which, as I suggested in my opening paragraph, he found so difficult to bear. Although Éluard always retained the Surrealist use of imagery, he moved, I think, a long way from its intention. For the Surrealists, imagery was the expression of a hidden, but for them, objective reality; for Éluard, it was the bricks and mortar of a totally different world of the imagination, beautiful and delightful. To put it bluntly, Éluard was an escapist, an 'incurable romantic'.

In some ways, the most important feature of Éluard's imagery is its universality. It has the universality of imagery drawn at one and the same time from everyday reality and from what is most continuous in the European poetic tradition. The best example of this in *L'Extase* is the image of the fire. Yet his secret lies in the fact that his imagery does not have the triteness of either everyday reality or a well-worn tradition. In this sense he renewed the French tradition of lyric poetry and it is in part at least the explanation of his great popularity.

The poem is clearly the work of a poet with a keen sense of structure. Its unity is mainly based, as almost everywhere in Éluard's poetry, on the principle of repetition. I have already shown how the poem is brought full circle by the repetition of the first and last two lines. *Devant* is repeated like a leitmotiv throughout the poem, emphasizing the contemplation theme and heightening the dramatic effect of the sudden change to *dans* in the last line. Apart from the simple repetition of words, the poet also uses balance and contrast, which are forms of repetition, as in lines 5, 8, 11, 13, 16, 17. Lines also echo one another structurally and verbally, as for example lines 5 and 17, lines 8 and 16, and lines 11 and 14/15. The structure of the poem reflects the image of the mirrors. There is not only the infinite reflection of the lover and the beloved in each other's eyes, the reflection of earth and sky, of the world outside and inside the poet's heart, but there is also the reflection of verbal patterns and sounds.

Assonance and alliteration are, in fact, two major features of the poem. It would be tedious to list all the sounds occurring in the poem, so I shall illustrate only one of them. The most predominant sound throughout is the nasal in *devant*. We have already seen the importance of this word, so this is yet another way of bringing it out. The two crucial words in the last two lines are *devant* and *dans*, and the second major innovation in the last line is *branche*: all of them contain this same nasal sound. The effect of changing from *devant* to *dans* is as if the word *devant*, and with it the whole poem, had been compressed into this one simple word, this dominant nasal sound. Another sound effect involving alliteration and assonance suggests a kind of vestigial rhyming. We have seen how *féminin* and *feu* are brought together in this way. Other examples are: *feu/yeux; s'éclairent/ saison; jamais/mêmes/miennes; saison/horizon; verte/ailes.* There is also an occasional hint of internal rhyme, with a similar effect of drawing words together: *s'embuent/nus; couvre/tout/nous* and *devant/branche.* This love of sound repetition produces at least one unfortunate jingle: 'le soleil au bout de tout venant de nous.'

The same sense of structure is observable in the stanza structure and in the use of metre. The first two stanzas each have six lines, while the third stanza, with seven lines, could be read as six lines, since lines 14 and 15, echoing the structure of line 11, could be taken as one line. The final two lines act as conclusion. The overall structure of the poem has a balance which is just not quite absolute, in much the same way as the rhyme is only vestigial. Similarly, the metre has a balance without establishing a completely regular pattern. One does not usually associate Éluard with the use of conventional metre, but in fact in his later poetry, especially after the war, he did tend towards a more frequent use of the alexandrine, as well as the other *vers pairs. L'Extase* contains nine alexandrines, which could be increased to ten if we count lines 14 and 15 as a single unit (lines 1, 3, 4, 5, 6, 11, 12, 19, 20); six octosyllabic lines, which could also be increased to ten if we count lines 8 and 16 as double octosyllabic lines since each has sixteen syllables (lines 2, 7, 10, 13, 18, 21); and two decasyllabic lines (lines 9 and 17). All but three of the alexandrines have a break after the sixth syllable, the exceptions being line 1: 4 + 8; line 19: 4 + 4 + 4; and line 20 – which repeats line 1: 4 + 8. The octosyllabic lines all have a break after the fourth syllable, and the two decasyllabic lines are divided 4 + 6, which is conventional. The use of *vers pairs* and the very conventional placing of the breaks gives the poem a rhythmic balance which underscores the theme of contentment, passivity and security.

Éluard continues his usual practice of making each line appear to be an independent statement, divorced from the others by the absence of punctuation and mostly lacking any kind of grammatical links except the most ordinary and unobtrusive (*et, où, ou, que*). Even these are sparingly used. *Et* seems to have the strongest effect, particularly at the beginning of line 19, where it emphasizes, in an almost Flaubertian manner, the culmination of the poem in the image of the sun contained in this line. The rational links between the lines are otherwise assured by the repetition of key words, such as *devant* and *raisons*. These are very characteristic features of Éluard's style and they make most of his poems immediately recognizable as being by him.

Éluard uses change in the length of line much the same way as poets have always done. We have already seen how the expanding sixteen-syllable lines express the vastness, fullness and exclusiveness of the poet's universe. In the last two lines of the poem, a dramatic effect is created by placing an octosyllabic line after an alexandrine; this device intensifies the suddenness and the finality of the action at the poem's climax.

I have already suggested that lines 14 and 15 could be read as a metrical unit. Yet they are set out on paper as separate lines. We have here the key to the nature of the line in modern French poetry, especially Éluard's. The eye, followed, not accompanied, by the mind, takes in the line as a unit of emphasis. In modern French poetry, where the *vers libre* is so popular, the line is no longer a metrical unit in the way it was before. In lines 14 and 15, Éluard wishes to catalogue equally important attributes of the *premier feu*, so he places them one under the other on the printed page, irrespective of the fact that they constitute a metrical unit. Whereas the earlier poet achieved emphasis primarily by rhythmical means, by relying, that is, on the mind's perception of rhythmical patterns and by placing key words at a suitable point in the metrical unit, the modern poet more frequently relies on the eye to perform this function. It just so happens that in this poem Éluard is using conventional metrical forms, which in this case he adapts to fit in with modern means of obtaining emphasis. If this is not true, there can be no reason why much modern poetry should not be written as prose. Perhaps my point can best be illustrated in relation to Éluard and this poem by comparing the use of this visual technique in lines 14 and 15 with the more conventional rhythmical technique used, as already shown, in the last two lines of the poem.

*L'Extase* is one of Éluard's so-called simple poems. Difficult Surrealist-type poems predominate in his early poetry, and simpler poems predominate in his later poetry, but he wrote both kinds throughout his life. This poem reveals two of the most striking features of Éluard's poetry: his sense of structure and his delight in a simplicity which belies a complex interplay of theme, metaphor and poetic technique. Moving away from a Surrealist technique which, in other poets, led to what was frequently an almost completely inaccessible personal poetry, Éluard's poetry re-joins the tradition of French lyric poetry, while revitalizing it through his adoption of contemporary use of imagery and poetic techniques.

*Source*
Paul Éluard (1895 – 1952): *Œuvres complètes*, Bibliothèque de la Pléiade, 1968, t. 11, p. 107.

*John Cruickshank*

# *CAMUS*
## Extract from *La Chute*

« Tiens, la pluie a cessé! Ayez la bonté de me raccompagner chez moi. Je suis fatigué, étrangement, non d'avoir parlé, mais à la seule idée de ce qu'il me faut encore dire. Allons! Quelques mots suffiront pour retracer ma découverte essentielle. Pourquoi en dire plus, d'ailleurs?
5 Pour que la statue soit nue, les beaux discours doivent s'envoler. Voici. Cette nuit-là, en novembre, deux ou trois ans avant le soir où je crus entendre rire dans mon dos, je regagnais la rive gauche, et mon domicile, par le pont Royal. Il était une heure après minuit, une petite pluie tombait, une bruine plutôt, qui dispersait les rares passants. Je
10 venais de quitter une amie qui, sûrement, dormait déjà. J'étais heureux de cette marche, un peu engourdi, le corps calmé, irrigué par un sang doux comme la pluie qui tombait. Sur le pont, je passai derrière une forme penchée sur le parapet, et qui semblait regarder le fleuve. De plus près, je distinguai une mince jeune femme, habillée de noir.
15 Entre les cheveux sombres et le col du manteau, on voyait seulement une nuque, fraîche et mouillée, à laquelle je fus sensible. Mais je poursuivis ma route, après une hésitation. Au bout du pont, je pris les quais en direction de Saint-Michel, où je demeurais. J'avais déjà parcouru une cinquantaine de mètres à peu près, lorsque j'entendis le
20 bruit, qui, malgré la distance, me parut formidable dans le silence nocturne, d'un corps qui s'abat sur l'eau. Je m'arrêtai net, mais sans me retourner. Presque aussitôt, j'entendis un cri, plusieurs fois répété, qui descendait lui aussi le fleuve, puis s'éteignit brusquement. Le silence qui suivit, dans la nuit soudain figée, me parut interminable.
25 Je voulus courir et je ne bougeai pas. Je tremblais, je crois, de froid et de saisissement. Je me disais qu'il fallait faire vite et je sentais une faiblesse irrésistible envahir mon corps. J'ai oublié ce que j'ai pensé alors. 'Trop tard, trop loin . . .' ou quelque chose de ce genre. J'écoutais toujours, immobile. Puis, à petits pas, sous la pluie, je
30 m'éloignai. Je ne prévins personne.

Mais nous sommes arrivés, voici ma maison, mon abri! Demain? Oui, comme vous voudrez. Je vous mènerai volontiers à l'île de Marken, vous verrez le Zuyderzee. Rendez-vous à onze heures à *Mexico-City*. Quoi? Cette femme? Ah, je ne sais pas, vraiment, je ne
35 sais pas. Ni le lendemain, ni les jours qui suivirent, je n'ai lu les journaux. »

THIS PASSAGE occurs almost exactly midway through Camus' short novel, *La Chute*. The fact that it is placed in such a position becomes all the more appropriate once we have realized its central significance within the overall intellectual framework of the book (the narrator himself refers to 'cette aventure que j'ai trouvée au centre de ma mémoire'). Indeed, the placing of this particular passage in relation to what precedes and what follows ensures that its full import can only emerge from a discussion of the structure and meaning of the whole *récit*. The incident recounted here by the narrator, Jean-Baptiste Clamence, represents a crucial turning-point in his life. It refers to a vital moment of self-confrontation in which Clamence's assumption of his own innocence and virtue was replaced by a sense of irremediable guilt. What happened on the Pont Royal one November night in the past transformed both his view of the world and his assessment of his own place in it.

Briefly, the broader setting of the incident is as follows. Clamence now holds court in the Mexico City bar in Amsterdam and tells the story of his life to an anonymous listener whose own comments are not recorded though they are sometimes suggested in an indirect way. At an earlier period in his life Clamence enjoyed a successful career as a Parisian lawyer. More particularly, he specialized in the defence of the relatively defenceless – 'la veuve et l'orphelin, comme on dit' – and outside his professional life he also made good works his chief concern:

> Par exemple, j'adorais aider les aveugles à traverser les rues. Du plus loin que j'apercevais une canne hésiter sur l'angle d'un trottoir, je me précipitais, devançais d'une seconde, parfois, la main charitable qui se tendait déjà, enlevais l'aveugle à toute autre sollicitude que la mienne et le menais d'une main douce et ferme sur le passage clouté, parmi les obstacles de la circulation, vers le havre tranquille du trottoir où nous nous séparions avec une émotion mutuelle.

The same traits of character ensured that Clamence was the first to offer directions to an enquirer in the street, the first to give help to a motorist whose car had broken down, the first to lift a woman-traveller's luggage on to the overhead rack. With an almost professionalized goodwill he gave up his seat to others in a crowded bus or underground train and offered his place in a taxi-queue to those more pressed for time than himself.

Incidents such as these happened well before the narrative present of the novel. Moreover, the irony with which Clamence recalls his earlier altruism implies that he has somehow 'seen through it' and rejected it. His present circumstances make the same point. He now leads a very different life – in the dock area of Amsterdam rather than in the legal circles of Paris, and surrounded by the sailors, prostitutes and underworld fringe of the Mexico City bar rather than among his eminent and respectable Parisian colleagues. On several occasions he hints at an intriguing story, and a specific event, lying behind this radical change in his circumstances. The explanation of how the change came about is in fact the substance of his protracted monologue ('Je suis bavard, hélas! et me lie facilement') which constitutes Camus' *récit*.

In the passage with which we are concerned here Clamence finally brings himself to describe the crucial incident that transformed his life. He reveals that one evening in Paris he saw a young woman contemplating suicide on the Pont Royal, heard her cry as her body struck the water, and continued on his way after some moments of hesitation and inner struggle. In a novel which contains many biblical allusions, both implicit and explicit, one is reminded of the parable of the good Samaritan in St Luke, chapter 10. In this case, however, it is as though the story had been told by the priest or the Levite who, unlike the Samaritan, 'passed by on the other side' when they came upon a stranger robbed and beaten by thieves. No doubt there is an element of shame present in the third sentence of the passage when Clamence says: 'Je suis fatigué, étrangement, non d'avoir parlé, mais à la seule idée de ce qu'il me faut encore dire.' Yet the adverb 'étrangement' suggests a more complicated reaction than straightforward guilt at his own cowardice or indifference. Earlier in the novel there are several anticipatory references to the incident which hint at its nature and 'strange' significance. At the end of his first encounter with his hearer Clamence uses the term 'étrange' in this same connection when he says:

A demain donc, monsieur et cher compatriote. Non, vous trouverez maintenant votre chemin; je vous quitte près de ce pont. Je ne passe jamais sur un pont, la nuit. C'est la conséquence d'un vœu. Supposez, après tout, que quelqu'un se jette à l'eau. De deux choses l'une, ou vous l'y suivez pour le repêcher et, dans la saison froide, vous risquez le pire! Ou vous l'y abandonnez et

les plongeons rentrés laissent parfois d'étranges courbatures.
This last phrase suggests a vital significance lurking in some incident which Clamence has not yet described to his hearer. Its full meaning will only become clear sometime after the account of the suicide in the passage with which we are dealing. The same is true of some other comments by Clamence which also occur at a relatively early point in his story of his life:

Ne croyez pas surtout que vos amis vous téléphoneront tous les soirs, comme ils le devraient, pour savoir si ce n'est pas justement le soir où vous décidez de vous suicider, ou plus simplement si vous n'avez pas besoin de compagnie, si vous n'êtes pas en disposition de sortir. Mais non, s'ils téléphonent, soyez tranquille, ce sera le soir où vous n'êtes pas seul, et où la vie est belle. Le suicide, ils vous y pousseraient plutôt, en vertu de ce que vous vous devez à vous-même, selon eux.

These lines refer to the perverse nature of chance. They also suggest a possible link between the girl's suicide, which Clamence happened upon by the merest accident, and the resultant suicide of a part of himself – another kind of 'moral' suicide to which the 'physical' suicide he ignored eventually gives rise. Indeed, as a result of having failed to help the young woman on the Pont Royal, he is haunted by what he believes to be the sound of mocking laughter behind his back. A major occasion on which this laughter occurs – as he crosses the Pont des Arts one evening some years later – is referred to in this passage when he speaks of 'le soir où je crus entendre rire dans mon dos'. This conviction that he hears mocking laughter proves much stronger than his attempt to forget the suicide incident ('Cette femme? Ah, je ne sais pas, vraiment, je ne sais pas. Ni le lendemain, ni les jours qui suivirent, je n'ai pas lu les journaux'). In the end, the laughter brings about the moral suicide of the 'friend of the widow and orphan'. Clamence (a name, he tells us, which he only assumed later) kills this part of himself by various means including, initially, debauchery and drink. This is perhaps neither an imaginative nor an unusual reaction. The 'strange' consequences, to which he refers several times in advance, only begin to grow clear when he adopts the new personality of 'Clamence' and, later in the novel, moves out from an awareness of personal guilt to an assertion of universal culpability.

More must be said about this point shortly. First of all, however, attention should be drawn to a feature in the setting of this passage that makes the impact of the drowning incident all the more powerful in its effect on Clamence. He tells us that, as he approached the Pont Royal, he had just left a mistress and was returning home ('Je venais de quitter une amie qui, sûrement, dormait déjà'). Now shortly before this passage, in the course of describing his character and temperament, Clamence had referred to his liking for a number of 'liaisons simultanées' and added: 'Aussitôt aimé, et ma partenaire à nouveau oubliée, je reluisais, j'étais au mieux, je devenais sympathique.' In other words, it is precisely at the moment when he is particularly self-satisfied and apparently impervious to adversity ('le corps calmé, irrigué par un sang doux') that his moral strength is put to the test as chance strikes suddenly and unexpectedly. In these circumstances the double sense of Camus' title, La Chute, also becomes clearer. The fall of the young woman's body into the Seine is eventually followed by the 'fall' of the successful Parisian lawyer from a state of innocence to a state of guilt, from his view of himself as a man of good works and delicate moral sense to his realization that he is a coward who evades responsibility when there are no onlookers.

It is significant, too, that Clamence agrees, towards the end of the passage, to show his hearer the island village of Marken next day. This fishing village is one of the most picturesque in Holland with its costumed inhabitants and attractively painted houses, but when Clamence and his companion go there on the following day Clamence says: 'Mais je ne vous ai pas conduit dans cette île pour le pittoresque, cher ami. . . . Je suis un des rares, au contraire, à pouvoir vous montrer ce qu'il y a d'important ici.' They go out on the dike connecting Marken with the mainland and gaze at the grey, monotonous levels of the shore, the dike itself, and the Zuider Zee. This represents, for Clamence, 'le plus beau des paysages négatifs' and the transition from 'le pittoresque' to 'le néant sensible' again reflects, in physical terms, the transformation which Clamence is to undergo from complacency to inescapable guilt.

It is as a result of the Pont Royal incident, with its revelation of his own moral failure when confronted by acute human need, that Clamence submits all his previous actions to a searching scrutiny. He concludes that 'la modestie m'aidait à briller, l'humilité à vaincre et la vertu à opprimer'. This is the first major shock which he attempts to neutralize with sex and drink. He fails to 'cure' himself, however, and sometime later, during a cruise, he has another experience which reinforces his growing conviction that the effect of the Pont Royal incident is ineradicable:

Soudain, j'aperçus au large un point noir sur l'océan couleur de fer. Je détournai les yeux aussitôt, mon cœur se mit à battre. Quand je me forçai à regarder, le point noir avait disparu. J'allais crier, appeler stupidement à l'aide, quand je le revis. Il s'agissait d'un de ces débris que les navires laissent derrière eux. Pourtant, je n'avais pu supporter de le regarder, j'avais tout de suite pensé à un noyé.

Yet if innocence and peace of mind are unattainable for Clamence, he realizes that they are also unattainable for all men. All men are guilty, and guilty in purely humanist, non-theological terms. This is a theme already adumbrated in *L'Etranger* ('De toutes façons, on est toujours un peu fautif') and *La Peste* ('. . . chacun porte la peste en soi'), but in *La Chute* it becomes a central preoccupation. Furthermore, if Clamence recognizes 'la culpabilité de tous' he also insists on 'la duplicité profonde de la créature'. This duplicity is activated by the fact that in a post-Christian world increasingly lacking belief in God 'le plus haut des tourments humains est d'être jugé sans loi'. Men therefore employ duplicity to escape judgment, but as they fear judgment so they also fear freedom. Pure freedom, without moral or social constraint, is the commonest contemporary form of guilt: 'Ah! mon cher, pour qui est seul, sans dieu et sans maître, le poids des jours est terrible.' Clamence himself has experienced something of this terror. Near the end of *La Chute*, in a further reference to the Pont Royal incident, he says: '. . . sur les ponts de Paris, j'ai appris moi aussi que j'avais peur de la liberté. Vive donc le maître, quel qu'il soit, pour remplacer la loi du ciel.' The second sentence here is echoed by a number of others in which Clamence accuses certain contemporary ideologies of the will to enslave, in the name of freedom, by emphasizing human guilt. Many critics have pointed out Camus' irony in *La Chute* at the expense of those ubiquitous phenomena of our time – the overtly authoritarian left-winger or the temperamentally intolerant 'liberal' – and he sums all this up in a trenchant phrase: 'Quand nous serons tous coupables, ce sera la démocratie.'

As far as Clamence is concerned he manages to escape final judgment by condemning himself simply in order to judge and condemn others. He indulges in calculated confession and plays the rôle of what he calls a 'juge-pénitent'. As a result, the severe self-portrait which he offers becomes a mirror in which his hearers see themselves, recognize their own guilt, and are therefore 'judged' by his 'penitence'.

The stratagem of the 'juge-pénitent' is not explicit in the particular passage under discussion. Nevertheless, it throws light on it, and is at least present as a possibility. The reader will be struck, for instance, by the contrast between the self-dramatization with which Clamence approaches the recounting of this particular incident ('Je suis fatigué, étrangement . . .') and the abruptness with which he ends it and continues: 'Mais nous sommes arrivés, voici ma maison, mon abri!' It is only when he has apparently been prompted by a question from his companion that he comes back to the story with the air of a man who has already forgotten it: 'Quoi? Cette femme? . . .' This can only be a simulated forgetfulness, simulated for some purpose, and indeed there is a disturbing air of deviousness and moral ambiguity about the whole passage. Incidentally, this impression is if anything reinforced by the physical setting of a dark, drizzling November night ('. . . une petite pluie tombait, une bruine plutôt . . .'). In the end, one suspects that there is a clever paradox embedded in the narrator's manner of telling his story: he uses the supposedly revelatory form of the confession, yet part at least of his purpose is to hide behind it.

The effect of this narrative method, and of the ambiguity which hovers over it, is to arouse the curiosity of the listener or reader. The passage we are discussing prompts questions not only because of straight factual inadequacy but also on account of the manner in which the incident is recalled. We are bound to be struck by the omnipresent first-person references in the passage ('je', 'me', 'moi', 'mon' and 'ma' occur over forty times in 400 words) and indeed Clamence had said earlier: 'Moi, moi, moi, voilà le refrain de ma chère vie. . . .' Yet we remain unsure about him, even while reading of the Pont Royal incident, and there are moments when we even begin to suspect that we might easily learn rather more about ourselves than about Jean-Baptiste Clamence. This is precisely the effect, of course, at which the 'juge-pénitent' aims. He reveals only enough of himself to launch his hearer into self-scrutiny. A stylistic device

which he uses to assist him in this purpose is, he tells us, to slide
imperceptibly in his narrative from the first-person singular to the
first-person plural, from 'je' to 'nous'. Once he has managed to do
this acceptably he has involved the listener in complicity with his
own guilt. It is significant therefore that in his last reference to the
Pont Royal incident – a reference which also forms the closing words
of the novel – Clamence quite explicitly implicates his listener in the
incident as he finally replaces 'je' by 'nous':

'O jeune fille, jette-toi encore dans l'eau pour que j'aie une
seconde fois la chance de nous sauver tous les deux!' Une seconde
fois, hein, quelle imprudence! Supposez, cher maître, qu'on nous
prenne au mot? Il faudrait s'exécuter. Brr . . .! l'eau est si froide!
Mais rassurons-nous! Il est trop tard, maintenant, il sera toujours
trop tard. Heureusement!

What began as a confidence in the Pont Royal passage itself is here
coming close to being an interrogation. Confession is fast giving
way to judgment. These final words of *La Chute* also convey something of the terrible pessimism – and clarity – which preside over it.
Clamence himself admits that 'il ne suffit pas de s'accuser pour
s'innocenter'. He knows that it is impossible for him to receive a
second chance on the Pont Royal and he regards this as fortunate
because, if faced a second time with such an incident, he would act
just as he had acted on the first occasion. Clamence, who does not
believe in grace, is not deceived by the sentimental consolations of a
'second chance' doctrine. Indeed, properly speaking, there cannot be
second chances in life.

As regards the style of the passage little needs to be said. Camus
has caught the tone of the self-obsessed talker. Even if he has not
wholly followed natural speech rhythms the monologue is at least a
literary rendering of actual speech – rather like the style employed
by Dostoevsky, for example, in his *Notes from Underground*. Incidentally this type of monologue, in which the speaker is sometimes less
than frank, also allows the writer to maintain a rather ambiguous
relationship between himself and his fictional character. With Camus,
as with Dostoevsky, there are times when he is speaking through his
narrator and times when he undoubtedly disagrees with him. Camus,
again like Dostoevsky, adopted a very ambiguous attitude to the
prevailing intellectual currents of his day and Clamence, like the
underground man, is a typical figure of his age – a hero of his

times with all that this implies of praise and blame on Camus' part.

Two final points, closely related to one another, should be made. One of them concerns the nature of Camus' *récit* while the other has to do with the whole question of literary commentary on a short passage as a critical exercise. It will be noticed that in the comments made on the passage selected above I have not 'kept to the text' in a rigorous manner. Rather than deal only directly with it I have, for much of the time, sought to illuminate it obliquely from other parts of the book. I have even gone in the opposite direction and used the passage, in some measure, as a stepping-off point for some general remarks about *La Chute*. However, I would want to claim that this was inevitable in the circumstances; the tightly-knit and interdependent nature of this work by Camus made such an approach unavoidable. This is true of almost any passage that one might have chosen from this particular *récit* and the difficulties just mentioned serve to emphasize how closely Camus organized the details of this book – how carefully thought out and worked out it is. Even what looks on the face of it like a set-piece – the Pont Royal incident – is closely integrated into the overall pattern of the work. It is both essential to the whole and relatively meaningless in itself when separated from the whole.

A second point follows. It is clear from what has just been said that the literary commentary or *explication de textes* – particularly where a passage from a novel is concerned – cannot follow a single general pattern however broad in scope. One can of course exemplify a prior procedural pattern by choosing one's passages for demonstration rather carefully. This, indeed, is what most handbooks on textual analysis do, and I myself have done just this in the past. The difficulty existing here has prompted a certain amount of criticism of the whole undertaking of *explication de textes*; where the close observance of rules of method has not led to triviality it has often limited the number of texts suitable for such treatment. Now I myself would not wish to see the *explication* approach rejected on such grounds. Instead, rather than consider it as a complete and autonomous critical method, I would much prefer to regard it as one of a number of related, 'text-based' approaches varying from the strict technique of a Rudler to the much looser, and perhaps ultimately more creative, technique of an Auerbach. To focus attention on a short passage still seems to me to be an admirable exercise, but it can as legitimately be the starting-point for an outward movement through the whole work (which ultimately illuminates it further) as for an inward-turned analysis that attempts to keep as completely as possible within the confines of a couple of paragraphs.

*Source*
Albert Camus (1913–60): *La Chute*, Gallimard, Paris, 1956, pp. 81–3.

# SELECT BIBLIOGRAPHY

*The following titles represent a highly personal choice*
*of works dealing with literary analysis*

I. Books containing examples of literary commentary

AUERBACH, E.: *Mimesis* (English translation, Princeton University Press, 1953; paperback ed. by Doubleday Anchor Books, 1957).

BARRÈRE, J. B.: *Explications françaises de licence* (Delalain, n.d.).

CRUICKSHANK, J.: *Critical Readings in the Modern French Novel* (Macmillan, 1965).

DHENIN, F.: *De l'Explication de texte au sujet général* (Bordas, 1964).

FROHOCK, W. M.: *French Literature. An Approach through Close Reading* (Schoenhof's Foreign Books Inc., 1964).

GALLIOT, M.: *Commentaires de textes français modernes* (Didier, 1965).

HATZFELD, H.: *Initiation à l'explication littéraire* (Max Hueber Verlag, 1957; 2nd ed., 1966).

LE HIR, Y.: *Analyses stylistiques* (Armand Colin, 1965).

NARDIN, P.: *Le Commentaire stylistique aux rendez-vous littéraires* (Dakar, 1958).

POUGET, P.: *L'Explication française au baccalauréat* (Hachette, 1952).

ROUSTAN, M.: *Précis d'explication française* (Mellottée, 1911).

RUDLER, G.: *L'Explication française* (Armand Colin, 1948).

SAREIL, J. (ed.): *Explication de texte* (Prentice-Hall, 1967).

SCHLUMBERGER, B.: *L'Explication littéraire* (Harrap, 1951).

SPITZER, L.: *Linguistics and Literary History* (Princeton University Press, 1958).

— *Cahiers d'analyse textuelle* (Sociéte d'Editions 'Les Belles Lettres', 1959–).

II. Theoretical works

BOOTH, W. C.: *The Rhetoric of Fiction* (University of Chicago Press, 1961).

COOMBES, H.: *Literature and Criticism* (Penguin Books, 1963).

CRESSOT, M.: *Le Style et ses techniques* (Princeton University Press, 1947).

FAYOLLE, R.: *La Critique* (Armand Colin, 1964).

GRAMMONT, M.: *Le Vers français, ses moyens d'expression, son harmonie* (Delagrave, 1937).

— *Petit Traité de versification française* (Armand Colin, 1947; Collection U, 1965).

LANSON, G.: *L'Art de la prose* (Payot, 1908).

MAROUZEAU, J.: *Précis de stylistique française* (Masson, 1950).

POULET, G. (ed.): *Les Chemins actuels de la critique*
(Le Monde en 10/18, 1968).

SAYCE, R. A.: *Style in French Prose. A Method of Analysis*
(OUP, 1953).

ULLMANN, S.: *Style in the French Novel* (CUP, 1957).

WELLEK, R. & WARREN, A.: *Theory of Literature* (1949; Penguin
Books, 1963).

WIMSATT, W. K. Jr.: *The Verbal Icon. Studies in the Meaning of Poetry*
(Noonday Press, 1966).

BARNWELL, H. T.
> Professor of French, The Queen's University of Belfast; author of *Les Idées morales et critiques de Saint-Evremond*; editor and translator of *Selected Letters of Madame de Sévigné*; editor of Corneille's *Writings on the Theatre*; and author of various papers on seventeenth-century topics, notably the thought of the *Libertins* and tragic drama.

BARRÈRE, J. B.
> Professor of French Literature, University of Cambridge; author of *Hugo; La Fantaisie de Victor Hugo; Victor Hugo à l'œuvre*; and of various books on modern French literature.

BOWMAN, Frank Paul
> Professor of Romance Languages, University of Pennsylvania; author of *Prosper Mérimée: Heroism, Pessimism, Irony; Montaigne: Essays; Eliphas Lévi, Visionnaire romantique*; and various articles mostly on French Romanticism.

BRÉE, Germaine
> Vilos Professor, Institute for Research in the Humanities, University of Wisconsin; author of *Marcel Proust and Deliverance from Time; The World of Marcel Proust; Gide; Camus; An Age of Fiction*; and various articles on contemporary French fiction, poetry and drama.

BRUMFITT, John H.
> Senior Lecturer in French, St Andrews University; author of *Voltaire, Historian*; editor and translator of a number of works, mainly by Voltaire.

CALLANDER, Margaret M.
> Lecturer in French, University of Birmingham; author of *The Poetry of Pierre-Jean Jouve*.

CARDINAL, Roger
> Lecturer in French, University of Kent at Canterbury; author of a number of articles on Surrealism.

CASTOR, Grahame
> Lecturer in French, Cambridge University; Senior Tutor, Gonville & Caius College; author of *Pléiade Poetics*, and articles on Ronsard.

CRUICKSHANK, John
> Professor of French, University of Sussex; author of *Camus and the Literature of Revolt* and *Montherlant* and editor of *The Novelist as Philosopher – Studies in French Fiction 1935–60* and *French Literature and its Background* (6 vols.).

HACKETT, C. A.
Professor of French, University of Southampton; author of *An Anthology of Modern French Poetry; Rimbaud; Autour de Rimbaud,* and articles on nineteenth- and twentieth-century French poetry.

HALL, H. Gaston
Senior Lecturer in French, University of Warwick; author of *Molière: Tartuffe,* an edition of *Le Bourgeois Gentilhomme,* and other studies, mainly in French baroque and classical literature.

KNIGHT, Roy C.
Professor of French at the University College of Swansea; author of *Racine et la Grèce,* and articles on Corneille, Racine and the teaching of French Literature; editor of *Nicomède* and *Phèdre.*

LOCKERBIE, S. I.
Senior Lecturer in French, University of Stirling; author of several articles and of a forthcoming monograph on Apollinaire; co-editor of *Charles Cros* (*Poètes d'Aujourd'hui*) and editor of H. Becque: *Les Corbeaux.*

MCFARLANE, I. D.
Professor of French Language and Literature, University of St Andrews; critical edition of Scève's *Délie,* contribution to *The Age of the Renaissance,* articles on comparative literature and Neo-Latin literature.

MYLNE, Vivienne G.
Senior Lecturer in French, University of Kent at Canterbury; author of *The Eighteenth-Century French Novel* and various articles on fiction and aesthetics.

NURSE, Peter H.
Reader in French, University of Kent at Canterbury; editor of Des Périers's *Cymbalum Mundi*; Corneille's *Horace*; Molière's *L'École des maris* and *Le Malade imaginaire*; and author of various articles on French Classicism, shortly to reappear in book form.

RAITT, A. W.
Fellow of Magdalen College, Oxford; author of *Villiers de l'Isle-Adam et le mouvement symboliste* and *Life and Letters in France: The Nineteenth Century*; editions of texts by Villiers de l'Isle-Adam and Balzac, and various articles on Mallarmé, Flaubert, etc.

SCARFE, Francis
Director of the British Institute in Paris, Professor in the University of London; author of *The Art of Paul Valéry, The Penguin Baudelaire, André Chénier, his life and work,* etc.

SCREECH, M. A.
Professor of French, University College London; author of *The*

*Rabelaisian Marriage, L'Évangélisme de Rabelais, Marot Évangélique;* editor of Rabelais's *Tiers Livre,* Du Bellay's *Regrets* and *Antiquitez de Rome,* Lefèvre d'Etaples's *Epistres et evangiles des 52 sepmaines de l'an;* articles on French Renaissance authors.

STEELE, A. J.
Professor of French, University of Edinburgh; has published the anthology: *Three Centuries of French Verse, 1511–1819,* and articles mainly on French poetry.

WAKE, C. H.
Lecturer in French, University of Kent at Canterbury; editor of *An Anthology of African and Malagasy Poetry in French;* joint editor/translator of *L. S. Senghor: Selected Poems* and *Prose and Poetry;* articles on modern African Literature.

WEIGHTMAN, John
Professor of French, Westfield College, University of London; author of *On Language and Writing,* and various essays on aspects of French literature.